STAR-CROSSED

STAR-

★————————————

The Story of

BOOKS BY BEVERLY LINET

STAR-CROSSED
The Story of Robert Walker and Jennifer Jones

DUKE: A LOVE STORY
*An Intimate Memoir of John Wayne's
    Last Years* (With Pat Stacy)

SUSAN HAYWARD
Portrait of a Survivor

LADD
*The Life, the Legend, the Legacy
    of Alan Ladd*

CROSSED

★

ROBERT WALKER

and

JENNIFER JONES

Beverly Linet

G. P. Putnam's Sons
New York

G. P. Putnam's Sons
Publishers Since 1838
200 Madison Avenue
New York, NY 10016

Typeset by Fisher Composition, Inc.

Library of Congress Cataloging-in-Publication Data

Linet, Beverly.
  Star-crossed.

  Includes filmographies.
  1. Walker, Robert, 1918–1951.   2. Jones, Jennifer, 1919–
3. Moving-picture actors and actresses—
United States—Biography.   I. Title.
PN2287.W244L5   1986   791.43′028′0922   [B]   86-12349
ISBN 0-399-13194-9

Printed in the United States of America
1   2   3   4   5   6   7   8   9   10

Acknowledgments

This book could not have been written without the generous cooperation of James Henaghan, Robert Walker's closest friend and constant confidant during the last six years of Walker's life. Jim spent countless hours talking with me at his Century City, California, apartment, candidly revealing everything he knew about Walker's life and sharing heartbreaking eyewitness details concerning his untimely death. Although a brilliant writer himself, Jim told me he was emotionally unable to write a book on Bob, but gave me his blessings after exacting a promise for "the first copy."

Jim's death from emphysema on April 1, 1984, was a great loss, but I was proud to have known him and grateful for his encouragement.

I am beholden to former MGM producer Sam Marx, director Mervyn LeRoy, and publicist Ann Straus for their personal recollections.

And to Walker's fellow performers, Van Johnson, Farley Granger, Barry Nelson, Audrey Totter, Joan Leslie, and June Lockhart, who also contributed valuable insights, as did actress and dancer Gwen Verdon— the first Mrs. James Henaghan—and Marie Windsor.

Keenan Wynn, who knew Bob from his radio days and later worked with Bob and Jennifer Jones, was interviewed extensively. Sharlee Hudson Wynn, who, coincidentally, dated Bob before her marriage to Keenan, supplied her impressions, as did Phyllis Thaxter, who met Jennifer Jones when both were aspiring young actresses and who later worked with and dated Bob when the two were at MGM, and Ann Richards, who worked with Jennifer in *Love Letters* and years later came into contact with Bob.

I spoke with Barbara Ford, Bob's second wife, prior to her death (June 27, 1985) and admired her candidness and lack of bitterness as she spoke about her difficult marriage, and concluded her testimony with a poignant "I still love him." Barbara was happy for the opportunity to clarify the many distortions about their very short-lived union.

Actress Augusta Dabney and actor Don Keefer were fellow students of Bob and Jennifer (then Phylis Isley) at the American Academy of Dramatic Arts and they talked to me of the time the two teenagers met and fell in love. My thanks to them and to the Academy, who dug into its archives and sent copies of their audition tests and other records pertaining to the class of 1937.

The distinguished John Houseman took time from his busy schedule to discuss Jennifer's first California stage appearance at the Lobero summer theater in Santa Barbara, which was a showcase for David O. Selznick's players and an early milestone in Jones's career.

Barbara Rabe, Walker's "favorite cousin" and early confidante, supplied essential information about the entire Walker family, Bob's difficult childhood years, his various returns to Ogden, and so much more. She was there "back when," and remembered and shared her memories.

Professor Raymond Ede (retired), Bob's language teacher at the Army and Navy Military Academy at Carlsbad, California, talked freely about Cadet Walker, and the academy sent yearbooks and exclusive school photographs documenting the formative period of his life.

The recollections of the late Alfred Hitchcock, Henry King, John Cromwell, Tay Garnett, Dore Schary, Richard Whorf, George Sherman, writers Hedda Hopper and Kirtley Baskett, and actor Peter Lawford were essential in my effort to recreate the story of two very private people, as were the reminiscences of June Allyson, Shelley Winters, Mrs. Irene Selznick, Vincente Minnelli, John Huston, Gregory Peck, and Joseph Cotten.

Sandra Acevedo neglected home and family to type my manuscript in completed form. I'd be remiss not to thank her for her effort and her interest.

On a more personal level, my love and deepest appreciation to my dear friend and peer Douglas McClelland, who was always at my side or just a phone call away when I needed someone trustworthy, supportive, and understanding with whom I could talk. In addition, Doug zealously helped me with my extensive research, put his photo collection at my disposal, assisted me in tracking down elusive people, and so very much more. When they made Doug, they broke the mold.

And finally, as always, my gratitude to my longtime editor Neil Nyren, not only for his patience and practical emotional assistance but also for his sharing my belief in the story of Robert Walker and Jennifer Jones from the very first day I presented it to him.

For Albert Delacorte—for many reasons

CONTENTS

A Personal Note

The first and only time I met and talked with Robert Walker, I knew neither his name nor anything about him. Some thirty minutes earlier, however, I had fallen completely under his spell.

The year was 1942, and I was a stagestruck kid who spent all of her time and allowance at the movies or theater, and, weekends, attended free radio broadcasts.

One of my favorites was *The Camel Caravan*, which aired from CBS Playhouse #2 on West Forty-fifth Street in New York and starred Xavier Cugat.

To provide relief from the incessant Latin rhythms, *The Camel Caravan* inserted brief, self-contained playlets under the overall title of *Our Town*.

One Friday evening I was so totally enchanted by the male juvenile that I waited at the stage door until he emerged, to tell him how absolutely wonderful he was and how certain I was that he was going to become a big star. My gushing enthusiasm must have startled him, but as I recall, he seemed pleased, although slightly embarrassed. We chatted a few moments, then walked up the alley together. After he headed west and I came down to earth, I realized I had forgotten to ask him for his autograph or even his name.

I continued attending *The Camel Caravan*, hoping to see him again. I never did. I thought it absurd that such an appealing, talented actor couldn't get a job. But radio actors (with the exception of the major stars) were an anonymous breed: voices with no names and no publicity.

The following June, I went to the Capitol Theater to view a war film called *Bataan* and was deeply moved by a newcomer who played the lone sailor. There was something vaguely familiar about the young man, but I couldn't make a connection. From the credits I learned that his name was Robert Walker, and I scanned the fan magazines for additional information.

I found a brief article which mentioned that Walker was a former soap-opera actor who'd also appeared in prime-time shows such as *The Camel Caravan*. Something clicked. I had found my "lost" actor.

After that, I took a proprietary interest in Robert Walker's life and career. His delightful *See Here, Private Hargrove* sent me into gales of laughter. I was deeply moved by his performance as the gentle soldier-suitor opposite Judy Garland in *The Clock*. I was astonished by his trans-

formation into a psychotic killer in Alfred Hitchcock's *Strangers on a Train*.

Like all of America, I fell in love with the story of his sweetheart marriage to a young girl named Phylis Isley, renamed Jennifer Jones, whom he had met in drama school. They were Hollywood's dream couple, so young, so clearly in love, so excited about the careers that had seen them get their first bit parts and movie breakthroughs together. Everyone agreed, these two would blaze a path to the stars. Instead, their lives blazed into ashes—because of the obsession of one man.

Only later would the harrowing details start to come out, and only now, I think, in this book, has the full story of this tragic triangle been fully told.

Star-Crossed is the story of three people: Robert Walker, the unloved son who became the boy every woman wanted to mother; Jennifer Jones, the eager, blushing girl whose first starring role catapulted her to an Oscar—and into the attentions of a man more powerful than she could have dreamed; and David O. Selznick, the lord of the cinema, domineering, persuasive, and determined to do anything in that power to make Jones his own.

The consequences of that passion would be terrible for all, sending each life crumbling into ruins, and utterly destroying Walker—but at the time none of us knew about that. Certainly I was stunned at the news that Jennifer Jones had left Robert Walker. With all the naiveté of youth, I couldn't fathom how or why she could let him go, after seeing their love scenes together in *Since You Went Away*.

At that time, I was employed as *Modern Screen*'s "Information Desk" editor, a job that required answering thousands of questions monthly. I thought I knew everything about Hollywood and its stars. And although privy to much of the current scuttlebutt, I had no idea why the two had divorced; nor was I aware of her intimate relationship with David O. Selznick.

In mid-1948 I was in California. Bob Walker was on loan-out to Universal at the time, appearing opposite Ava Gardner in *One Touch of Venus*. By a happy coincidence, a dear friend, the late Billy Daniel, was the choreographer on the film and invited me to spend an afternoon on the set. When we arrived, Ava Gardner was before the cameras, gorgeous in a white, filmy Grecian robe, filming the last moments before the "living" Venus again becomes a marble statue.

Bob Walker was nowhere in sight. "Not working today," Billy informed me. When I asked if Billy could arrange for an informal cup of coffee with Bob at the Universal commissary before I left town, he replied grimly, "I'd rather not. You might be very disillusioned. He's usually

hung-over these days." I didn't care. But Billy, whom I'd never heard say an unkind word about anyone, dismissed my request: "Forget it."

I had read and heard that Bob Walker was an extremely unhappy man, but I didn't realize the extent of his misery until I saw a grotesque photo in *Life* taken of him in a Los Angeles jail, his hands balled into fists, his face contorted with rage. Shortly afterward I read that he had been committed to the Menninger Clinic for the mentally disturbed, where he remained for six months.

Three years went by. It was now 1951, and I had left *Modern Screen* to become an editor at *Photoplay*. I was on my way to Hollywood to supervise the magazine's annual Pasadena Playhouse Scholarship contest. I recall sitting in the club car of the streamliner, *City of Los Angeles*, planning my schedule. After the contest, I'd be interviewing the "new boy" on the Twentieth Century-Fox lot, a young man named Robert Wagner. But then—and for me this was a long-awaited plum—*Photoplay*'s veteran photographer Hymie Fink and I were to shoot a home layout of Bob Walker and his boys—Robert Jr. and Michael. I'd been mulling over a couple of title ideas when, through a noisy barrier of crackling static, I thought I heard a newscaster say, "Actor Robert Walker is dead." Robert *Walker*? Impossible. Absurd. I told myself he was too young to die. I must have misheard. And I began to concentrate again on my notes.

All the morning papers told me I had not misheard. It was true. He was dead. And for the first time in my life I began to cry inconsolably over the loss of someone I didn't even know. Bob's was such a premature, tragic, and, as I would learn, *unnecessary* death. It would haunt me in the decades to come.

A dozen years later, I was introduced to Bob Walker Jr. during rehearsals of two one-act plays, *The Stronger* and *Rope*, which had been booked for a brief run at the Fourth Street Playhouse, a dingy Greenwich Village mini-theater, which charged no admission and for which its actors worked gratis.

Bobby Jr. had already launched a professional career: he was on television in a *Ben Casey* episode and in *The Picture of Dorian Gray*, and he had made an auspicious film debut in MGM's *The Hook*, which coincidentally was produced by William Perlberg and George Seaton, who had been the producer and screenwriter of *The Song of Bernadette*, the 1943 movie in which his mother, Jennifer Jones, had become an instant star and for which she had won an Oscar.

He talked very little about his father. When I showed him old photographs and crumbling clippings, he studied them carefully but insisted that he remembered nothing about those early years.

He told me, "I'm not superstitious, but I do believe in ghosts."

I had always been superstitious but had never believed in ghosts. Never, that is, until I spent seven hours that day with one. For Robert Walker Jr. looked, sounded, and acted just like his father. What had it been like for Jennifer to see him grow up like that, his face before her eyes, his voice in her ears?

It was twilight when we parted on Forty-seventh Street and Third Avenue. I wished Bobby luck and told him that his father would have been very proud of him, and predicted he would become a star.

I vividly recall his parting shot. With a touch of sadness he said, "You seem to know and remember so much more about my dad than I do."

I thought I did. Until I began probing into Bob Walker's and Jennifer Jones's pasts for this book. There was so much I didn't know—so much mystery that engulfed their lives, so much heartbreak. In every way, they were, indeed, star-crossed.

Beverly Linet
New York City

LITTLE
BOY LOST

★──★

*I basically felt inadequate, unwanted, and unloved
since I was born. I was always trying to make an
escape from life. I was an aggressive little character,
but what nobody knew but me was my badness was
only a cover-up for a basic lack of self-confidence, that
I really was more afraid than frightening.*

—ROBERT WALKER

Chapter

1

The first words Robert Walker recalled hearing from his angry mother's lips were "Bad boy!"

The incident that provoked these harsh words was, in retrospect, minor. One morning, when he was still in the skirts little boys wore in the 1920's, he scurried out the kitchen door of the Walkers' home on F Street in Salt Lake City to explore the world outside.

After following the postman for blocks until his legs gave out, Bobby curled up on a local resident's lawn and promptly fell asleep.

The lady of the house spotted the slumbering child. Recognizing him as the Walkers' youngest, she called Zella Walker, who had been oblivious of her baby boy's disappearance, and requested her to come fetch him. Instead of being relieved that her son was safe and in good hands, she was embarrassed and infuriated by Bobby's adventure. As she carried him back to F Street, she repeated as in a chant, "Bad boy, bad, bad boy." To make sure the episode would not happen again, she took her hairbrush in hand, slung Bobby over her lap, and administered what she considered a therapeutic spanking.

The punishment didn't cure his wanderlust. Although Zella Walker took precautions to see that the door was always closed, Bobby usually contrived to find a way to reach the knob and wander off—later to be returned either by a neighbor or by a local policeman. Neither spankings nor scoldings altered his errant ways. It was not Zella's straitlaced fashion to see his actions for what they were—an innocent form of acting out on the part of a little boy starved for the mothering Zella didn't know how to give.

And as he grew older, the defiance grew bolder. Classmates, teachers, neighbors joined his mother in dismissing Bobby as a rebellious and incorrigible brat—little knowing and little caring that they were inflicting wounds from which the vulnerable child would not recover . . . ever.

Decades later, when his life was in a shambles, Bob would publicly admit: "I basically felt inadequate, unwanted, and unloved ever since I was born. I was always trying to make an escape from life."

Robert Hudson Walker's life began at the Salt Lake City Hospital in Utah on October 13, 1918, the night of the Big Fire, when flames scourged the downtown streets and sprayed angry red embers high into the glowing desert sky as far as the Wasatch Mountains which rimmed the city of the Latter Day Saints.

His father, thirty-five-year-old Horace Walker, then city editor of the *Deseret News*, Salt Lake City's leading newspaper, was unable to leave his desk to be with his wife when their fourth child was born. It was only after the fire extra was rolling that he managed to steal a few minutes to call the hospital to inquire about Zella's condition and be informed that she had given birth to a healthy seven-pound son.

He found it difficult to conceal his disappointment. Both he and Zella, then thirty-two, had fervently prayed for a sister for their three sons. Wayne, twelve, had been born a year after the Walkers married; Walter followed two years later. Eight years passed before Dickie came into the world. When, in February, Zella became pregnant again, the couple was confident that the odds favored the child's being a girl. On Horace's salary, a fourth baby was a luxury. Neither Walker had wanted to increase the family any further, although both had come from traditionally large Mormon families themselves.

Zella McQuarrie was from a family of eight—three girls, five boys—and Walkers were sprinkled all over Utah. There were dozens of Walker and McQuarrie cousins, aunts, uncles, and "kissin' kin" spread all over the state—staunch Mormons all.

Zella was a plain girl in her late teens when she met Horace Walker. Even her few living relatives can't provide details of the courtship. Horace was also unprepossessing, but he was innately

intelligent and a good writer. She was determined to marry him, and after a comparatively brief courtship, he proposed. Theirs was a placid if passionless union which lasted until his death at eighty-one on January 13, 1964. Zella survived until July 9, 1976, a month after her ninetieth birthday.

Bobby was less than a month old when the armistice ending World War I was declared, and Horace Walker found himself working overtime as the *Deseret News* was inundated with stories. His sons were almost always asleep when he arrived home at night, and he saw little of them, except on Sundays, when the family, with the exception of the baby, attended church together and later had guests for an early dinner.

Of his elder sons, he favored Walter, a solid student, robust, healthy, and active in sports. Although never overly demonstrative toward any of her children, Zella focused her attention primarily on Dickie, who clung tenaciously to her apron strings as she went about her daily chores. She ran her house efficiently, and Horace allowed her a free hand and bent to her will where the children were concerned.

According to Robert Walker, when Zella first started complaining to her husband about Bobby's willful and unpredictable behavior, Horace merely laughed away his son's escapades with the era's comforting cliché, "Boys will be boys. He'll outgrow it." But when Zella insisted that none of her other sons ever acted like Bob, Horace just shrugged. "By the time he's ready for kindergarten, he'll be just like every other youngster his age."

Bob, however, didn't live up to his father's prediction. After his first day in kindergarten, Zella Walker received a visit from his teacher, who informed her that Bob had caused chaos in the classroom by tormenting several timid little girls.

"First he pulled their hair; then he hugged them so hard they went into hysterics. I was forced to send him to the principal's office. I've seen some pretty wild children in my day, but Bob is totally unmanageable. When asked why he did those things, he just laughed and replied, 'Because I felt like it.' I'm afraid he is going to be quite a problem to us unless you and your husband discipline him severely."

After that, Bob kept his distance from the girls, but he couldn't stay out of trouble. Because he was small for his age and severely

handicapped by bad eyesight, he felt compelled to take on the bigger and stronger kids, provoking fistfights in the playground. Inevitably he came out second-best, but just as inevitably, the black eyes, bloody noses, and bruises he suffered didn't diminish his fighting spirit. His behavior was still showing no improvement when, at age seven, he was enrolled at Lowell Grade School, a short distance from his home. Only his tactics had changed. Aware that he couldn't lick the school's bullies and bad guys, he decided to join up with the worst of them.

He was at school less than a week when he and about a half-dozen of the other "bad" kids bolted from the courtyard during recess and made for the hills. Late that evening, the principal and a posse of teachers uncovered Bob and his gang hiding up in the canyon, dragged them out by their ears, and threatened the boys with expulsion. The next day, Bob ran off again.

In desperation, Horace visited the principal and pleaded for a reprieve for his son. It was undoubtedly Walker's prominent position on the *Deseret News* that kept Bob from being expelled.

Although Walter, whom Bob adored, offered to help him with his homework, Bob showed no interest in his studies. At the end of his first term at Lowell, he came home with a report card bristling with demerits. In addition to black marks in deportment, his grades were disastrously low; he was within a hairbreadth of being held back.

It was about this time that Wayne, seventeen and equally as unhappy at home as Bob, although more adept at concealing his feelings, shocked his family by dropping out of high school and taking a menial job in order to be able to afford to marry the girl he loved.

Even Walter, the brilliant, favored son, was eager to escape from his confining life, but Walter had more practical plans. He would finish high school, enroll in a distant college, study for a law degree, then possibly move to New York where Zella's wealthy sisters, Ann Hatch and Hortense Odlum, had powerful connections. Walter was determined to become a successful man before he'd even consider marriage. He was as stunned as his parents by his older brother's impulsive decision, but kept those feelings to himself.

As for young Bobby, he had nothing but envy for Wayne's new freedom, and yearned to be seventeen and able to do as he pleased.

After Wayne left home, the Walkers were encouraged by an improvement in Bobby's behavior. Although he was still vocal about hating school and continued to get the lowest grades in his class, he stopped playing truant and provoking fistfights in the schoolyard. He ignored his schoolmates, and they, in turn, made no overtures to court his friendship.

Bobby was preoccupied with other matters. At age eight he was seized with an urge to earn his own money. With Horace's help he snagged a *Liberty* magazine subscription route, then, when school recessed for the summer, he pestered his neighbors to hire him to root out dandelions and mow the lawns. He hoarded dimes and quarters with a definite goal. Someday he'd have enough stashed away to make good his escape from F Street.

When he was about nine, an incident occurred which he would always remember with unabated bitterness.

Looking for new fields to conquer, he wandered off to a nearby neighborhood in search of unmowed lawns and unclipped hedges.

He found just what he was looking for in front of the largest house on the block. Spotting the owner about to enter his car, he rushed over and asked breathlessly, "Cut your lawn for fifty cents, sir?"

"Sure, son, if you want to," the man replied as he drove away. So Bobby spent all of a hot Saturday afternoon shoving the heavy mower back and forth across the big lawn until the job was completed to his satisfaction. He then waited for the owner to return, eager for a compliment, hoping for his wages and maybe a tip.

"But," as Bob recalled years later—still angered at the memory—"he never paid me. Not even a dime. I'll never forgive him."

That wealthy, anonymous man did far more damage than just cheating an impressionable child out of a half-dollar: he undermined the boy's trust in people, in "older men" particularly, for decades to come.

When Bob was about eleven, Horace got an offer to join an advertising agency in Ogden, thirty miles down the Union Pacific's main line. Realizing he'd never get rich on a city editor's check, he decided to make the move.

He and Zella found a comfortable brick house at 2504 Eccles Avenue in a respectable neighborhood, enrolled Bob and Dick in Madison Grade School, and settled down in their new home. Walter had by now left to attend George Washington University in Washington, D.C. Later, Horace would leave advertising and join the First Security Bank in Ogden.

No longer encumbered by his reputation as the "bad boy" of Lowell, Bob improved his disposition and grades during his first year at Madison. He was neither an A student nor an angel, but he stayed out of trouble socially and scholastically.

His first acting appearance dates from that year. The school staged a minor operetta, and Bob tried out for and won the lead as the major of a pixie army. Outfitted in a suit of dyed-black underwear with enormous epaulets, he talked-sang and strutted about the stage in what he thought was a terrific performance. He was excited to see his name in print in the Ogden *Standard Examiner*, where his antics were singled out for special mention by Alice West, who worked on the paper's drama desk. At this juncture, the only thing he wanted when he grew up was to be free, to live his life without any binding restrictions.

The summer following the Walkers' move to Ogden, Zella learned that Walter did not plan to return to Utah during his summer break and decided to visit him and show her two younger sons the nation's capital.

The trip east was uneventful, but Walter remembered an incident that occurred the morning after his family's arrival in Washington:

"Mother and I planned to take Bobby and Dickie sightseeing, starting with the Capitol building. Bobby was the first to arise, and after waking Mother and Dickie, insisted that they take off *immediately*. Mother said something about going after breakfast. With that Bobby's hair-trigger temper went into action.

"'I don't want to wait,' he stormed. 'I'm going right now.'

"'No, you're not!' Mother said firmly.

"'I am too!' Bobby screamed. When Mother, who hadn't completed dressing, ignored his demands, Bobby said, 'Okay, then I'll jump out of the window.'

"They were on the fifth floor of the hotel, but within seconds Bobby had bolted over to the window and out onto the ledge,

poised to leap. Mother was petrified, afraid to do or say anything that might result in an accidental fall. Then, just as suddenly as he had hopped on the window ledge, Bobby turned and jumped back into the room.

"Mother was still trembling when I arrived to pick up the family."

Later, when they were alone, Walter asked Bobby, "What in the world possessed you to do a thing like that?"

"'I just felt like it.' He grinned mischievously. What he felt like doing he did. Although Mother had written that he seemed happy in Ogden, that incident indicated that he was still a holy terror, and I kept a close eye on him, and I saw to it that the rest of their tour was not marred by any further misadventures."

Nevertheless, when Zella Walker returned to Ogden, she was forced to face the painful truth that her youngest son's unpredictable moods were more than either she or Horace could understand, much less cope with.

She consulted her sister Hortense McQuarrie Odlum, who, divorced from millionaire Frank Odlum, now headed New York's chic department store Bonwit Teller. Mrs. Odlum, or "Aunt Tenny" as she was known to the family, owned a beautiful summer home in Logan Canyon and the Walkers were frequent visitors.

It was at Aunt Tenny's suggestion, and through her considerable influence, that Zella Walker, though skeptical about "the good of such things," arranged to have Bob see a child psychiatrist practicing at the University of Utah.

Mrs. Walker spent an hour with the doctor, and, the following day, dragged Bobby to the university for a private session. Bobby proved himself an adept actor. Afterward, Zella Walker was assured by the eminent therapist, "The only thing wrong with your son is that he wants to grow up too fast. Nature will take care of that in time."

Bob had been too proud and too private to reveal his feelings of inadequacy, his loneliness, and his desperate need to be loved.

But he *did* indeed want to grow up fast, to be capable of running his life independently of his parents. To Bob, the house on Eccles was a prison from which he dreamed of escaping.

The summer preceding his thirteenth birthday, Bob boarded the train to Salt Lake to visit an old friend named Adrian.

He had earned the fare and one silver dollar for spending money. He kicked around his childhood haunts with Adrian, and they wandered down to the freight yards where they used to watch the trains. A loaded freight was crawling slowly out of the yards, headed for California. "I wonder what California's like?"

"It's wonderful," said Adrian. "I've got a rich brother there. Let's visit him."

In a second they had hopped the iron ladder of a freight car and crawled inside. The train rocked through the mountains and ground to stops at other Utah towns. At each one, the door was furtively pushed open and ragged men climbed in.

Just outside of Las Vegas, Nevada, a flashlight came swinging down the line of cars. The hoboes slipped off into the night and Bob and Adrian closed the door.

But the door slid open. A railroad cop leapt inside and grabbed them by the collars and heaved them off into the cinders. "Beat it, kids," he growled. They slept that night in a city park, padding their thin clothes with newspapers to keep out the biting desert cold. Next day, they went from door to door, getting odd jobs and buying food with their pay. Days later, Bob and Adrian jumped a freight headed back to Salt Lake City and Ogden.

Bob wasn't punished. By now, punishment was useless. He resolved never to yield to temptation again, but that was a hard resolve to keep.

He had another spell of industry and hard work and saved up enough money to buy an old Star touring car on time. That made him a person of consequence at Central Junior High, which he was now attending, but the car was too handy a means of escape when he felt unrest coming on, and pretty soon, after an argument he had with his dad and mother over staying out late, he packed up blankets and food in the car and disappeared again. This time he drove out in the desert and camped, skipping school and getting himself into hot water again. After a painful session with the principal, the Walkers decided something drastic had to be done.

At her wits' end, Zella wrote to her sister Hortense, baring her despair, repeating her decade-long lament, "I simply don't know how to handle him."

Bob's favorite cousin, Barbara Rabe, recalls, "Aunt Tenny, who was very well-to-do and concerned about Bob, decided that the

most practical solution would be to send the young rebel to a military academy, away from Utah. There he would not only receive an excellent high school education, but would be subjected to an impersonal kind of discipline that would shape his character. But the Great Depression was still in full swing, and such schools were beyond the Walkers' means.

"Aunt Tenny, however, insisted that she would be willing to pick up the bills, in addition to supplying Bob with whatever spending money he might need. Aunt Zella was delighted to accept her generosity.

"With the assistance of one of her influential friends in California, Aunt Tenny managed to get Bob admitted to the freshman class of the very prestigious Davis San Diego Army and Navy Academy.

"Bob was always a restless soul. He had this unquenchable craving to get up and go, and from what I can remember, he jumped at the chance to finish his schooling in California."

No freight trains this time! Mrs. Odlum provided him with a first-class ticket to the Coast. He traveled light, since the school provided uniforms modeled after a West Point cadet's, and his "civilian" garments would not be required.

What Bob's well-intentioned aunt and mother had failed to reckon with was that it would take far more than a change of venue and a change of uniform to tame his rebellious soul.

Chapter

2

Bob arrived in San Diego a few weeks before his four-teenth birthday, one of the school's fourteen "rats," as the freshman were known. After some of the glamour of the military ambience had worn off, he began to hate the academy regimen, and he rebelled against having to carry himself like a ramrod and to drill like a wooden soldier.

It was the same old story. He broke rules, talked back to his officer-teachers, was sloppy at drill, neglected his studies, fought with his fellow "rats."

Over and above his bad eyesight and his almost pathetically skinny frame, Bob was also plagued with acne, and his face seemed in constant danger of erupting in a dozen directions. This concatenation of shortcomings, vastly magnified by his teen imag-ination, did nothing to diminish the chip on his shoulder—and he actually began to *court* trouble.

Dining-room regulations called for a new boy to be appointed head of the table each day. As head, it was Bob's duty to super-vise manners at the table; the dishing-out and passing of the food was also his responsibility. Bob kept himself aware of the culinary dislikes of his fellow cadets, and when it was his turn to sit in the chair of command he would see that nobody got what he wanted. If he knew a boy hated potatoes, that is all he would put on his plate. And if the boy complained, Bob suggested that they settle it outside—after the angry one had eaten all of his potatoes.

Yet his language professor, Raymond Ede, now retired, recalls, "Overall, Walker appeared to be a fairly normal kid, although he seemed a bit on the aloof side. He wasn't a man's boy or a boy's

man. He did nothing in athletics, and of course that didn't endear him to too many of the other boys. And the fact that we were a military school gave him lots else to rebel against."

Just when all seemed lost, two fortuitous events intervened to transform Bob—magically—from belligerent outsider to sought-after insider.

Wandering into the school's empty auditorium one afternoon, he saw an uncovered set of snare drums. Idly he picked up a stick, gave a tentative tap, liked the bounce provided by the taut skin, began to experiment with simple rhythms. Before he knew it, he was banging the hell out of the hide—inexpertly, but with an unmistakable beat and, he realized later, an indignation and an abandoned rage he had never been able to express. When he set the sticks down, the sweat was pouring off his face. He felt, he remembered, so good afterward that he decided to master the drums and applied for special lessons. By the end of his first year he was so proficient that bandleader Bill Atkinson assigned Bob to replace a departing cadet as lead drummer.

The following semester, Bob attracted the attention of Atkinson's wife, Virginia, the lone female on the faculty, who taught the drama class. Mrs. Atkinson was the first teacher to recognize the sensitivity and uniqueness dormant beneath Bob's brash exterior.

A warm and affectionate woman who had been with the academy since 1924, she quietly persuaded him to read for a small role in a production she was preparing for her Masque and Wig group. When Bob finished the reading, he anxiously awaited her verdict.

It was totally unexpected. Instead of the minor part for which she had had him in mind, she decided to award him the lead in the tragedy titled *The Other Side*, which she intended as the academy's entry in the annual San Diego high-school dramatic contest.

In January 1935 *The Other Side* won the trophy as Best Play. Cadet Robert Walker received the title of "Best Actor in San Diego County." Suddenly the problem cadet was a hero at the academy. "You will go far in the theater," Mrs. Atkinson predicted. Nevertheless, the inbred insecurities remained. He was convinced that he was not really liked for himself—Robert Hudson Walker—but rather for what he "pretended" to be: an invented character. And

he didn't think he wanted to spend the rest of his life playing make-believe.

Unfortunately, Bob's astonishing aptitude for acting and his perfect performances with the school orchestra didn't extend to his academic work, which he continued to find tedious.

Professor Ede notes, "He couldn't master a foreign language, and I think his absorption with theatricals interfered with his studies. His grades were always quite low, D's and F's, although he was an intelligent boy and certainly could have done better if he had been properly motivated."

Although Bob's band and drama activities had made him a campus celebrity, and thus potentially popular, he remained aloof from the other cadets—with one notable exception. In the person of Creighton Horton he found a close friend and roomed with him in 1935, and then again in 1936, when the academy moved to nearby Carlsbad, California.

Creighton's parents, Chelta and Meade (a successful insurance executive), were not unlike Zella and Horace: reserved and undemonstrative Mormons. Creighton had taken an instant liking to Bob, who, in turn, admired his intelligence and was flattered by the fact that the handsomest boy at the academy showed such interest in him and his life.

On the surface, the two were an odd couple: Creighton, so studious, serious, and confident about what he wanted to do with his life, which was to go on to a good college, study medicine, and become an internist; and Bob, still floundering and confused. Yet Creighton, like Mrs. Atkinson, was aware of the sensitivity and goodness in Bob and was genuinely impressed by his talent.

"I wish I could be just like you," Bob confided after lights-out one night.

"Don't sell yourself short," Creighton chided. "You've got more going for you than you think."

Mrs. Atkinson continued to nurture Bob's dramatic talent. When it came time to choose a one-act play for the annual high-school competition again in 1936, she selected a grim drama titled *Just 'Til Morning*, based on its author's actual experience in a state prison. It was the story of two embittered criminals who shed their veneer of hardness to pray on their knees for the life of the older

convict's little son, near death in a hospital. Mrs. Atkinson cast Bob in the lead role of Chick Dugan, and though the play itself lost the competition by one point, Bob tied with one Jose Orozco, a youth from San Diego, as Best Actor, and, to his amazement, was offered a scholarship at the prestigious Pasadena Playhouse to continue his dramatic training after his graduation from the academy.

He was, in his own words, "flabbergasted" by the unexpected offer. In addition to the lift to his ego, the scholarship would enable him to remain in California for two additional years, without depending on Aunt Tenny for support.

He and Creighton eagerly looked forward to graduation: Bob was to be featured in the orchestra as well as the floor show at the senior prom. After the Easter holidays, however, he plummeted to earth with a thud.

Professor Ede recalls, "Because of his constant D's and F's, the faculty decided it couldn't permit him to graduate. He would have to repeat his senior year with passing grades. We had warned him repeatedly to pay more attention to his studies. He was an intelligent young man with the ability to learn his lines in a play perfectly and the notes of his sheet music; there was no logical reason he couldn't master math or history—if he had only set his mind to it."

When Bob heard the disheartening news, his immediate reaction was to take off, but he didn't want to disgrace himself any further. He sent word to the Pasadena Playhouse that he would be unable to attend the following fall and received a letter back that the scholarship would be waiting for him the following year.

Bob was seized by a fit of depression as he watched his fellow cadets receive their diplomas on graduation day. He was heartsick when he was forced to say good-bye to Creighton, who promised to keep in touch and prophesied that "One day I'll be proud to tell my friends that I knew that great Broadway star Robert Walker."

Bob smiled wanly. When Creighton returned to Los Angeles, Bob was desolate, thinking: What's the point of becoming close to anyone? It hurts so much when you lose them.

Reluctantly he returned to Utah for the summer to face Zella's unconcealed disappointment and Horace's indifference, but this time determined to study. He had obligations to Aunt Tenny and

Virginia Atkinson to fulfill, and he was determined not to disappoint them again. He finally had his motivation—and it paid off.

Bob's grades improved the next year. He started getting B's and C's in contrast to the previous D's and F's. Far more astonishing than that, however, was the fact that the new group of seniors voted him their class president, the last thing he ever expected.

When he wrote home, his father, Horace, still very much the newspaperman at heart, phoned the Ogden *Examiner*, and on October 7 Ogdenites read the short piece that made the local news:

PRESIDENT VOTED TO ROBERT WALKER

Cadet Corp. Robert Walker, son of Mr. and Mrs. H. H. Walker of 2504 Eccles, Ogden, has been elected president of the senior class for the year of 1936–37 of the Army and Navy Military Academy, Carlsbad, Calif. Walker has also been elected president of the drama department of the same institution.

Following the Christmas vacation, Mrs. Atkinson began rehearsals on the play she had chosen for the annual competition. It was called *I Am a Jew.* Even by 1937, those four short words bespoke yellow armbands and ruthless segregation into cramped ghettos. The lead as a Jewish scientist in a play so charged with the high emotions of the era was a role in which the young actor could make either an ass of himself or a hero. Bob's performance was, said a reviewer, "stunning"—and once again the judges awarded first prize to the academy, and the Best Actor medal to now-Cadet Captain Robert Walker.

With his graduation assured, Bob became undecided about accepting Pasadena Playhouse's offer of a scholarship. When he wrote to Aunt Tenny for advice, she replied that in spite of the excellent reputation of the Playhouse, she had other—and even more ambitious—plans for him.

She wanted Bob in New York, where she could keep an eye on his progress. Walt and Dick, who had moved to New York to start classes at Columbia University, shared an apartment at 2 Beekman Place and had agreed to make room for him if he accepted Aunt Tenny's offer to finance his tuition at the American Academy of Dramatic Arts, home of such distinguished graduates as Spencer

Tracy and Ruth Gordon (and later Robert Redford, Lauren Bacall, and Grace Kelly).

Bob discussed the alternatives with Virginia Atkinson, who urged, "By all means go to New York. The exposure to live theater will prove invaluable—and the Academy courses are the best to be had."

So the Academy it was to be—if they accepted him.

When Bob arrived at Grand Central Station in early October, Walter was at the arrival gate, eager to show his kid brother the sights of the great city before Bob settled down to work on his audition scene, a recitation from a one-act prison play called *Allison's Lad*.

In spite of his honors at military school and the fact that the American Academy was in dire need of male students—there were seventy-five would-be actresses applying for the junior year, in contrast to a meager thirty-nine men—Bob still had to pass muster with the Academy's faculty before gaining admission. On October 18, five days after his nineteenth birthday, he faced the ordeal.

After he completed his audition scene, his judges noted that "his reading was very intelligent; he had a sensitive and pleasing personality, a fairly good voice, good stage presence, and a definite dramatic flair," concluding: "a fine boy of ability, good juvenile type, should develop fully."

His classes in the Carnegie Hall Building on West Fifty-seventh Street began the following week and Bob was caught up in a whirlwind of stimulating activity.

In addition to acting, there were speech courses, voice lessons, improvisation, body control, dancing, fencing, breathing exercises, makeup, and a course in the interpretation both of drama and of "dramatis personae."

The classrooms were scattered all over the building, and the students would jam the elevators to get from one to another. Below, in the basement, was a small auditorium where students could practice scenes with one another and where the end-of-semester plays were performed. The entire setup was under the control of Charles Jehlinger, general stage director and director of instruction.

With such an imbalance between boys and girls, there was terrific competition among the young ladies for the attention of the

male students. The girls were often forced to choose "unisex" practice scenes. The boys, of course, had their choice of the prettiest and best actresses with whom to work.

Diana Blythe, a Barrymore and, like her father, John, an outrageous flirt, could and did get any boy she wanted—much to the envy of her female classmates. However, she completely ignored Bob Walker, who was definitely not her type. Bob was unable to keep track of the number of girls with whom he practiced, but he found none of them even remotely interesting.

On some mornings, rushing to catch the elevator, he'd notice a tall, dark-haired, big-eyed beauty, usually accompanied by a cute red-haired ingenue. She was in none of his classes, and often he wouldn't catch sight of her again for weeks. Nevertheless, he couldn't get her out of his mind.

One afternoon, just prior to the Christmas break, he wandered down to the basement auditorium, where he spotted the girl rehearsing a scene with another youth. He sat mesmerized in the back row until it was time for him to return to one of his own classes.

He daydreamed of her throughout the holidays, meeting her in his fantasies in any number of romantic ways.

But when he returned to the Academy on January 2, 1938, he saw her again in a small corridor, summoned all his nerve, approached her, and, with an appealing grin, said, "I've seen you perform. Gosh, you're a wonderful actress. I'd love to work on some scene with you—if you're not tied up.

"My name is Robert Walker."

"I'm Phylis Isley," she replied.

It began as simply as that.

"PHYL"—
A LOVE STORY

We were both in love with acting and were mutually attracted. I was only nineteen but even then I knew there could never be anyone else. I didn't consider myself "good enough" for her. She made me want to be somebody. We were happy. Or at least I thought we were.

—ROBERT WALKER

Chapter

3

If Phylis Lee Isley wasn't literally born in a trunk, she *was* born into an atmosphere of trunks, touring, greasepaint, and all the accoutrements of third-rate show business.

Phylis was the only child of Flora Mae Suber and Philip Isley, and her earliest memories were of traveling with her parents, owners of the Isley Stock Company, a summer tent show that made the rounds of rural communities in the South Central states.

Admission was a dime, and the play was often complemented by a film—pleasant diversion for entertainment-starved customers.

Acting was always in Philip Isley's blood. As a bachelor he had had dreams of conquering Broadway, which never materialized. Flora Mae, known as "Dolly," worked in an office that booked tent shows. After their marriage, Phil started his own stock company, which enabled him to alternate a comedy and a drama with the leading man's role tailored to *his* talents. Flora Mae was often called upon to appear as his leading lady. The rest of the company consisted of stage veterans grateful for their twenty-five-dollar-a-week salaries. Phil even put his mother, Flora Belle Isley King, to work—as cashier.

Phil Isley added to his income by operating a movie theater in his home town during the winter months and was therefore in Tulsa when his daughter, Phylis Lee, was born on Sunday, March 2, 1919.

Phylis was always well-behaved, obedient, and often lost in a world of her own making. An extremely beautiful child, with huge dark eyes and wavy dark hair, she'd blush furiously whenever members of the company made a fuss over her.

Yet, when she was only six, she blithely informed her parents that she intended "to become a great actress when I grow up." Neither of them was surprised or alarmed.

In September 1925, after a summer on the road, the Isleys moved to Oklahoma City and Phylis entered Edgemere Public School. School, however, was just something to endure until tent-show time began again.

By the time Phylis was ten, she was working as the company's ticket taker and candy seller. Phil wasn't trying to save on staff, but was hopeful the experience would help his daughter become less shy and easier around people.

That was the summer preceding the Wall Street crash and the great depression which followed. Business was booming along the Isley circuit, but although Phil Isley did not deny his wife and daughter any necessary comforts, he banked the bulk of his profits with an eye toward the future.

He was determined that his family have a pleasant home, his daughter a good education, and that he'd never end up—as did so many actors in his company—sleeping in fleabag hotels located along the tracks.

Consequently, on the Wednesday following Black Tuesday of October 29, 1929, when Phil Isley picked up the copy of *Variety* which whimsically noted the crash with the headline "WALL STREET LAYS EGG," his main interest was with the town-by-town movie grosses and the latest developments in "talkies," which were by now proving to be more than just a passing fancy. Although the major studios controlled the movie palaces, there were many smaller houses throughout the Southwest that were still not equipped for sound. Isley dreamed of controlling his own mini-chain of theaters—and ironically, the Depression helped make that dream come true. Theater owners, bankrupt because of bad investments or in desperate need of cash, searched for buyers. Isley had the cash necessary to purchase the theaters and to install sound equipment. Within a few years he became one of the most suc-cessful movie-house operators in the Oklahoma-Texas area.

Although the theme song of the period was "Brother, Can You Spare a Dime?" he didn't lack for patrons who could spare a dime to lose themselves and forget their problems for three hours watch-

ing a double feature, a couple of cartoons, and a newsreel at an Isley theater.

Twelve-year-old Phylis was fascinated by talking pictures, and her parents continued to encourage her interest in acting. Each time she'd return from a movie, she'd ape the mannerisms and inflections of its leading lady. She was particularly taken by Sylvia Sidney and studied her intense manner, her low, throaty voice and lingering look. "Some kind people said I looked like Sylvia Sidney, so I guess all that wistful business, the lost quality—so effective in *Street Scene* and *An American Tragedy*—really works," she'd later say.

(It's ironic to note that during the time Phylis was emulating Sylvia Sidney, who was eight years her senior, the "wistful" Miss Sidney was damaging the long time marriage of Paramount chief B. P. Schulberg—according to Schulberg's son, Budd—and that Schulberg was the man who, in 1928, had hired a twenty-five-year-old whiz kid named David O. Selznick to serve as a major producer and eventually his executive assistant at Paramount Studios.)

Phylis was less interested in the actors she saw perform on the screen, had no dreamy schoolgirl crushes on male movie stars, nor for that matter on any of her male schoolmates. After dinner, homework completed, she'd lose herself in a book or read a play, her favorite being Rudolph Besler's *The Barretts of Wimpole Street*, the love story of poets Robert Browning and Elizabeth Moulton Barrett, which the legendary Katharine Cornell both produced and starred in in 1931. In time, Phylis knew every line by heart and entertained dreams of playing the role herself some-day—after she had become a great actress. There was no doubt in her mind that she would become one.

Phil Isley continued to prosper. When Phylis graduated from grade school, she enrolled at Monte Cassino Junior College, a private school of the Benedictine Sisters in Tulsa. It was at Monte Cassino that Phylis began to emerge from her shell and form close ties with girls her own age. Two of her closest friends were Mary Birmingham and Ruth Bowers.

Together with a few other students, they formed an intimate

club called the Toppers, and Mary Birmingham recalls that Phylis "cared little about social events. Whenever she went out with us she was always the most popular, but she didn't care for anything but acting. When the other girls daydreamed about the future, most of them agreed that they'd get married when they were twenty-five.

"'Not me,' Phyl would break in. 'I'm going to wait until I'm thirty-five!'"

With her theatrical background, no one was surprised that Phyl was almost always cast in the lead in the school plays. She was so effective in one such play, the title long since forgotten, that, in a scene where she was supposed to take poison, she played it so realistically that some youngsters actually jumped from their seats shouting, "Don't let her do it—don't let her!" When the curtain fell, they were sure she was dead. Phyl was also popular among the teachers at Monte Cassino—always punctual, up on her grades, never requiring stern discipline or lectures.

Her favorite teacher was her French instructor, Marie Giel Barrett, who'd later remember being invited to the Isleys' Tulsa home at 301 East Twentieth Street, where Jennifer would perform for her—on a bench under an elm in the backyard. No one had more faith in her future than this French teacher, who would recall her work as being "inspired."

The years at Monte Cassino flew by. Although much of Oklahoma was now strangled in the grip of the Depression, with farmers losing land and livestock to the beat of the auctioneer's gavel, and jobless city residents wondering where next month's rent would come from, the Isleys were personally immune to the chaos surrounding them. They were aware of it, though. The girls at Monte Cassino contributed money from their allowances for the holiday baskets which the Benedictine sisters distributed to the "less fortunate."

By the spring of 1936, Phylis had developed into a lithe five-foot-eight beauty, and Phil Isley, convinced his daughter was ready for Hollywood movies, offered to get her a start through his industry connections. However, he couldn't resist her pleas for tuition to Northwestern University outside Chicago. Northwestern was reputed to have the best drama department of any college in the country, and Phylis felt she still had a great deal to learn about her

intended profession. Her close friend Ruth Bowers opted for the University of Texas, and she recalls that although both were sad about the impending separation, they vowed they'd remain "best friends forever" and see each other during vacations.

Another of Ruth's fond recollections centers around the period shortly before graduation. Phyl was chosen May Queen for her class, but rather than feeling joy about the honor, she told Ruth, "This is silly. I don't want it. You should be queen." She couldn't dissuade the judges from their selection, so she attended the ceremony resplendent in a white satin gown with an Elizabethan collar, while Ruth sat beaming at her side as "one of the court."

Phyl, however, got her way when she was offered the honor of becoming valedictorian. "No," she said firmly. "Let Mary [Birmingham] do it. I'm doing so many things already."

When Phylis entered Northwestern as a drama major in the autumn of 1936, she quickly discovered that her tent-show background put her light-years ahead of her fellow freshmen, most of whom were starry-eyed novices—an advantage which did not sit well with the other girls in her class.

The Northwestern experience was not an altogether happy one. The nonacting courses, mandatory for a B.A., bored her. She found no one with whom she could duplicate the rapport she had had with Ruth Bowers and Mary Birmingham. She missed her friends and family and often wondered if she shouldn't have followed her father's advice and gone to Hollywood to pursue a professional career in films. Her dream, however, was to become a great *stage* actress—so she endured the boredom . . . and the loneliness.

Although determined not to become romantically involved with anyone, she found herself impressed by a handsome blond male drama student, Andy McBroom. (McBroom would later achieve a modest success at Universal Pictures under the name of David Bruce.) McBroom was enchanted by Phylis, she was fond of him, and his companionship helped relieve feelings of isolation.

Shortly after Thanksgiving, Phil Isley phoned to tell Phylis not to plan on returning to Tulsa for the Christmas break. Since he had business meetings in New York in connection with his theaters, he and Dolly had decided to pick Phylis up in Chicago and take her east with them—"so you can see your precious Broadway at last."

Phyl was dazzled by New York. Despite the Depression, the

theater was booming. Years later, she'd recall the thrill of seeing Ruth Draper's name in brilliant lights above a marquee—Miss Draper was starring in a one-woman show—and the excitement of watching Katharine Cornell (her Elizabeth Barrett Browning) in Maxwell Anderson's *Wingless Victory*. In that play, the first lady of the theater played a Malay princess, and although Brooks Atkinson would later write in his book *Broadway* that Cornell "looked and behaved like a cultivated American," to Phyl her performance was sheer magic—so much so that Phyl would later admit that she had attended five performances of the show during her short stay in New York, but had lacked the courage to try to get backstage to meet her idol. Instead, she wrote her first fan letter, one in which she also asked for advice on how to become a great actress.

Miss Cornell's reply was short—and pointed:

"There's only one way to become a great actress and that's never to give up trying to be one."

By the time Phylis returned to Northwestern for the spring semester, she had decided to leave college at the end of the term and seek admission to the American Academy of Dramatic Arts in New York, where she could concentrate exclusively on acting.

She told her family of her plans when she came home for the Easter break. Isley, aware of the Academy's prestige, agreed to foot the bills for both tuition and a respectable place to live, adding, "You may turn out to be an actress, but you're not going to be a bohemian."

Ruth Bowers was also back in Tulsa for Easter, and she and Phylis were inseparable. Later Ruth recalled that "Phyl was on fire with enthusiasm, and when she discovered I had two additional vacation days, she deliberately missed her train so we'd be able to drive out to the country for a long excursion together."

The girls had no idea when they'd be seeing one another again. Phil had already made plans for his daughter's summer. He had backed a stock company run by Richard Mansfield Dickinson, a well-known drama coach, and arranged for Phylis to be hired as the Mansfield Players' young leading lady. She, in turn, had extolled the talents of young Andrew McBroom, who joined the group as its juvenile.

Phylis worked diligently during that Southwest tour of the Mansfield Players in a repertory that included *Smilin' Through*,

The Family Upstairs, and *This Thing Called Love*, admission thirty-five cents. She knew how valuable the experience would be when she tested for admission to the Academy. Classes were not due to begin until late October, but the Isleys came to New York after Labor Day to investigate suitable lodgings. They decided upon the Barbizon Hotel for Women, located on East Sixty-third Street and Lexington Avenue. Its rooms were scarcely larger than closets, but the hotel was within walking distance of the Academy and the protection it offered more than made up for the cramped quarters. Men were not permitted beyond the lobby.

On September 10, 1937, Phylis underwent her "evaluation" audition. She shrewdly selected a poignant scene from *Wingless Victory*.

The staff's appraisal was that she was "promising" in the areas of spontaneity, versatility, distinction, and pantomime: "has attractive personality, a good stage presence, an above-average voice, a sensitive temperament, and definite dramatic instinct."

Their summation concluded: "A fine girl of ability, intelligence, and sensitivity—should do something worthwhile."

Once classes began, Phylis devoted herself passionately to her studies. Within a few days she became acquainted with a cute little redhead in her group named Estees Potter; within a few weeks the two had become devoted friends, sharing confidences and ambitions, spending weekends exploring the city or taking in a show. Broadway was buzzing that fall of 1937, the marquees lit up with such hits as *Golden Boy*, *Of Mice and Men*, *Amphitryon 38*, starring the celebrated Alfred Lunt and Lynn Fontanne, and John Gielgud portraying Shakespeare's Richard II. (It's unlikely that in her wildest dreams she could foresee the day when she'd be receiving star billing over *him*—as she would in MGM's *The Barretts of Wimpole Street*.)

For the first time in her young life, Phylis did not look forward to the Christmas holidays; they were an intrusion. She wanted to keep on working—and growing.

She eagerly returned to the Academy on January 2. Early that afternoon she was approached by a gangly youth with an appealing grin, who said, "I've seen you perform. Gosh, you're a wonderful actress. I'd love to work on some scenes with you—if you're not tied up. My name is Bob Walker."

Chapter

4

By the time Phyl celebrated her nineteenth birthday—
two months after their initial meeting—she and Bob were vir-
tually inseparable.

He had saved enough from his allowance to send her flowers
and denied himself lunch so he could afford to take her for a
decent dinner.

Both were constantly on the lookout for scenes to do together
and, after formal classes, hurried down to the small auditorium
located in the basement of the Academy to rehearse—lost in their
work and one another.

Actress Augusta Dabney, the former wife of Kevin McCarthy
and presently Mrs. William Prince, recalls:

"To my regret I never got to know either Bob Walker or Phylis
Isley in our junior class, but in every class there's a student or two
destined for stardom and there was a great deal of favorable talk
about their ability, and talk, too, that they were very much in love.
One afternoon, after I had finished with my lessons, I went down
to the auditorium and sat in the shadows to watch them work.
There was no doubt about it, they *were* special. There was a
quality in their work which was beautiful to behold."

Actor Don Keefer, another junior, also retains memories of his
AADA days:

"We were all off in different groups. Whom you met and
worked with depended entirely upon what group you were in.
Phylis was in my group and we did scenes together early in the
term. All kinds of scenes. In one she even played my *mother*. Even
at that age she had a technique which surpassed the other students.
She was well *above* the rest of us.

"Once she met Bob, she worked exclusively with Bob. They were totally inseparable, two terribly enthusiastic kids. I didn't think of it as love, but I was such a child myself, what did I know about love? None of the rest of us were romantically inclined; it was a very innocent time.

"I thought it was their ambition, high intellect, and talent that formed the bond between them. She was a leading lady and seemed very womanly and older. He seemed terribly boyish—that was part of his charm. Just looking at Phylis' great beauty and maturity made me think of her becoming interested in and marrying an older man when the time came."

Most evenings they would stop for a hamburger (which Phyl favored) and a glass of milk (she never touched coffee), then slowly stroll uptown to the Barbizon, where, under the watchful eye of the desk clerk, they'd say good night, until the next day.

Then he'd walk the near-mile back to Beekman Place in order to save bus fare.

His brother Walt remembered "suddenly seeing a radical change in Bob's demeanor. Always a sort of casual dresser, he began to take endless pains with his clothes, began laboring with his hair.

"Finally, I asked him, 'Okay, who is she?'

"Bob remained mum, but I kept teasing him. I knew there was *someone,* and envisioned something very blond and vaguely hussy-ish.

"Finally Bob broke down and admitted her name was 'Phylis Isley and she's beautiful, eyes like . . . I don't know. You can't describe Phyl.' Then he started rhapsodizing about her acting, and after that we couldn't shut him up. But he was reluctant to bring her to the apartment and was evasive when I suggested he and his girl join Dick and me at some classy restaurant. Finally I stopped asking, figuring we'd meet this mystery girl eventually—if the relationship lasted."

Although he was always on his best behavior with Phyl, Bob was disturbed about his strong feelings. He was a nineteen-year-old kid without a dime, and in less than two months he was positive he wanted to spend his life with her. Yet he was in no position to support himself, much less a wife, and agonized as to whether she'd be patient and willing to wait until he was.

Whenever he dropped Phyl off at the Barbizon, he'd see attractive young men of obvious means escorting their dates home, and began to see *every* attractive young man as a potential threat, though Phyl had assured him she wasn't interested in seeing anyone else or going to fancy places or parties.

So they continued going out on the cheapest of dates: a fifteen-cent local movie—or to one of the posh Broadway movie palaces where admission was a quarter before noon. Occasionally they'd splurge fifty-five cents to buy a ticket for a play, and whatever theater they'd attend, they'd look at the stage and think: Someday *we'll* be up there.

When spring arrived they'd take long walks in Central Park, as safe as one's own living room at the time. Bob would later recall, "We never seemed to run out of things to talk about."

A subject that occupied a great deal of their conversation was their presentation of acting excerpts to be performed before Charles Jehlinger and members of the faculty, which would determine whether they'd be invited back for a second year at the Academy.

Aware of Phyl's passion for *The Barretts of Wimpole Street*, Bob went along with that choice, although physically and vocally he was a most unlikely Robert Browning. The two worked on their scenes until they were letter-perfect.

Bob later remembered that he was "scared to death on the day of the exam." He was certain Phyl would be wonderful and invited back, but he was unsure of his own performance. When it was over, "Jelly" Jehlinger came backstage and tore Bob's performance into little pieces. He pointed out every flaw, told Bob he'd have to develop.

"You haven't enough strength. You've got to get guts." It seemed obvious from his ruthless commentary that Bob would not be back for the senior year.

Bob left his dressing room totally dejected. When he received congratulations from a member of the faculty, he blurted out Jehlinger's reaction. The teacher just laughed.

"Do you want to know something? Jelly thinks you're one of the most talented students here, and so do I. Don't you know that the ones he murders most are the ones he likes best?"

Bob thought the woman was being kind, but the following morning the bid to return to the Academy was in his mailbox.

Phylis received an identical bid.

The first person to be called was Aunt Tenny. She was delighted, though not surprised by the news, and reaffirmed that her gesture to sponsor him at the Academy was for the complete two-year course. She offered him a check for the round trip home to Ogden for the summer.

He had already decided, however, to remain in New York and try to find a job that would provide him with money of his own.

He dreaded the coming summer. Phylis' father had booked her for another season in stock, and to Bob the thought of the impending separation was painful and depressing. The only way he felt he could endure it was by keeping busy.

He tried to be cheerful when he escorted Phyl to Pennsylvania Station, assuring her and himself that the summer would fly by. He was, however, miserable and insecure. What if he couldn't find a job? What if Phyl was swept off her feet by an attractive young man in the stock company or came to the realization that he had nothing really to offer her?

Walt Walker remembered Bob's return to Beekman Place, "lost and confused, unable to eat, and too restless to sleep.

"'Oh, come on, kid,' I told him, 'no girl is that great to get sick over. Besides, she hasn't gone to China to become a missionary. She'll be back in the fall.' But he was—irrationally, I thought—beyond consolation."

Bob spent the next few weeks wandering around the city looking for a job, any job. One afternoon he stopped by Walgreen's drugstore, an actors' hangout in midtown, to inquire if they needed an extra counterboy. Unfortunately, quite a number of young, hungry would-be actors had had the same idea long before he did; there were no openings of any kind.

He was sipping a cup of coffee, reading the "help-wanted" ads, when he was approached by a personable young man who said, "My name is William Bowers and I'm a playwright. My show is about to go into rehearsal, and my friends and I were wondering if you were an actor."

Bob surveyed Bowers coldly. He had heard all the stories about

young actors or models being approached by strangers with a pitch that was a prelude to a proposition.

"So what if I am?" he replied.

"How would you like to read for a part? We've been looking for someone your type—thin and sensitive—to play a college student. And no one who has read has been suitable."

Bob turned back to his paper. "Get lost," he said.

Bowers recalls, "I was shocked at the brusque attitude, but I pressed the matter. When I was still unable to convince Walker I wasn't a phony, I suggested he follow my friends and me out of the drugstore. If we didn't go into the stage door of a theater, Bob could keep walking. If we did, he could come in, and we'd discuss the matter further. Reluctantly Bob agreed, and that's how it was done."

Bowers, who later became a well-known Hollywood screenwriter, did indeed have a college play titled *Where Do We Go from Here?*, which, if it survived the mandatory out-of-town tryouts, was due to open on Broadway in late fall. One of the men with him was Dwight Taylor, the producer's casting director.

Bob was given a copy of the script, asked to do a cold reading of the part, and breezed through it. The fact that he had neither an agent nor an Actor's Equity card didn't seem to faze Bowers or Taylor. Getting the role meant he was eligible for Equity; Taylor assured him the salary scale was the same offered to Equity members with *agents*, and that, once he was seen on Broadway, every "flesh peddler" in town would be clamoring to sign him.

Bob was dazed by the sudden turn of events. *Where Do We Go from Here?* was no *You Can't Take It with You*, but it was a cheerful comedy, lots better than a great many he had seen or read, and even if it had only a moderate run, he'd be able to save enough to ask Phyl to marry him. It seemed too good to be true. He couldn't shake the feeling that it would all blow up in his face. He didn't rush to the phone to break the good news to Aunt Tenny or his family in Ogden. He didn't even tell Walt or Dick when he returned to Beekman Place. He wanted to wait until he was well into the role before making any announcements, and then he wanted Phyl to be the first to know.

Unfortunately, his lucky break turned into a heartbreaker.

According to Equity rules, an actor—star and bit player alike—

could be replaced in a role anytime within five days of the rehearsal period, without the producer being forced to pay him "run-of-the-play" compensation.

On the crucial fifth day, Bob was called aside by his director.

"Look, kid," he said, "you're giving a fine performance, but we've decided the role would come off a great deal funnier if it was rewritten for a fat guy. Don't let this get you down. You're a fine actor, and you're going to have a great future if you just stick with it. You're not the first actor this has happened to. God knows you won't be the last."

The play's title turned out to be ironically prophetic. After leaving the theater, grateful that he didn't have to face sympathetic farewells from the other members of the cast, he wandered the streets aimlessly wondering "Where the hell do I go from here?" He passed Carnegie Hall and decided that he never wanted to see the Academy again. What good was all the training in the world if—on a whim—someone decided he wanted "fat," not "thin"? He hated New York, the theater, and acting. He loved Phyl but felt unworthy of her.

He didn't want to talk to Aunt Tenny or his brothers, nor did he want to return to Ogden. He just wanted to disappear and never be seen or heard of again.

Having nothing to do with himself, he struck out crosstown to the Hudson River docks to work off his anger and frustration. As he later recalled, he stepped into a ramshackle diner for a cup of coffee and overheard a conversation between two longshoremen which revealed that the United Fruit Company was still short of manual workers for their banana boats. He found the address in a local directory, applied for a job, and although he'd never be specific as to how a skinny, inexperienced kid managed to persuade the personnel department to hire him, he was signed on as a general helper aboard the SS *Pastore*.

Aunt Tenny, Walt, and Dick were stunned by what they considered a rash decision, but he was determined to go through with it.

"Maybe I'll be gone two months, maybe two years," he said defiantly.

"Maybe you'll grow up," Walt replied angrily. "And just how do you think your girl will feel about this?"

"She'll be better off without a born loser" was Bob's only comment.

The SS *Pastore* carried bananas as her main cargo. She stopped at all the Central American banana ports and loaded on the gargantuan green bunches, stowed them in the hold, and then cruised her way north through the Gulf of Mexico and up the Atlantic Coast back to New York.

In addition to the drab and dirty jobs such as cleaning the engine room, polishing brass, painting, and helping in the galley, there were times when Bob had to descend into the inky hold to check the temperature and see to it that the cargo was in good condition and riding well.

He spent his free time reading or writing letters to Phylis—some mailed, some not—and she was thoroughly bewildered over this turn of events and deeply disturbed by hints that he might not return to the Academy.

Bob made four voyages to Central America and back, exposed to the seamy side of life, before deciding to chuck the whole thing. The fact that Phylis was due back from Tulsa obviously had a great deal to do with his decision, but he was still determined not to return to the Academy.

He headed back to Walt's Beekman Place apartment, muttering fiercely, "The only way to be an actor is to act."

Although Walt didn't throw him out bodily, he made it clear to Bob he could remain only until he was able to find a place of his own, and suggested he try the YMCA. Aunt Tenny, also angered by what she considered Bob's defiance and lack of gratitude and common sense, let it be known she was cutting off future financial assistance.

Bob had saved most of his seaman's pay, but without a job or family subsidy, he knew he couldn't get by for more than a couple of months.

He pored through the rooms-for-rent and employment ads until a specific one caught his eye.

"Wallace Cooperative Lodge. Inexpensive room and board for young men. Apply YMCA." Bob headed for the Y, explained his situation, and was referred to a remote address in Yonkers, New York.

The "Lodge" was in reality a rambling old building which oper-

ated on the principle "No work, no food." For fifty cents a day, its boarders were provided with tiny rooms furnished with a cot and a dresser. "Work" involved washing dishes, tending the lawn, and doing whatever odd jobs were necessary to keep the ancient building in condition. Dinner usually consisted of ground beef and potatoes; chicken on Sunday. Bob, however, was rarely home for dinner.

When he'd completed the morning chores, he'd dash for a trolley car, then switch to the IRT subway line for the tedious ride to midtown Manhattan, where he tackled the business offices of all the eatery chains—Horn and Hardart, Child's, Schrafft's—where he felt he could land an evening job that didn't require any skill, experience, or training. But, as he should have learned from his earlier experience at Walgreen's, dozens of other young actors and actresses had the same idea.

It was still a Depression year in 1938, and even the lowliest of part-time jobs was almost impossible to get.

Actually, Bob was marking time until Phylis returned from Tulsa. He had written her that he had moved to the Wallace Co-op but deliberately avoided mentioning he would not be returning to the Academy. He wanted to break that news personally—at the right time, in the right place.

He was at Penn Station when her train pulled in, and they cabbed to the Barbizon together. He waited in the lobby while she checked in and unpacked; then they strolled over to Central Park to catch up with each other.

He anticipated her surprise; he even hoped she'd express some disappointment, but never did he expect her reaction, immediate and firm:

"If you're not going back, I'm not going back either. We'll just make the rounds together and see what happens."

When Phyl phoned home the following morning to explain her sudden change of plans, the Isleys took the news philosophically. They insisted she remain at the Barbizon, however, and continue to accept a regular weekly allowance to cover all her general expenses. Mr. Isley was still determined that his daughter would not "become a bohemian."

So Phyl and Bob tackled Broadway as a team, touring the heartless agencies and casting offices all day, leaving résumés and photographs, bravely facing rejection after rejection.

Then they heard of the Cherry Lane Theater down in Greenwich Village, run by one Paul Gilmore, who had worked on Broadway as an actor, director, and producer a decade earlier with little success before starting his own little playhouse, both to keep busy and to give budding performers a chance to be seen.

The Cherry Lane had acquired a good reputation in spite of its antiquated appearance. The stairs were rickety, the stageboards creaked, and backstage, rats and mice kept house—and multiplied. It was a non-Equity showcase, and the actors were paid fifty cents a performance for appearing in such revivals as *Springtime for Henry* and *Three Men on a Horse*. However, all Phylis and Bob cared about was the fact that they were working together; their sparse audiences liked them and there was always the possibility that an important agent or producer might come down, be impressed, and open all the right doors.

None did.

Phil and Flora Mae came east in mid-autumn with a twofold purpose: they wanted to meet the young man about whom their little girl had spoken so glowingly and they wanted to see her perform on a New York stage.

Having operated tent shows and acted in them, Phil should have been immune to tacky small-time theater. Nevertheless, he and Flora Mae shuddered at the dingy conditions in which his daughter was working. Of his initial meeting with Phylis' parents, the only detail Bob would vividly remember Isley saying to him was, "Now, you make sure Phylis gets home safe every night," and his replying, "But I do, sir, always."

On the way back to Tulsa, the Isleys decided something had to be done about the situation. They wanted Phylis out of Greenwich Village and away from the young man who, though ingratiating and a capable-enough young actor, seemed in no position to offer their daughter much of a future.

Isley realized he had to act cautiously and subtly. A close friend of his who operated the Mutual radio station, KOME, had been mulling over the possibility of presenting a Sunday afternoon half-hour show, and it took little arm-twisting to persuade him that Phyl, whom he had used in the past, would be an ideal leading lady.

The offer was dispatched to New York. She'd receive twenty-five

dollars a week, with the added inducement that the program would be tagged *The Phylis Isley Radio Theater*, and she would have a say in selecting her own material. It was an irresistible offer, but one Phylis strongly resisted *unless* Bob Walker was part of the package, at the same salary, as her leading man.

Once again, Phylis exhibited a will of iron beneath her sweet exterior. Bob got the job.

Gilmore was sorry to see them leave, but he knew he'd have no problems finding suitable replacements. He auditioned and hired an ingratiating twenty-two-year-old freckle-faced redhead from Newport, Rhode Island, named Charles Van Johnson, whose boyish charm compensated for his lack of experience.

Van recalls attending Walker's closing night.

"I went backstage afterward to see my new dressing room and to ask Walker if he had any tips that might be useful to me at the theater.

"'Just one,' he replied tersely. 'Watch out for the mice and rats.' Then he was gone."

A few days later Bob and Phylis left for Tulsa.

Although there was an unused bedroom in the large house on East Twentieth Street, the Isleys did not invite Bob to move in with the family. Instead, Bob found an inexpensive room in a boardinghouse downtown from the Isleys, which was primarily used as a place to sleep, shower, and change clothes. Other than that, he and Phylis were together constantly and Phil and Flora Mae had to accept the fact that if they wanted to see their daughter for dinner, there had to be an extra service laid out for Bob. Within a few weeks, they too were captivated by his boyish charm, impressed by his performances on the radio show, and convinced that he could have a bright future as an actor. Their reaction to a marriage, however, did not change: Bob and Phyl were simply too young. In a few years, perhaps—but why rush into a lifelong commitment?

Phylis by now had completely forgotten her girlish determination not to "marry until I'm thirty-five." She wanted to be Mrs. Robert Walker as much as he wanted her to be. They talked about little else, pooled their salaries to build a "nest egg."

Phylis, however, didn't even confide her romantic plans to her best friend. Ruth Bowers King later admitted: "I had no idea of what was brewing until a week before the wedding."

It was during the Christmas holiday, and Phylis and Bob decided upon a date. They had just completed their radio commitment and romantically agreed it would be perfect if they married on January 2—the first anniversary of their initial meeting. A new year and a new life.

They took vows early that morning at Christ's King Church, a private family affair with only ten people present.

Phylis made a dazzling if unusual bride, wearing a Peter Pannish hat and the red velvet suit she had always felt brought her good luck. Bob splurged twenty-five dollars for a new suit for the occasion.

Philip Isley had decided, however, to give the newlyweds' luck a little push in the right direction. Firmly informed that they would not accept any financial aid from the family once they were married, he presented them with a smashing Packard convertible as a wedding gift, in which they could drive to Ogden—where they planned to spend part of their honeymoon.

Together with the automobile came the sage advice that the couple continue on to California after their visit with Bob's family.

"You've knocked yourselves out in New York," he commented. "It's freezing there now; there's no reason to return. I have friends in Hollywood who can open doors. Why not give it a try? You have nothing to lose."

Bob, who had been to Los Angeles on many occasions during his military-academy days, left the decision to Phyl.

"I always wanted to see California," she said simply. "And if nothing happens, we can always leave."

Bob shared Phil Isley's sentiments that Phyl would knock them dead as a movie actress. She photographed like a dream, had proven dramatic talent and more experience than most girls her age.

He had a great deal less faith in himself. He knew he wasn't the movie-star "type," with his offbeat face and scrawny frame. He had good comedy timing, however, and had seen enough films to know that, given the opportunity, he could always provide what was known as "comic relief." Of one thing he was certain: he'd never be cast as Phyl's leading man in a movie, and he wondered about the effect it would have on him to see her being made love to

by some gorgeous Adonis. The old insecurities again. He shrugged them off.

What the hell, he thought. *She loves me. She wanted me. She married me.*

As Bob and his bride set off on their trip west, he experienced a rare sense of exhilaration. Whatever the future might bring, of one thing he was absolutely self-confident: never again would he feel unwanted and unloved.

Chapter

5

The Walkers arrived in Hollywood with four hundred dollars, an envelope packed with Phil Isley's letters of introduction to his influential friends, and the address and telephone number of a respectable boardinghouse run by a middle-aged, motherly lady known as "Aunt Daisy," who catered to struggling young performers. She had a room for the honeymooners and an inexhaustible fund of advice and encouragement. The room was inexpensive, the advice free, and the comfortable old house, located on La Brea Avenue just north of Hollywood Boulevard, was in close proximity to most of the major studios.

After getting settled, they decided to give the nearby Paramount Studios a try. Paramount had formed what it called a "Golden Circle" of young hopefuls and was constantly on the lookout for promising talent, whom they could sign cheaply, and own cheaply, should the performer click with the public. The Walkers were called in for an interview, offered a test, and given the opportunity to choose their own material.

The latter "advantage" proved to be a grievous disadvantage. Instead of picking something youthful and lighthearted, Bob and Phylis decided on scenes from the sophisticated *Tovarich* and Ibsen's morbid *Ghosts*, in which Phyl portrayed her husband's *mother*. Had the plays been less highbrow, the young couple might have had a chance. Frank Freeman, head of Paramount, came on the testing stage to look them over, but all the "artistic" acting turned him off—that wasn't what he had in mind for the stock company. Still, the studio did not reject them on the spot. They found Phyl appealing and there was a part in a Henry Aldrich film for which Bob had the right build. For several weeks the Walkers

awaited a phone call. When it finally came, the decision was negative.

With their funds rapidly dwindling and summer approaching, Phylis reluctantly decided to use her father's letter of introduction to his friend at Republic Pictures. Considered the second lowliest of all the studios, a "factory" noted for hoss-operas and quickie serials that were "fillers" on a Saturday matinee, Republic had a male contract list of singing cowboys like Gene Autry and rugged sluggers on the order of John Wayne. Bob was definitely not their type of leading man.

Phylis, however, was considered decorative and unobtrusive enough to serve as a utility player. On June 25, 1939, she half-heartedly signed a six-month contract with Republic for a meager seventy-five dollars a week, and within a matter of days—the studio had no wish to waste a dollar by keeping a contractee idle— she was cast in the role of Celia Joslin, John Wayne's romantic interest, in a Three Mesquiteers feature, *New Frontier*, a potboiler whose plot revolved around a conflict between hardworking ranchers and evil construction-company bosses who wanted to convert the ranchers' lush valley into a reservoir. George Sherman, who went on to better westerns in his long career, recalled that "Phylis Isley seemed to have much more talent than her role called for. And she was a real lady. Not timid, really, but quiet. Like she was determined to learn everything she could, and she didn't miss much. When not working, she took in every phase of the filming technique, which was obviously new to her."

Actually, Phylis didn't have time to take in much of anything. *New Frontier* was completed within a week, and that was immediately followed by the only female role, with fourth billing, in a fifteen-chapter serial, *Dick Tracy's G-Men*. Although she was to appear in thirteen episodes, her work was again done within a week's time; her scenes consisted of talking to Tracy by radio, answering the phone, and forwarding messages to the boss, the sum total of which added up to 204 words of spoken dialogue.

When Phylis signed with Republic, she and Bob moved from Aunt Daisy's to a cozy thirty-five-dollar-a-month cottage in Laurel Canyon, a few minutes' drive to the North Hollywood studio, and Bob continued job-hunting. He connected with a story editor named Dave Bader, who paid him thirty-five dollars weekly for

reading and synopsizing scripts; then he began doing bit roles. He played the undergraduate who asks Ann Sheridan for a dance in Walter Wanger's *Winter Carnival*; another college-boy role in Lana Turner's picture *These Glamour Girls*; and a walk-on part in Lana's distinctly B picture, *Dancing Co-Ed*.

Bit players usually lunched at the MGM coffee counter, adjacent to the commissary, and occasionally Bob would sneak a peek inside to catch a glimpse of such reigning favorites as Mickey Rooney and Judy Garland, James Stewart, Eleanor Powell, Hedy Lamarr, and Nelson Eddy. One lunchtime, even the legendary Louis B. Mayer brushed by him en route to the executive dining room, but Bob could just as well have been the invisible man. However, it provided conversation when he returned home at night.

"You have more to offer than anyone on that lot," he told Phylis one evening.

"Tell that to the great Louis B." She laughed.

They desperately needed to find things to laugh about, since they shared the feeling they were on the road to nowhere.

Phylis was assured by her bosses at Republic that they had several roles in mind for her, but by late July all she wanted was her freedom, and she boldly requested release from her contract, claiming she wanted to return to New York with her husband.

After being turned down, she spoke to her father, who in turn called his friend at the studio, assuring him that Phylis had not been approached with a better offer but that she simply did not find film work interesting and was bored and unhappy. He would consider it a personal favor if they tore up the contract. Since Isley now controlled twenty-three theaters in areas where Republic films were widely shown, his goodwill was of more importance than retaining an unhappy twenty-year-old girl with no public following, one who could easily be replaced by any number of starlets eager to work for seventy-five dollars a week or less, and willing even to "entertain" visiting exhibitors. They let Phylis go without further argument.

Although the Walkers had earned some money in Hollywood and had lived frugally, their financial situation was shaky. Their most valuable asset was the Packard, which they knew they had a better chance of selling in California than in New York.

They received one thousand dollars for it, which paid the fare back to New York, with enough left over to cover rent and food bills for several months—if they were careful.

Later, Bob recalled, "We found a little apartment on West Tenth Street—and get this—with all the luxury Phylis had been used to, when we wanted to take a bath, we had to climb a little ladder to the large kitchen sink! Anything to avoid using the dreary bathroom we shared with all the other tenants."

Fall casting was at its peak by the time the Walkers had returned to New York, and enthusiastically the two started making the rounds again. Their résumés seemed far more impressive now than they had before: the Cherry Lane, the radio serial, Hollywood film credits, new photographs.

They were certain they couldn't miss—but missing was a lot easier than they thought. They missed for four long weeks with agents, producers, and casting directors. It was the old chestnut again: "Don't call us; we'll call you."

During their second week in town, Bob noticed that Phylis appeared uncharacteristically moody and listless. One morning, after she had hardly touched her breakfast, he wondered if she was feeling okay.

"You're not coming down with a cold or something?" he asked.

"No," she replied hesitantly, "I don't think so."

Actually, by now Phylis was beginning to suspect the cause of the malaise, and a local doctor confirmed her suspicions: she was pregnant.

Bob reacted to the news with genuine elation, but an elation tempered with concern. He and Phylis were just managing to get by on their own. They had no money for the little luxuries of life, and he was hardly in a position to support a child. He had dreamed that someday they'd have a family. That "someday," however, was always part of the distant future, at a time when he would be firmly established and mature enough to take on the responsibilities of fatherhood. However, at the moment, he had just turned twenty-one and had no prospects whatsoever.

The Isleys, he knew, could always come to the rescue, pay the hospital and medical bills, buy the layette and crib and any other necessity, but that prospect was humiliating. The only alternative

was to abandon acting and attempt to get a nine-to-five job. Phylis, however, refused even to discuss that.

They managed to get through the winter on what little money they had. Phyl stopped accompanying Bob on the rounds—who'd hire a pregnant actress?—but her almost fanatical belief in her husband's talent made him keep trying, despite the plethora of rejections.

By now there were practical matters to consider. Their damp flat was no place for an infant. They needed a larger but inexpensive place—which couldn't be found in the city. While searching through the classifieds one day, they noticed an ad for a small house in Long Beach, near the ocean, which offered an extra two months rent free before the summer season. The house was little more than a shack, but it was affordable, and it offered an escape from a hot Manhattan summer as well as plenty of fresh sea air for their expected baby.

Bob picked up an old jalopy for seventy-five dollars, and it took just a weekend to lug their entire household furnishings—a chair, a love seat, a table, two lamps, a chest of drawers, and the bed—to Long Beach.

They were only halfway through unpacking when Phyl whispered to Bob that she'd better stop.

At five A.M., April 15, 1940, their son Bobby Jr. was born in Jamaica Hospital, Queens. Even at one week old, Bob's son was a replica of every baby picture Bob had ever seen of himself.

The coming of Bobby seemed to reverse the Walkers' streak of bad luck—or perhaps it motivated Bob to try his luck in another area of show business. Since he was unwanted by stage and screen, he decided to try radio, where it made no difference how he looked.

At the time, the networks held weekly open auditions for unknowns, to use in small parts, at scale: twenty-five dollars a performance. Bob applied, decided against being arty or dramatic at his audition, and chose instead a touching scene from Thornton Wilder's *Our Town*.

Within a week he received a call from NBC to report for a five-line role in a "soap" called *Yesterday's Children*. Though he earned only twenty-five dollars for this, it was a breakthrough. Indeed, it turned out to be far more than just a breakthrough. A

celebrated agent named Audrey Wood was at the studio looking after another client and became taken with Bob's reading and his appealing quality.

In the past, Bob and Phylis had never been able to get past the Audrey Wood–Bill Leibling reception desk. Wood, a petite bundle of dynamite, who was called by Leibling, her husband, "the little giant of the American stage" and was responsible for discovering and encouraging a fledgling playwright named Tennessee Williams, told Bob she thought he had a "great future in radio." Wood's recommendation was a passport to the world of steady employment. Within a few months he was working almost every day in such soap operas as *David Harum, John's Other Wife, Stella Dallas,* and *Myrt and Marge.* Producers quickly realized he had the halting soft speech needed to drag a sad drama to infinity, and he became much sought-after—so much so that he would do one show on NBC in Rockefeller Plaza, dash over to CBS on East Fifty-second Street and start playing another character almost before he had a chance to catch his breath. He actually ate when he was on the air, grabbing a bite of sandwich or a gulp of coffee during a fellow actor's dialogue.

It was an exhilarating time for Bob, a lonely one for Phylis. Her life consisted of watching over baby Bobby and taking time out to listen to the various shows on which his dad appeared. Her "acting" was limited to going over Bob's lines with him. Since radio actors read directly from scripts, it was not necessary to memorize lines, but he was a stickler for proper characterization and enthusiastically responded to all of Phylis' suggestions.

Working steadily sent his self-esteem soaring. By summer's end he had saved more money than he had ever had in his life, and although it was no great fortune, he knew he could finally afford a proper home for his family.

Although a shorter commute would have been more convenient for him, he and Phylis decided against a move back to the city. They found, instead, a lovely two-story house with three bedrooms and a sunroom at 151 Brompton Road in the affluent Nassau County community of Garden City.

Phylis still clung tenaciously to her dream of "becoming a great actress," but wanted to wait until Bobby was a little older before resuming her career. Bob was certain his agents would take her on

as a client—he had talked incessantly about his wife's brilliance—and once properly represented, he was confident she'd have no difficulty in securing a wonderful role in a hit play.

However, the Walkers had barely settled down in Garden City when Phylis realized she was pregnant again. Two babies within a year's time was a stunning turn of events. The house in Garden City was large enough to accommodate another child, however, and Bob's bank account—together with his reputation as a radio actor—continued to increase.

He began getting called in for juvenile leads on prime-time radio without the formality of an audition. Although he was still an anonymous voice as far as the public was concerned, there was talk at CBS of finding him a show of his own.

Socially the Walkers remained loners. They had little in common with their neighbors in Garden City, nor were they the "partying" type. Still insanely in love, they zealously spent whatever free time Bob had alone—together.

Phylis' second pregnancy meant her abandoning any plans of returning to work, at least for another year, and there were times when she seriously considered forgetting about acting entirely. That, however, was the last thing Bob wanted her to do. Optimistically he pointed to the advantages of having two babies in record time. They'd have their family, and when Phylis got a play, they'd hire a nurse to look after the sleeping youngsters when she was at the theater. Other actresses did it all the time, and they weren't accused of being bad mothers, and he'd make sure he was home on matinee days, since he was now in a position to turn down a job if he desired. As far as he was concerned, the rough times were a thing of the past.

In early November 1940, Bob did, in fact, inform his agents to turn down all jobs for a few weeks, since he planned to take Phylis and six-month-old Bobby to Ogden while Phyl was still up to traveling. Obviously still eager for their approval, he wanted his parents to see their young grandchild and the other tangible evidence of his success. Bob, Phylis, and Bobby spent the week at the house at 2504 Eccles—their visit and departure recorded by the Ogden *Standard Examiner*, which made a point of listing all of Bob's radio credits.

As Bob would later tell a friend, if his mother, Zella, felt any

pride in his accomplishments, she was unable to express it, nor was she able to show any deep affection toward Phylis. She accepted the news of Phylis' pregnancy with detachment, her only comment to Bob being a cryptic, "Well, at least you can afford a family." (Bob's oldest brother, Wayne, had fathered four daughters and was struggling to make ends meet as a bartender.)

The week in Ogden was hardly joyful. It was an obligation Bob felt had to be fulfilled, but he regretted having put Phylis through the ordeal, though she never said a harsh word against her frigid in-laws, who were such a contrast to her own demonstrative parents.

Phil and Flora Mae Isley were thrilled about having a little boy in the family, delighted about the prospect of another grandchild, and naturally pleased that Bob had come up in the world and was now able to provide their daughter with the kind of life she had known growing up.

Phil's business affairs brought him to New York regularly; his theater chain was thriving, and he was planning a permanent move to Dallas, where the major part of his operation was now centered.

As for the interruption in his daughter's career, his attitude was cheerfully optimistic: "You're only twenty-one, and you don't look a day over seventeen. Having a family now won't interrupt your career once it gets going"—and it *would*, he assured her.

The Isleys had had a very efficient housekeeper working for them for years. "When I return home," he said, "I'll see if I can persuade her to come east and work for you after the new baby is born. She's crazy about children, and I think she'll welcome the change."

The Walkers' second son, Michael, arrived March 13, 1941, eleven days after Phylis' twenty-second birthday. As with Bobby, he bore a striking resemblance to his father. Within a month, Phil Isley's housekeeper, Henrietta, had joined the family, enabling Phylis to drive into the city with Bob in his new Buick convertible, "just to see what was going on."

When Bob wasn't working, the two would have dinner in town and catch a Broadway show: *The Doctor's Dilemma*, with Phylis' adored Katharine Cornell; Gertrude Lawrence in *Lady in the Dark*; Paul Lukas in *Watch on the Rhine*; and Rose Franken's

Claudia, starring a charming but hitherto unknown actress named Dorothy McGuire.

Phylis was enthralled by *Claudia*, a funny yet poignant comedy about a childlike bride who reaches maturity only after learning, as a result of her habit of listening in on an extension phone, that her mother is dying of cancer. She returned to the Booth Theater to see it on three different occasions, and when she joined Bob in the early evening, could talk of little else except, "I must play that role."

Phylis wasn't alone in her admiration for *Claudia*. The show was playing to packed houses, and producer David O. Selznick had paid $187,000 for the film rights and had put author Franken and her husband, William Brown Maloney, under option to write the screenplay at a salary of twenty-five hundred dollars a week. However, the man who had launched a nationwide search for Scarlett O'Hara hesitated to sign Dorothy McGuire to recreate the role on the screen until he had had an opportunity to see and test other young girls.

Simultaneously, John Golden, who had produced *Claudia*, was also on the lookout for an equally appealing actress for a projected Chicago company. There wasn't an ingenue in New York or Hollywood that season who wasn't convinced that she was the definitive Claudia.

Phylis' determination to play the role, however, bordered on obsession. Bob agreed that she'd be perfect, although his heart sank at the possibility of her auditioning for the Chicago company. They hadn't been separated since the summer he had spent on the banana boat, and he didn't know how he could get by without her for any length of time.

Simultaneously, he chided himself for his selfishness, aware of her eagerness to return to work and her desire to play *Claudia*. He spoke to his agent, who promised to do what she could for Phylis.

The outcome was that Phylis, together with another aspiring *Claudia* named Phyllis Thaxter, was invited to spend a few days with the author.

Phyllis Thaxter vividly recalls: "We both tried out for the Chicago company. I was the first to be picked out by Rose Franken. We rehearsed at Miss Franken's farm at Old Lyme, Connecticut, and in fact roomed together while we stayed there. She talked

about her actor husband Robert Walker often, and he phoned her every night, which I thought was lovely. Then I replaced McGuire for one matinee in New York, and John Golden told me he wanted me for the Chicago company."

According to Miss Thaxter, it was around the same time that Katharine Brown, who was in charge of David O. Selznick's New York operation, became aware of Miss Franken's interest in both Phyllis Thaxter and Phylis Walker. David Selznick was scheduled to be in New York the week of July 20, and Miss Brown set up appointments for the two girls to read for her on succeeding days. Selznick arranged to be in the 630 Fifth Avenue office—but out of sight. If either (or both) impressed him, he would make his presence known. If not, the diplomatic Miss Brown would dismiss the girls as gently as possible. After *Gone with the Wind*, she was an expert in such matters.

Phylis Walker's appointment was scheduled for the afternoon of July 21.

She was well-rehearsed for her scene—but the importance of the audition obviously overwhelmed her. She read, but as she would later say, "I knew I was very, very bad." Then she burst into tears and, mortified by her lack of control, rushed from the office before Miss Brown could say or do anything to comfort her.

Paradoxically, Selznick was not turned off by either Phylis' reading or her emotional outburst. Instead he was deeply moved by her sensitivity and a rare quality he found difficult to define.

"I want to talk with her myself," he told Kay Brown. "Call and have her return tomorrow."

When Phylis returned to Garden City, miserably depressed, she was given Miss Brown's message asking her to appear at the office the following afternoon. As she would later relate, she thought Miss Brown wanted to see her to let her down easily, and so ignored the message.

When she didn't appear at the office at the appointed time, she received another phone call from Miss Brown, who informed her that Mr. Selznick was waiting to see her. Phylis had just finished washing her hair, and it was still wet, but she dressed in record speed, called a cab, and made the trip into the city with her long hair dangling from the window to dry. She arrived a few minutes after Phyllis Thaxter had departed, and was immediately ushered

into Selznick's private office. She wasn't asked to read again. He just wanted to talk informally.

She told him of her background, of her work in the tent shows, that she was married and the mother of two young sons. She became intensely animated when she discussed her passion for acting and the role of *Claudia*.

When Phylis left the Selznick offices that afternoon, she was confident that this time she had made a good impression. Kay Brown assured her they'd be in touch.

At dinner that evening, Phyl told Bob about her interview in detail, adding, "I think he liked me."

Her evaluation was correct—even though the preoccupied producer was somewhat confused as to her identity. In a note to Kay Brown later that afternoon, he wrote:

"Regarding *Phyllis Thaxter*: Whether or not you should test should depend entirely on whether or not you think she is a good bet for the future apart from *Claudia*. Is this the big-eyed girl we saw . . . who had two children? Incidentally, if it is the big-eyed girl, I certainly think she is worth testing."

Three days later, however, Selznick was enraged by the sum of money Phylis' agent suggested during contract negotiations: two hundred dollars as her initial weekly salary, with option-renewal clauses over a seven-year period escalating the amount to an outrageous three thousand dollars.

"We wouldn't dream of paying her any such figure," Selznick roared.

Phylis didn't think the figure *that* exorbitant. If she failed to come through, she knew she'd be dropped after the first six months or year. What was two hundred dollars a week to a man who spent millions on his films? And she *had* received seventy-five at the lowly Republic. That latter point was not brought up, however. In fact, when discussing her background with Selznick, she had deliberately avoided mentioning ever having faced a camera before, certain that that bit of information would do her more harm than good. Naively, she thought no one would ever uncover her "secret."

Within twenty-four hours the mercurial Selznick adjusted to the salary request. Spending ten thousand dollars for a year's commitment was less than he often blew at the gaming tables in a night—

Selznick was an inveterate gambler—and he intuitively felt that with Phylis Walker he might hold a future star. He wanted the girl under personal contract. He wanted the girl.

With the two words "Sign her" he triggered a chain reaction that would turn Phylis' wildest dreams into reality, Robert Walker's life into a nightmare, and his own distinguished career into a whirlwind of self-destruction.

PRODUCED BY DAVID O. SELZNICK

With Mr. Selznick, I don't have to worry. I have no feeling of fright because anyone can place complete confidence in his good judgment.

—JENNIFER JONES, 1945

My personal life has been completely wrecked by David Selznick's obsession for my wife. What can you do to fight such a powerful man?

—ROBERT WALKER, 1945

David's love for Jennifer was very real and touching. . . . Everything he did was for Jennifer . . . to the detriment of his good judgment. . . .

—JOHN HUSTON

6

David Selznick was born on May 10, 1902, the third son of Lewis and Florence Sachs Selznick. When he was eight, his father, a jeweler by trade, relocated to New York City, with grandiose plans of competing with Cartier and Tiffany, but his jewelry business fizzled out within two years. He optimistically looked for new worlds to conquer, and in 1912 he informed his astonished wife he was entering the movie field, claiming, "Less brains are necessary in the motion-picture business than any other."

Lewis Selznick, however, had brains, imagination, and nerve. A natural-born wheeler-dealer, he maneuvered himself into (and out of) key positions at Universal Pictures and World Film. He promoted himself with as much zeal as he did his stars and product, and after leaving World, decided to take a giant step forward by forming his own company. His slogan, "Selznick Pictures Make Happy Hours," was emblazoned on Broadway for years.

Although his eldest son, Howard, was uninterested in films, both Myron and David shared their father's enthusiasm for the lucrative industry. When David was fourteen, he'd rush from classes to his father's office, where he'd compose thoughtful critiques of directors, stars, movies, and stories. By the time he was eighteen he was running Selznick Studios' publicity department and publishing a weekly newsmagazine for Selznick employees. An avid reader, he aimed to become a distinguished writer after completing college, while his older brother Myron aspired to join the company as a producer, which, in time, he did.

In 1923, however, the Selznick empire collapsed, due in part to Lewis' extravagances and a conspiracy among his powerful en-

emies in the industry to prevent the "happy" Selznick pictures from receiving proper distribution.

Lewis and Florence Selznick were forced to sell off their treasures and move from a twenty-two-room Park Avenue apartment to a three-room furnished flat, a nerve-shattering decline for a man whose gambling losses reached a high of a million dollars during his halcyon days. Gone were Florence Selznick's sables and jewels. Gone, too, was Lewis' mistress, silent screen star Clara Kimball Young, which Mrs. Selznick surely did not mind.

Two years later, the Selznicks moved to California, where Myron joined them, hell-bent on destroying the moguls responsible for his father's downfall. David remained in New York an additional year producing successful "short subjects" and used the profits he made from them to produce his first motion picture, ironically titled *Roulette*.

Then, with his savings of five thousand dollars he decided to join his family. He was twenty-four, fired with optimism, and as determined as Myron to restore glory to the Selznick name.

In the autumn of 1926, the only position offered him was as a reader in MGM's story department, and that on a trial basis. In record time he had been elevated to assistant to producer Harry Rapf, whom he besieged with proposals about possible productions. Rapf was highly impressed with the young man's intelligence, imagination, and energy.

Rapf, in fact, recruited David to escort Irene Mayer, Louis B.'s twenty-year-old daughter, to the posh Mayfair Ball on New Year's Eve, 1926, a chore David deeply resented. He spent the evening getting drunk, drove Irene back to the Mayer mansion, Ocean Front, in Santa Monica, and expressed no desire to see her again.

However, when the two met at director Edmund Goulding's beach home a few months later, something seemed to click. This time he *did* want to see her again, and after several Sundays spent at the home of mutual acquaintances, the two had their first "official" date—an evening of dinner and dancing at the Coconut Grove.

Irene recalled David being "solicitous, responsive, and totally engaging. I was riveted." Within a few months they were unofficially "going steady."

David was a young man in a hurry. He ached to achieve the greatness and stature which Irving G. Thalberg took for granted as an executive producer at MGM. Any suspicion that David was using Louis B.'s daughter as a stepping-stone was dispelled when, after a clash with Thalberg, David refused to apologize. He was told to clear out his desk and leave.

David didn't remain unemployed for long. In mid-December he was hired by Ben Schulberg, general manager of Paramount's West Coast production, on a "trial basis." Within a few weeks Schulberg had named David his "personal assistant."

During his three-and-a-half-year tenure at Paramount, Selznick either produced or assisted in the production of a dozen films. During those years he utilized the directorial services of the brilliant William Wellman, Merian C. Cooper, and John Cromwell, all of whom would figure prominently in his future.

On April 29, 1931, David and Irene took their marriage vows in Louis B. Mayer's spacious living room and were off for a six-week honeymoon in Europe. Shortly after he returned to Hollywood, David and other top Paramount personnel were asked to agree to a substantial pay cut. The Great Depression, together with some box-office busts, had had a dire effect on the studio's financial resources. Refusing to "pay" for the mistakes of others, David handed in his resignation.

Depression be damned. He'd start his own company, one in which he'd have total control of product and performers.

Obtaining financial backing was more difficult than he anticipated. He put his dream on hold and told his brother Myron, now a powerful agent, to be on the alert for an opening at the major studios. He didn't wish to return to either MGM or Paramount; the brothers Warner were a family operation, opposed to independent production. Fox was in trouble and Universal was facing bankruptcy. The last remaining possibility was the minor RKO, whose only distinction was the fact that it was owned by RCA and controlled by Radio Corporation of America's visionary pioneer, David Sarnoff.

Sarnoff wanted a "class" studio. In October 1931 he placed Selznick under contract with the starting salary of twenty-five hundred dollars a week and the prestigious title of vice-president in charge of production. David also received a guarantee that any

films made under his personal supervision would be billed on screen and in ads as "A David O. Selznick Production."

Selznick remained with RKO until late January 1933. During this period he was personally responsible for twenty films, including *A Bill of Divorcement*, which turned a young New York stage actress named Katharine Hepburn into an overnight star; *Westward Passage*, with youthful English actor Laurence Olivier; and *Bird of Paradise*, directed by King Vidor. He also signed a brilliant young Viennese composer named Max Steiner to write the scores for nine of those twenty films.

However, many felt he was gambling away his future by insisting the New York brass permit his friend Merian Cooper to go ahead with his dream of directing a bizarre "ape movie" requiring a budget of a half-million dollars. He even went one step further, promising Cooper complete control of the project, without any executive "interference" unless Cooper requested it.

The "ape movie," *King Kong*, was sneak-previewed the final week of January 1933, a few days after Selznick gave notice that he would not sign again with the then-faltering studio. *Kong* had dual openings in New York, at Radio City Music Hall and the Roxy, on March 16. Selznick was not there to participate in the glory, although without his support there would have been no *King Kong* to save RKO from bankruptcy. He was back where he had started—on the MGM payroll.

The previous December, Irving Thalberg, MGM's creative genius, had suffered a serious heart attack. His doctors prescribed a long rest and Louis B. Mayer was given no indication if or when Thalberg would be able to resume his duties.

Mayer approached his son-in-law with an offer to return to the studio, tempting him with a four-thousand-dollar weekly salary for a two-year term and his own independent unit to produce class pictures, with the added inducement that he'd be given priority on any stars, directors, stories, and writers he wanted. Hesitant at first, fearing the possible insult of nepotism, Selznick finally acquiesced.

Selznick's return to MGM inspired the classic line "The Son-in-Law Also Rises" in the trade journal *The Hollywood Spectator* and enmity within the Thalberg ranks.

However, after David produced the smash all-star *Dinner at*

Eight, featuring Marie Dressler, Jean Harlow, John Barrymore, and Wallace Beery, among others, within a record twenty-four days at the modest cost of $387,000, he won the grudging respect of everyone on the lot. And by the time Thalberg returned to Culver City on August 19, even the past grievances of the two young geniuses were forgotten.

Selznick's accomplishments at Metro were staggering: *Viva Villa, David Copperfield, Anna Karenina*, and A *Tale of Two Cities* were among the eleven films he turned out within his contracted two-year period.

Nevertheless, he still nurtured the dream of running his own studio.

At age thirty-three he finally secured the necessary financing to start his company, with facilities at the old Thomas Ince Studios on Washington Boulevard, just a half-mile east of MGM.

Just outside the colonial mansion which housed his offices hung the modest but memorable sign which proclaimed: Selznick International Pictures.

After launching his company with *Little Lord Fauntleroy*, he went on to produce *The Garden of Allah, A Star Is Born, The Prisoner of Zenda, Nothing Sacred, The Adventures of Tom Sawyer, Made for Each Other, Intermezzo: A Love Story* (with his Swedish discovery, Ingrid Bergman), his ultimate triumph, *Gone with the Wind*, and *Rebecca*.

He accomplished all that with an obsessiveness that drove everyone with whom he worked to distraction. No detail was too small for Selznick to oversee, no decision so minor that it could not inspire one of the famous memos that he sat up late into the night—sometimes to dawn—dictating to a shifting corps of secretaries. "My function is to be responsible for *everything*," he said, and indeed he was, often to brilliant effect, but sometimes forcing directors or technical staff to resign, so fed up were they with his constant interference.

To give but one example of the single-minded attention of which he was capable, during the filming of *Intermezzo* he bombarded his production executive, director, director of publicity, makeup artist, advertising manager, story editor, and stars with memos on everything from Ingrid Bergman's height (did they think they would have to use a stepladder with Leslie Howard?),

hair, eyebrows (they should be left unplucked), and a possible change of name, to camera setups, publicity angles (the dentist husband "doesn't help any"), saving money on the musical arrangements, and the amount of light and shading on Bergman's face (as important as the performances). He fiddled with the title, he rewrote the script, he roamed the set. Ultimately he replaced both the original director, William Wyler, and the director of photography, Harry Stradling.

This kind of behavior made for excellent pictures, but also won him a certain reputation—"egotistical" and "overbearing" were the words most often used—especially after *Gone with the Wind* and *Rebecca* won back-to-back Best Picture awards for 1939 and 1940 and the pressure grew steadily more intense for him to find a suitable follow-up. Once on a certain plateau, the thought of any lessening of prestige was unbearable.

Such pressure also required suitable methods of release away from the office. As noted, Selznick had acquired the gambling habit from his father, and he could drop several thousand dollars in a single night. Also like his father, Selznick enjoyed chasing pretty women, and he had many casual affairs. Louella Parsons recalls Selznick being deeply interested in actress Nancy Kelly, a beautiful redhead, in the period immediately preceding his discovery of Phylis. Actress Evelyn Keyes remembers him chasing her around his office. Virginia Field says that while filming *Little Lord Fauntleroy*, she was ushered into Selznick's office: "When he got off the phone, he rose without a word, walked around to the front of the desk, grabbed the front of my dress, and ripped it down. I grabbed a decanter from his desk, hit him on the head with it, and ran out." And so on.

None of these sexual contacts meant anything important to Selznick, however. They were all just a way to ease the tension in his work, to add a little excitement to his life. To none of them did he bring the kind of obsessive attention that so overwhelmed his coworkers on the job.

And then Phylis Walker entered his office and his life.

After signing her contract with David O. Selznick, Phylis alternated between exaltation and bewilderment. She had been given no specifics as to how or when or where she would start working—

in anything—just generalities about eventually testing for *Claudia*.

Bob was as ecstatic as his wife about the contract, but equally disturbed about the lack of details. CBS wanted him for his own New York-based radio show, *Maudie's Diary*, for which he would receive on-the-air star billing and a four-hundred-dollar weekly salary. The thought of being separated from Phylis, however, was unendurable.

There was no reason for her to stay in Hollywood unless she was working on a movie, Phylis suggested. Between films she could resume her life in New York. That idea, however, didn't sit well with Bob.

"Look," he said, "if you're going to be making movies in Hollywood, we'll just move west again. There are plenty of radio jobs in California. Now that I'm established, I shouldn't have any difficulty getting work. I only wish I knew what that man has in mind for you, so we could make some definite plans."

In early August, Phylis received word she was needed on the West Coast by mid-month for a brief but unexpected assignment.

According to producer John Houseman, "David Selznick had decided to initiate a gala month-long season of summer stock at the Lobero Theater in Santa Barbara as a showcase for his contract players."

Anna Christie, starring Ingrid Bergman, was scheduled for a week-long run, to be followed by the little-known *Lottie Dundass*, starring Geraldine Fitzgerald (a Houseman favorite since their Mercury Theater days), and *The Devil's Disciple*, with Selznick contractees Alan Marshal and Janet Gaynor.

When *Anna Christie* moved to San Francisco for a week's run, Houseman encountered William Saroyan, who had just completed a one-act play called *Hello, Out There*.

Houseman decided to present *Hello, Out There*, a compact drama about a jailed man and the girl cook who tries to help him escape a lynch mob, as a curtain raiser to *The Devil's Disciple*, and Selznick insisted that his newest discovery, Phylis Walker, be cast as the girl. Then he would be able to gauge audience reaction to Phylis and get a better idea of her dramatic talents. At the conclusion of the play's one-week run, he'd set up a series of screen

tests. After being tested, she'd return to New York and her family. In all, she'd be gone less than a month.

This was the Walkers' first separation since their marriage. With so little notice, there was no way Bob could accompany Phylis to the Coast. His work kept him busy, but he missed her terribly. Their nightly phone conversations provided the only relief from his loneliness.

Houseman recalls: "Phylis gave a beautiful performance" opposite Henry Bratsberg (later to be known as Harry Morgan), and the audiences responded enthusiastically during the curtain calls. The *Hollywood Reporter* said she was "a natural for pictures." However, when Houseman invited her to join a party with the Los Angeles press after the opening performance, she did not appear. She said she had to call her sons. She may also have been concerned that the press might recognize her as the girl who had appeared in *New Frontier*.

Houseman also recalls, "It was evident that Selznick was interested in her personally as well. I would say that she and Selznick were romantically involved as early as that summer."

That soon? Nobody knows for sure, but it is doubtful. What is for sure is that she discussed Bob at length with Selznick. Selznick worried about her family. He "wouldn't want to give her the big opportunity and make her a star, only to find we had problems later as a result of her family being back East," he said.

"Oh, we've talked about that," she assured Selznick. "My husband is prepared to make the move, if necessary."

Selznick obviously had been giving a great deal of thought to "the husband." He asked Katharine Brown to interview Bob and advise whether she thought he should also be placed under contract, as an element of protection. If so, it should be done right away, "so it doesn't look later as though we are buying him just because we are giving her *Claudia*," and thus injure Bob's pride.

If such an interview ever transpired, it was never discussed publicly by Bob, Phylis, or Selznick. Kay Brown has no recollection of meeting Bob. Whatever the reason, he was not signed with Selznick Studios.

On September 5, 1941, Phylis was screen-tested for the first time: a brief scene from *Claudia* to gauge her on-camera personality. Wearing a simple blouse and little makeup, a sleeveless

sweater, a pleated skirt, and flat-heeled shoes, with her dark hair parted in the middle and flowing loosely to her shoulders, she was a vision of innocent loveliness. When Selznick saw the film in the privacy of his projection room, it confirmed his initial instincts that the girl had a radiant appeal which could make her an overnight star. Other tests were set up, which, Selznick later told a less-than-enthusiastic Rose Franken, "knocked everyone for a loop."

"I am aware of the girl's shortcomings," he informed her. "I have seen her rehearse, I have seen her perform, I have seen her before audiences—and I know the excitement that she causes in audiences. . . . We mustn't underestimate the value to any picture of an electric screen personality—as I believe I've uncovered one in the person of Phylis Walker."

One of the very few things Selznick felt his newest contractee *did* lack was a memorable screen name. Remembering his own confusion the day of their meeting, he felt Phylis Walker was too similar to Phyllis Thaxter, in addition to being "undistinguished." He wanted a first name that was fairly unique and at the same time not too fancy, and a one-syllable last name that had some rhythm to it and was easy to remember. He sent out a directive to his staff requesting suggestions.

It would take him four months to decide upon the name Jennifer Jones—the "Jennifer" being his personal inspiration.

Before Phylis left California in mid-September, she was reassured by her employer that his faith in her was absolute; he'd be in touch regularly and would undoubtedly be seeing her back east, since his business affairs involved a great deal of shuttling between New York and Hollywood. For all the firmness of this assurance, she was still left in the dark as to whether or not she'd be his Claudia.

Bob was relieved to have Phylis back. Although they had spoken nightly, he had found her absence intolerable—and he'd been keeping a surprise for her return. While she'd been away, he had spent his Sunday afternoons taking the boys on excursions to various resorts on Long Island. On one such trip, he had seen an enchanting colonial house set in four green acres in the posh Sands Point area. "You'll love it and it will be wonderful for the boys. I'm going to be stuck in town for another year, and God only knows when you'll be called back to the Coast."

She was hesitant, but after seeing the house, she too fell in love with it and saw no reason to put off the move, since, Bob reasoned, she might not be needed in Hollywood for six months or more. She couldn't put her life into suspended animation while awaiting Selznick's decision. By now she had been informed by Kay Brown that it was a tossup between her and Dorothy McGuire, and that Rose Franken still favored the original star.

On September 19 Selznick dashed off another memo to Kay Brown, in which he confirmed that he wanted Walker to do *Claudia*, but added with some irritation, "Things have happened with the girl that were beyond her wildest dreams a few months ago, so she shouldn't be impatient. She has what may be her last opportunity for a long time to devote herself to her two kids, and she had better make the most of it.

"I am terribly afraid the girl is going to get spoiled. Already she has lost some of that eager, blushing quality that made her so enchanting when we first saw her. I am terrified that by the time we get *Claudia* in work she will be wrong for it, because the bloom will be off the peach."

Although Phylis was unaware of the memo, she *was* devoting most of her time to the family. They settled down in Sands Point, bought a shiny new Buick convertible, and splurged on a recording machine so that Phyl could wax Bob's radio programs at home. They'd replay them together and discuss what he'd done on the air that wasn't as good as it should have been, and she'd cue him on upcoming shows—an opportunity for her to keep in practice. They played tennis, took long walks along the beach, and occasionally they'd have friends to the house for dinner or drive into town to catch a play.

They never lacked for things to talk about, but whenever the subject was the future, the name David Selznick was prominent in the conversation. Selznick called regularly, as vague as ever about *Claudia*, but he repeatedly assured Phylis that no matter what film he chose for her screen debut, it would be one that would send her soaring to stardom.

Phylis was panicked by Selznick's repeated reference to "screen debut," and in a constant dilemma as to whether to tell him about her Republic Pictures "quickies" or chance that they would never be associated with her.

Although she was registered with the Screen Actors' Guild as Phylis Isley, there were dozens of people at Republic who'd recognize her instantly once she had made another film. Her secret would be out, the press would have a field day, and she was certain Selznick would never forgive the deception. She also realized that the longer she delayed her "confession," the more difficult it would be for her.

In late October, during one of Selznick's frequent trips to New York, she summoned up her courage and revealed everything about her first trip to Hollywood. To her relief, Selznick assured her the deception did not threaten her future with Selznick productions.

Privately, however, he confessed to being "seriously worried." Although she told him the contract had been terminated by mutual consent, he *was* concerned that there might have been a loophole which would prevent her from working for someone else, and assigned a member of his staff to ascertain that none existed. None did.

As for presenting his protégée as a bona fide newcomer, he was confident he and his high-powered publicity department could get around that when necessary.

Relieved by Selznick's attitude, Phylis and Bob enjoyed a peaceful, uneventful autumn at Sands Point. When Bob celebrated his twenty-third birthday on October 13, 1941, he considered himself "the luckiest guy alive."

World War II was raging in Europe and many of his fellow performers on Radio Row were being drafted, but Bob was free of that worry. His poor eyesight, which he had been so sensitive about as a youth, automatically placed him in the 4-F category. Although not politically inclined, he was aware of what was going on, but he, like many other young Americans, did not think the United States would become embroiled in the European conflict.

Bob and Phyl were spending a lazy Sunday afternoon at home when they heard the news that Pearl Harbor had been bombed by the Japanese. He later remembered that he had immediately thought of his brothers and how they'd be affected. At thirty-three, Walter was still single and practicing law in New York, and Bob saw him occasionally. Dick had moved to San Francisco, and Wayne, now thirty-five, was back home in Ogden.

Bob also thought of his classmates at San Diego and the irony that although he had received his education at a military academy, he stood no chance of being called into service.

He was at CBS the following day when the network preempted its regular program to broadcast Franklin D. Roosevelt's address to the nation which proclaimed to the world that a state of war existed between the United States and Japan. "I suppose," Bob prophesied to a director acquaintance, "that I'll be in a lot of war stories now."

Although as shocked as the rest of the country by the carnage at Pearl Harbor, Phylis was relieved her husband would be safe for the duration and that the war would have no immediate effect on her life—or her career. She was wrong about that. By sheer coincidence, David O. Selznick and his wife, Irene, were houseguesting with their close friends the William Paleys in Manhasset, a few miles away from Sands Point, on December 7.

As Irene recalled, David insisted upon returning to California immediately, with the intention of joining the army—as a private. Irene was amused by his impulsive burst of patriotism, noting that "his spirit was fine, his idea impractical—he was nearsighted, slewfooted, overweight, overage. He didn't need an enemy; he'd kill himself."

"You'll put someone's eye out in your first salute and trip over your rifle," she joked.

Selznick, however, was determined to save his country and beseeched his Washington friends to find him a suitable post. If he couldn't be a soldier, he wanted to make films for the armed forces, like Darryl F. Zanuck, John Ford, and Jack Warner were doing, but he found no takers. To Undersecretary of the Navy James V. Forrestal he sent a detailed twelve-page plan for the establishment of a Navy Bureau of Photography, but Forrestal, privately referring to him as an "egomaniac," took it no further. He did receive an offer to run a radio program, but that he simply termed "ridiculous." Finally, he confessed, "So far as I can see, the government is convinced it can do very well without me," but that didn't stop him from continuing to send suggestions of every kind to all branches of the armed forces, the State Department, and even the President. "He had one big job after another lined up," says Irene Selznick, "but he blew them. They couldn't deal with him and the war both."

Confused as to his role in the war, and in financial difficulties due to excessive taxation on his recent hits and to cost overruns, Selznick decided to liquidate Selznick International and re-form as his own smaller company, without outside partners—David O. Selznick Productions, Inc. That meant liquidating the properties he had owned as part of Selznick International, however. Gone was the *Claudia* he had spent so much time fussing over for Phylis—it, and half of Dorothy McGuire's contract, were bought by Twentieth Century-Fox, as were two other pet projects, A. J. Cronin's *The Keys of the Kingdom* (for which Phylis had also been considered) and *Jane Eyre*. His interest in Selznick International he sold to Jock Whitney for two million dollars. Whitney in turn sold the rights to *Gone with the Wind* to MGM.

He retained his stars and directors, however. Sometimes, to their distress, he made a small fortune by lending them to other studios for lucrative sums—pocketing all but their regular salary himself. Joan Fontaine, for example, received only thirty thousand dollars of the hundred and fifty Selznick extracted for her services. Often, these exorbitant profits went to pay gambling debts or to buy extravagant gifts for Irene.

Phylis, now officially on the Selznick roster as Jennifer Jones, knew little of Selznick's professional or personal life, but was heartbroken when informed that Selznick had relinquished his rights to *Claudia*, and unnerved by his evasiveness when she tried to elicit information about her future.

He merely reiterated his belief in her, implored her to be patient, and assured her he'd find a proper role for her, if not under his direct auspices, then with one of the major studios. He had no intention of releasing her from her contract; he was more convinced than ever that she had the potential of becoming a major star. He did not want her to become tied up in a Broadway play, but suggested that if she felt restless, she might take private acting classes with Sanford Meisner, who worked with professional performers as well as with neophytes. And he promised to keep in touch.

Bob later recalled that that spring and early summer was one of the most frustrating periods of Phylis' life.

When her first-year option expired in late July, it was immediately renewed and she received an automatic raise in salary,

although Selznick was still making an effort to obtain a post with the military for the duration of the war.

Bob's radio career was on an even keel. *Maudie's Diary,* though no blockbuster, was successful enough to keep the network happy, and other one-shot roles—like the lead in the *Camel Caravan/Our Town* segments—were his whenever he chose. He tried, however, to keep his weekends free to relax with Phylis and the boys at the Sands Point Country Club, painfully aware of the toll her career hiatus was taking on his wife's peace of mind.

On August 14, Selznick, alone in New York on one of his periodic business trips, impulsively called Phylis and invited her to dinner to discuss her career. If Bob thought it peculiar that the invitation did not include him, he kept his feelings to himself. Naively, it never occurred to him that a middle-aged (David had turned forty on May 10) family man—and a physically unattractive one at that—could pose a threat to his own idyllic marriage.

Dressed in her prettiest summer frock, her hair hanging loosely to her shoulders, Phylis drove into town to dine with her boss, determined not to pressure him about his plans. She was in high spirits that evening, brimming with charm and vivacity, and she allowed him to do most of the talking.

He said little that he hadn't said before—except for predicting that "the whole world will fall in love with you, just as it has with Ingrid Bergman: I'll make sure of that."

There'd be a notable difference, however. David Selznick hadn't fallen in love with Ingrid Bergman, but whether he was aware of it or not at the time, he was falling in love with the girl he had renamed Jennifer Jones.

The following morning he dropped a note to his production executive, Dan O'Shea:

"Mindful of how valuable I expect Jennifer Jones to be, I think that when the next option is taken up, or even before then, perhaps starting immediately, we should say we want a new seven-year contract starting immediately, so that the year or more she has been on payroll without doing anything isn't time out of the contract."

And then he was compelled to add, "I saw her last night and she looked wonderful and most charming."

Without hesitation, Phylis agreed to the terms of the new con-

tract. Her insecurity about her career seemed to vanish: she was now certain that Selznick had her best interests at heart.

Within two months she received a phone call which confirmed her feelings. She was to return to California immediately to test for the title role in *The Song of Bernadette*. Twentieth Century-Fox was adapting Franz Werfel's mammoth religious novel about the fourteen-year-old French girl whose claim to have seen a vision of the Blessed Lady on February 11, 1858, at a grotto outside of Lourdes led first to her prosecution, then to a general belief in the miracle of Lourdes' healing waters, and eventually to her taking vows and commencing her novitiate under the name of Sister Marie Bernard. The story ends as Bernadette finally dies of bone tuberculosis, refusing to avail herself of the Lourdes spring, because her Lady had promised, "I cannot make you happy in this world—only the next." Bernadette was canonized on December 8, 1933.

A member of Selznick's New York staff would immediately send over a copy of the novel for her to read en route to the Coast. Furthermore, Jennifer was told, the Selznick office had located and rented a charming place in Beverly Hills, within minutes of Twentieth Century-Fox, to ensure her comfort and privacy for however long she was needed on the Coast. Selznick overlooked no single detail.

According to Bob, Phylis was surprised but calm about this latest development. After the disappointment of *Claudia*, she wasn't about to set herself up for another awful letdown—especially since *The Song of Bernadette* was being produced by a studio over which David Selznick had no control, one which already had a long list of talented young actresses under contract.

Bob dreaded the thought of another separation, since neither was sure how long she'd be out there, and before Phylis' departure, the two formulated their plans for the future. He would remain at Sands Point and watch over Bobby and Michael until his *Maudie's Diary* went off the air in December. Simultaneously, he'd instruct his agent, Marcella Knapp, to line up radio work in Hollywood after the first of the year. When he was free, he'd give up the house in Sands Point, ship the Buick west, and the family would permanently relocate in California.

Even if *Bernadette* didn't work out, he felt certain that Selznick

would find something terrific with which to launch his wife's career. "He's not paying you all that money to keep you idle forever. This has been *my* big year." He grinned. "Now it's your turn. God knows you've waited long enough."

After seeing her off to the Coast, he was seized by an inexplicable feeling of melancholy. He attributed it to loneliness. He later insisted he had no foreboding that this temporary farewell was, in fact, the beginning of the end.

Chapter

7

When her train pulled into Union Station in Los Angeles, Phylis Walker—or Jennifer Jones, the name to which she had now become accustomed—was totally immersed in the otherworldly character of Bernadette Soubirous, fiercely determined to get the role, and curious as to just how David Selznick had been able to arrange the test, having only the *Claudia* footage as proof of her talent.

The role was a tour de force for which any established star would have sold her soul. Darryl F. Zanuck, who had bought the bestseller in 1941, felt that only an "unknown innocent" would be believable in the part, but after Zanuck temporarily vacated his position of vice-president in charge of operations at Twentieth Century-Fox to serve as a colonel in the army for the duration, William Goetz was assigned to that powerful post. Goetz was David O. Selznick's brother-in-law—wed to Irene's sister, Edith.

Aware of the project and that the title role was still "up for grabs," Selznick did no small amount of arm-twisting on Goetz and the film's projected director, Henry King, to test his newest discovery for the part, using Selznick's close friend Leon Shamroy as cinematographer.

As King would later recall: "The obvious test, of course, was the scene where Bernadette sees the vision of the Blessed Lady. All the other tests had been done with this material. To find out how Jennifer handled herself both physically and mentally, I filmed a scene of her crossing the brook on stones. This she accomplished very nicely. Then I did the vision scene. I looked at her test in the projection room, together with footage of other actresses we had tested, which would give us a better comparison. When I saw

them all together, I noticed one outstanding thing. All the others *looked*—Jennifer actually *saw* the vision."

King was convinced. He didn't have the final say, however. His decision had to be confirmed by *Bernadette* producer William Perlberg, as well as by William Goetz, and although the latter two were deeply impressed, there was still studio politics to consider: the understandable reluctance to take an unknown who was under exclusive contract to another man and make an overnight star of her.

All three were bombarded by phone calls, memos, and proposed deals by Selznick. He adamantly refused to relinquish half of her contract, as he had with Dorothy McGuire's. Reluctantly, however, he pledged Jennifer's services for one major picture a year over a period of five years in exchange for starring her in *Bernadette*.

And there the matter rested for what seemed, to Jennifer, an eternity.

David Selznick phoned her regularly, but he failed to realize that, having no friends in California, she was pathetically lonely. She missed her husband and children; she was not interested in shopping. She spent most of her days listening to music on radio, her evenings reading.

Oddly enough—or perhaps not so oddly—Selznick made no attempt to include her in his social circle. When Ingrid Bergman had arrived in Hollywood, leaving her husband and daughter behind in Sweden, she had been the Selznicks' houseguest before starting the American version of *Intermezzo*. Irene Selznick had held a dinner party in her honor and taken her to other parties to meet the major actors and directors of the period. No similiar gestures of hospitality were extended to Jennifer. Selznick was determined that she endure what was tantamount to a cloistered existence. She was advised to avoid the press, to discuss neither her husband nor her sons with anyone.

In New York, Bob was as lonely as she. Don Keefer, his former schoolmate at AADA, who, after two small roles on Broadway, had also turned to radio to make ends meet, says:

"I kept running into him on Radio Row. Bob had made it very big on radio by this time and he was trying to help me. I remember a little notebook in which he had all the agency people listed—the

casting people—and he was always giving me little tips. He was terribly generous, terribly enthusiastic about wanting to help other people.

"Then I saw him shortly after Phylis had gone to Hollywood to test for *Song of Bernadette*. He was still tops in radio and he was forced to remain here and he was terribly lonely.

"To my astonishment, he said, 'Don, why don't you come out and stay at the house with me'—he was *that* lonely. And I thought at the time: Gee, they got everything but he is lonely. His invitation was particularly surprising because we were never *that* close. He was disappointed that I couldn't take him up on his offer to spend some time at Sands Point, since I had obligations in the city, but he wasn't angry. He just wandered around Radio Row like a lost soul."

Selznick, agonizing over Twentieth's procrastination about making a firm commitment for Jennifer's services, was simultaneously brooding about what he considered "the husband problem."

Jennifer had told him of Bob's intention—to join her in California before Christmas—which Selznick considered a mixed blessing. According to reporter Bob Thomas, his relationship with Jennifer at the time was the same as with his other leading ladies. "He was domineering, persuasively overpowering. He attempted to impose his will over her in all matters, from simple elements of grooming to the conduct of her everyday life."

If anything irritated him more than temperamental stars, it was the mates of any of his stars who might vocally disagree with his decisions and edicts. He had never forgiven Laurence Olivier for taking Vivien Leigh back to England after the war broke out, although the decision to leave was as much hers as Olivier's.

He deeply resented Ingrid Bergman's husband, Peter Lindstrom, who, as Irene Selznick recalls, "was not a subtle man. . . . Righteous and strict, he was able to dominate his home in Hollywood as he had in Sweden, and had even refused to allow Bergman to buy a new evening dress for an important premiere."

Selznick had no idea to what degree Walker would interfere with his plans for Jones. Jennifer had told him, of course, that Bob intended to resume his radio career, but Selznick didn't think that would be enough to keep Walker out of his hair. If Walker was to

be in California, then the best thing was to keep him busy—and that meant getting him some acting jobs in films.

Jennifer had told him of Bob's early futile attempts to crash the movies, but the situation had changed markedly in three years. The majors were losing an alarming number of leading men and young actors to the war, and to aggravate the situation, all the studios were turning out films with military themes. Draft-exempt actors were at a premium, whatever the reason for the exemption. MGM was among the hardest hit—and from his father-in-law, Louis B. Mayer, down, David had powerful connections in the lion's den.

Among the properties being prepared at the most prestigious of all studios was a grim, realistic melodrama, *Bataan Patrol*, recounting the last days of the heroes who had endured one of the earliest World War II defeats in the Pacific. Robert Taylor, soon to enlist in the Navy Air Force, was to star, but there were twelve additional male roles still to be cast, representing the standard cross-section of fighting men.

One of the most appealing roles was that of a cocky young sailor—one of the last of the expendable servicemen to die in the defense of the peninsula. A twenty-seven-year-old Broadway actor, Richard Widmark, was a leading contender, despite his age, but suddenly, out of the blue, Bob's agent, Marcella Knapp, received a phone call from the head of Metro's New York casting office requesting that Bob audition for the part. If he possessed the right qualities, they'd set up a test in a Manhattan studio and then fly it to Culver City to be viewed by *Bataan*'s director, Tay Garnett, producer Irving Starr, and other MGM executives.

If he was given the role of Leonard Purkett, he'd be signed to the standard seven-year contract with options. His salary would be negotiated once a decision was made.

When Miss Knapp called Bob with the news, he was far from euphoric. "I've tested before. You should see my report cards. Ask any scout. I'm perfect for radio, but for pictures—no studio ever chanted, 'We want Walker.' I did two bit roles at MGM. Nobody even noticed me."

Miss Knapp refused to be put off by his pessimism. "We're going over to 1540 Broadway tomorrow," she said firmly, "and you're going to pour on the boyish charm. And, for God's sake, don't

mention those movies you did there, and be glad that nobody did notice you. If you're hired now, that'll be something to laugh about later."

"I still think you're wasting your time," Bob replied. "But what the hell, there's nothing to lose. I'm not desperate for a job."

Due in part to that lack of desperation, he gave a superb reading. A formal test was set up within the week. It seemed almost too easy, but the role of Purkett was a "natural," a scene-stealer, one that didn't require a matinee idol.

The studio, he was told, was looking for typical G.I. Joe and girl-next-door types now, people with whom audiences could identify. Most of the 1930s' glamour girls—Garbo, Norma Shearer, Joan Crawford—were slowly being eased out as relics of another era. White ties and tails were being replaced by khaki, satin and sequins by gingham and ruffled aprons, passion by patriotism.

Bob breezed through his test, projecting an irresistible combination of cockiness and wistful charm. Within a week Marcella Knapp informed him that MGM wanted to sign him. Due to commitments with the other actors in *Bataan Patrol*, later retitled *Bataan*, he'd receive only sixth billing. "But," Miss Knapp assured him, "if you click—and you will—the studio is practically guaranteeing a star buildup. Everyone there was very taken by you."

Throughout this crucial period, Bob was constantly on the phone with Phyl. Her delight over his big break was tempered only by her frustration at still being left dangling about *Bernadette*. Everyone was enthusiastic, but no deal was being consummated. She was as miserable as he, missed the children, and was so bored that she offered to test with performers up for other roles in the film—just to keep busy.

Bataan was scheduled to start shooting early in January. Bob still intended to be in California before Christmas. He and Phylis decided to have the boys' nurse, Henrietta, escort them west for the Thanksgiving holidays, while Bob used the intervening weeks to close down the house in Sands Point.

"In the meantime," he told Jennifer, "you can be looking around for a place for us. Maybe you can find something like the one we have here, where we can really enjoy the outdoor life." And because he couldn't resist it, he added, "Just make sure the bathtub isn't in the kitchen."

David Selznick, though, relieved that Bob had been signed by MGM, persuaded Metro's head of publicity, Howard Strickling, to avoid mentioning in any initial releases that Walker was married to Jennifer Jones and the father of two boys. He also maneuvered to keep Bob's name out of Jennifer's publicity, not wishing to damage the "virgin" image of Bernadette. Why mention it if it wasn't necessary? The less said about Bob, the better.

Jennifer spent Thanksgiving with her boys. Selznick, busy with his wife and sons, sneaked off for a few seconds to phone and wish Jennifer a happy holiday and reassure her that he intended to get a definite decision from Twentieth within the week.

On December 3 he called Bill Perlberg to ask him what the hell was going on about Jennifer. Perlberg told Selznick he had made up his mind, as had Henry King and Bill Goetz, but that they had promised Anne Baxter they would give her a test. Selznick told them to hurry up, for God's sake, pointing out that they had kept Jennifer idle—and on the payroll—for a long time.

Anne Baxter tested on December 5, a mere formality. When her footage was viewed together with Jennifer's, the three men's earlier opinions were only reaffirmed. Jennifer was the definitive Bernadette. Goetz phoned his brother-in-law, who in turn contacted Jennifer, beaming. "The role is yours."

Bob was home alone when her call came, her voice brimming with joy and excitement. "Darling," she exclaimed breathlessly, "I got it. I'm Bernadette. I don't believe it, but the role is mine."

Bob recalled sharing her elation and counting the remaining days until the two would be together.

On December 9, 1942, the press was informed that Jennifer Jones, an unknown actress under contract to David O. Selznick, would play "the most coveted role of the year."

Filming would commence on the back lot of the vast Twentieth Century-Fox studios on March 15. Principal photography was due to be completed by mid to late July, with an initial release set for Christmas week. The latter was considered perfect timing for *Bernadette*'s religious theme. It would also bring it under the wire to qualify for the 1943 Oscar nominations.

Because of George Seaton's 329-page screenplay, running time was estimated at between two and a half to three hours and the final budget set at two million dollars.

The press was also informed that at least two dozen powerful actors would be or had been selected for pivotal roles, among them Charles Bickford, Anne Revere, Lee J. Cobb, Vincent Price, and Gladys Cooper. William Eythe, a young stage actor being groomed for stardom, would be cast as Bernadette's pre-miracle "love interest."

Naturally the studio was besieged with requests for interviews with the lucky unknown, but even the three gossip queens, Louella Parsons, Hedda Hooper, and Sheilah Graham, were tactfully but firmly turned down. David O. Selznick emphatically decreed: "No interviews or gallery sitting until *The Song of Bernadette* is completed and ready for release." He wanted to build an aura of mystery around his fresh young discovery in order to make her Bernadette as believable as possible.

He also cautioned Jennifer to keep a very low profile, to avoid social functions, nightclubs, premieres, any place where she could be cornered and questioned. Since she was still very timorous and nervous in crowds (and would remain so), she was as relieved by that advice as she was by the fact that she'd be protected from the press.

In addition, he advised that she remain aloof from other members of the cast, lest her performance be influenced by unwise suggestions. With a single exception, Jennifer dutifully adhered to her mentor's request.

Shortly after they had met during the testing period, a warm rapport had developed between Jennifer and fifty-four-year-old veteran character actor Charles Bickford, cast as Peyramale, Dean of Lourdes, who after a period of doubt eventually becomes Bernadette's defender, protector, and champion.

Bickford, who had come to Hollywood from Broadway in 1930 and had a rough, tough screen image, was in reality a warm, compassionate man, happily married to the same woman since 1919, and the father of two grown children. Aware of the strain Jennifer had been under and sensitive to her insecurities, he was a pillar of strength and support, almost a surrogate father. Their friendship would last until his death in 1967.

Bob arrived in Beverly Hills the week before Christmas and he and Jennifer scurried around to give the boys a real Christmas with

a tree, toys, candy canes—everything they would have had back east.

They saved their gala New Year's celebration, as was their custom, for January 2, which now marked the fifth anniversary of their meeting and their fourth wedding anniversary. Bob made reservations for the best table at the most expensive restaurant in Beverly Hills. For three hours they forgot about their careers, their babies, everything—except how wonderful it was to be back together for good.

Bob had no presentiment that this would be the last Christmas holiday and the last wedding anniversary they would ever spend together.

Chapter

8

Later that week Bob received a call to report to MGM to start work on *Bataan*. His initial scenes were sent over by messenger with instructions to report to Makeup by seven A.M.

There was no welcoming committee awaiting him at the artists' gate. After locating his name, the strict security guard instructed Bob to park his car in the large lot opposite the administration building and return on foot—a usual procedure for studio employees and supporting players. Only the stars and executives were afforded their own private parking spaces inside the lot.

Bob was then passed through and directed to the makeup department, where, again, he had to identify himself and the film to which he had been assigned. With expert efficiency, his hair was deftly disheveled, his face covered with grime.

He was then sent to Wardrobe to be outfitted for his role. Throughout the film, his "wardrobe" would consist of well-worn navy fatigues and a battered sailor's cap, replaced in later scenes by a combat helmet. At that point a studio aide met him to escort him to the shooting site.

Bataan had been realistically recreated on indoor sound stage number sixteen: bridges, ravines, foxholes, tropical foliage, a native hut. As he was marveling at the sight, Bob was approached by a jovial, soft-spoken man who extended his hand and said, "Welcome to the war, Bob. I'm Tay Garnett, the director of this little epic. You did a great test. We're glad to have you. Now I want you to meet Bob Taylor and a few of the other fellows before the camera starts rolling."

Walker's first scenes were with Taylor. Being a quick study, he knew his lines perfectly. Garnett, however, felt that the scenes

were just not jelling. When the company broke for lunch, he asked Bob if they could speak privately for a few minutes.

"How old are you, kid?" he asked.

"Twenty-four. I never lied about it."

"I'm sure," Garnett replied. "But that's been the crux of our problem this morning. You're acting *your* age. Purkett is a green kid in his teens. With that boyish mug of yours, you can get away with that easily. But you've been coming across too mature. I'm not looking for Andy Hardy—but just play the part younger, and you'll be okay. You'll be more than okay. When Purkett goes, I want the audience heartbroken. Bob Taylor is the star of the film, but you can steal it right out from under him—and I'm not handing you any Hollywood bullshit."

Bob got the message. He played Purkett younger, more vulnerable, and the result was indeed a scene-stealing performance. Later Garnett would say of Bob: "I admired him deeply. He was a talented, sensitive, fey guy who combined the comic abilities of Jack Lemmon and Bob Montgomery with a heart-grabbing little-boy-lost appeal."

Bob, in turn, trusted and liked Garnett. He talked glowingly to him about Jennifer and their two boys, even voicing his disappointment that she had been forbidden to visit the set to watch him work.

"It's nutty," he confided to Garnett, "but Mr. Selznick doesn't want us to be seen together or linked together. It's as though we are clandestine lovers instead of a family. He keeps saying he wants Phyl to present a virginal image to the public. I don't understand that man."

"Relax, Bobby," Garnett advised, "and join the club. I don't think anyone understands Selznick, including our boss, and he's his father-in-law. But you won't have to endure this charade forever."

Apart from Garnett and Robert Taylor, Bob had little contact with members of the all-male cast. Though Taylor was well aware that Bob was outshining him in their scenes together, he was far too generous a person to pull rank and prevent the grand larceny. As an attention-grabber, Garnett had Bob chew gum throughout the action, and during the last few minutes of the film, the wounded gob would compose a letter to his mom awash with such

pathos that there was barely a dry eye on the set when the scene, played with Bob Taylor, was completed.

Taylor did everything possible to support Bob in front of and away from the cameras, and cognizant of the value of publicity to a newcomer, encouraged still photographers to shoot candids of them together which could be planted in newspapers or magazines.

Walker, who usually avoided superlatives, openly admitted that "Bob Taylor is the swellest person I've ever met. He's made everything so easy for me."

Other than Taylor, he made few friends among the cast, which also included George Murphy, Thomas Mitchell, Lloyd Nolan, Desi Arnaz, and Barry Nelson, the latter another eager young MGM contractee about to be drafted. Barry remembers only that, "Our paths seldom crossed, but we all heard that the studio was high on him. The world was opening to him. The bad things would come later."

Everyone agreed. When MGM executives Benny Thau and Eddie Mannix viewed the daily footage of his scenes, they decided to rush him into a prestige film as soon as possible. *Madame Curie*, the biography of the discoverers of radium, was in preparation: the role of Curie's young assistant and friend, David Le Gros, was still uncast. Director Mervyn LeRoy was convinced that Bob could readily be transformed from a cocky American sailor into a serious French scientist.

Bob was handed the script while still fighting the battle of Bataan. "This will give you the opportunity to prove your versatility," he was told by Benny Thau, "and you'll get fourth billing after Greer Garson, Walter Pidgeon, and Henry Travers."

The role of Le Gros was an undemanding one, but Bob felt he was miscast. He was in no position, however, to argue with the studio.

"I don't believe it," Bob told Garnett. "I'm from Utah, Phyl's from Oklahoma—and we'll both be playing in French roles." "Par for the course," laughed Garnett. "Just concentrate on *our* picture. Once the public and critics discover you, you'll be able to write your own ticket." Bob couldn't suppress his astonishment. The way things were progressing, he'd have two films completed even before Phyl started working in *Bernadette*. The only thing that

dismayed him was that after their long separation, they had so little time together—which was just the way Selznick had wanted it.

In order to alleviate her boredom and do something constructive, Jennifer enrolled in a nurse's aide training course at the Los Angeles County Hospital, with serious intentions of serving in that capacity when she wasn't before the cameras. She and Bob had only dinnertime to be with one another, and Sundays, which they usually spent driving around with Bobby and Michael in search of a suitable house—not easy to find at a time when there was both gas rationing and a shortage of small, comfortable homes at a reasonable distance from their studios.

Director Henry King eventually solved their housing problem. King, whose faith in the young Tyrone Power had been responsible for Power's ascent to stardom in *Lloyds of London* some eight years earlier, was still Power's favorite director and close friend. Aware that Power's former house in Bel Air was for rent, he suggested Jennifer and Bob look at it.

The gracious and elegant white villa, leasing for $225 a month, was more spacious and luxurious than anything the Walkers had seen to date. It featured a large backyard, where the boys could romp or ride their tricycles safely, as well as servants' quarters. Their household help, including a nurse and a part-time gardener, would come to an additional two hundred dollars a month, but with their combined salaries they could manage nicely.

Their other expenses were minimal. Once Jennifer started to work, there'd be no time for entertaining, and neither of them was interested in jewelry or fancy clothes.

Bob, who had brought a couple of business suits from New York, supplemented his wardrobe with several pairs of slacks and a half-dozen plaid shirts. Jennifer's "shopping spree" consisted of purchasing a few cotton pinafores, a half-dozen interchangeable peasant blouses, an afternoon dress, and a few pairs of flat-heeled shoes—shoes being among the items rationed during wartime.

Her only extravagance since arriving in Hollywood was the purchase of a new Mercury sedan to get her to and from the studio.

Shortly after signing the lease for the Bel Air house, Bob splurged four hundred dollars on a second-hand motorcycle because, as he later told a friend, "Phyl was not economical with gas, and we were not allowed enough for two large cars. She hated the

Robert Walker at 4, already a rebel. (The Academy of Motion Picture Arts and Sciences)

Walker found an outlet for his frustrations at the Davis San Diego Army and Navy Academy, where he became president of his senior class and three times won Best Actor honors in the state drama tournament. Below: Walker is second from left, next to drama teacher Virginia Atkinson. (Davis Academy)

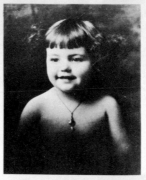

AGE 2

AGE 12

AGE 17
HIGH SCHOOL
GRADUATION
1936

PHYLIS TO-DAY

PHYLIS
ISLEY

MAY QUEEN
MONTE CASSINO

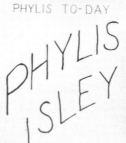

PHYLIS AND BLANCHE Y
AT PAWNEE BILLS RAN

A 1938 photo montage of Phylis Isley before her marriage to
Walker. The "Mr. Dickinson" of the dedication ran a stock
company in which she performed during the summer of 1937. (The
Museum of Modern Art/Film Stills Archive)

An early portrait of the "big-eyed girl." At this time, she attracted the interest of David Selznick. (Author's collection)

Phylis' second film role: 204 words in a fifteen-chapter Republic serial, *Dick Tracy's G-Men*. (McClelland Collection)

Simultaneous breakthroughs: Bob made a strong impression in *Bataan* (above) and *See Here, Private Hargrove* (with Donna Reed) (below, left) while, under Selznick's tutelage, the newly christened Jennifer Jones exploded into view with *The Song of Bernadette* (here, with Anne Revere) (below, right)—and won an Oscar. (McClelland/Jim Meyer Collection, Kent State University Libraries/McClelland)

The Hollywood "dream couple" at home with
their two sons, Bobby and Michael. Their
happiness had only months to go. (The Academy
of Motion Picture Arts and Sciences)

The storm breaks. Even while wooing Jennifer away from Bob, Selznick persisted in casting the two together as young lovers in his World War II epic *Since You Went Away*. A few days before shooting began, he threw a cast party on the set. An unsuspecting Bob posed with a smiling Jennifer. Soon thereafter, she dropped the bomb: she was leaving him. Their poignant love scenes became agony for both.
(Author/Tom Johnson Collection)

After receiving her Oscar for *Bernadette*, Jennifer docs a radio broadcast with Greer Garson. The next day, she filed for divorce from Bob.
(Academy) ▶

Bob's roles in *Thirty Seconds Over Tokyo* (above left) and *The Clock* (with Judy Garland) (above right) increased his popularity—but he still couldn't get over Jennifer. "It broke your heart to see the guy," said *Tokyo* costar Van Johnson. (McClelland)

At a birthday party for Van Johnson with, from left to right: Keenan Wynn, Evie Wynn, Johnson, Hume Cronyn, Judy Garland, and James Brown. (Author)

Talking to director Richard Whorf, who tried to shake him out of his melancholia. (Author)

Between takes.
The divorce was final now.
(Author)

A brief relationship with model/writer
Florence Pritchett ended in bitterness.
(Author) ▼

motorcycle. It was the only major bone of contention between us—I thought."

While Bob was working a ten-hour day at MGM, Jennifer busied herself by putting her house in order, and David Selznick was frantically attempting to cope with his tangled business affairs, find a property suitable for Jennifer which he could personally produce—and choose a gift that would mark the long-awaited starting date of *Bernadette*. The gift must be in impeccable taste— neither too intimate nor too impersonal.

After rejecting several possibilities, he finally decided to present Jennifer with a fine leather-bound first edition of *The Song of Bernadette*. With no little effort he located a first edition and the name of the best bookbinder in Los Angeles. When the elegant volume was delivered to him in February, he immediately shipped it to Franz Werfel, who was living at the St. Moritz Hotel in New York City. He enclosed a brief letter requesting the author to autograph it to Jennifer, so he could surprise her with it on the first day of shooting.

Werfel graciously complied and penned a note to Selznick informing him that he was planning an early visit to California so he could meet his "heroine" in the flesh.

Selznick had intended to keep what he considered an inspired gift a closely guarded secret until that long-awaited first day. However, his pleasurable anticipation of Jennifer's reaction gave way to a very different emotion when, almost simultaneously, a more explosive secret became public knowledge.

Aside from a few innocuous production items and the release of a few photographs, Howard Strickling and his staff at MGM had done nothing to launch either a major or a minor publicity buildup for Bob Walker.

In late February, however, when the publicity department received a call from Alice Pardoe West of the Ogden *Standard Examiner*—the same Alice West who had reviewed Bob's operetta at Madison Grade School—requesting an in-depth interview with their home-town boy, they discussed it with Bob, who thought it wise to comply. The *Standard Examiner*, he remembered, had published his photograph and devoted several paragraphs to him when he did his initial bit in *Winter Carnival*. The newspaper had also covered his trip to Ogden when he, Jennifer, and little Bobby

paid that week-long visit to his folks in November 1940. It would be impossible to ignore Mrs. West without creating ill-will back home. If he refused to see her, that in itself would be a story, one in which both he and Jennifer could be presented in a most unfavorable light.

Privately he was relieved, even grateful, to be able to put an end to the deception. "Have someone bring her to the set tomorrow," he told Howard Strickling. "I'll try to make a good impression. But if she asks about Jennifer and the boys, I can't say 'No comment.' She already has the material in her files."

That evening he told Jennifer about the forthcoming interview, and she was visibly distressed. "Mr. Selznick is going to be awfully upset. What can I tell him?" "The truth," Bob replied. "The paper knows all about us, and there was no way out. I'll try to keep the conversation centered upon my career. But I can't play the boyish bachelor forever."

Mrs. West arrived on Stage 16 as scheduled, and recalled: "As I walked on the MGM set, Bob was one of the first to greet me. He had just performed in one of the most touching scenes in the picture. The sequence was inspired and there were many moist eyes among the onlookers.

"'That kid has something!' and 'That kid's all right . . . he can really act' went around the group. And that's what Hollywood is saying now about young Walker. He is going places!"

Mrs. West interrogated Bob throughout the afternoon, filling her story with extensive biographical material about his youth, education, courtship, marriage, early struggles, radio career, and the events leading to *Bataan*. Once Bob started talking about his wife, the floodgate opened. He didn't, however, touch on their efforts to keep their marriage a secret. Thus, when Mrs. West asked about joint photographs, he was forced to admit that both MGM and Twentieth had put a ban on home layouts "for the time being." "Still," he added, "it's a wonderful break that we should have a chance to come to Hollywood together. If we can only keep our careers here and not too scattered. I'm keeping my fingers crossed!"

Mrs. West should have been satisfied with the interview—but she felt her story needed something more, that something being a few paragraphs from Jennifer to round things out.

"You'll have to have her studio arrange that," Bob said apologetically. "But I'll put in a good word."

Jennifer, however, didn't want to be interviewed. An angry David Selznick was violently opposed. The head of publicity at Twentieth, furious that their "virgin" would soon be exposed as a married woman with two children, was initially dead set against it, but the damage had been done, and Mrs. West was a persistent journalist—so a compromise was arranged.

The studio would set up a brief interview if Mrs. West gave her word to limit the conversation solely to the picture and role of *Bernadette*. Mrs. West, eager for anything from Jennifer to flesh out the Walker story, promised to stick to those subjects.

The little that Jennifer had to contribute sounded like a prepared statement:

"An actress plays all types of roles. When I play Bernadette, I will become Bernadette, but when I'm off screen I'm again Jennifer Jones. No girl could fail to want her life to be so exemplary that she can be worthy of a role like Bernadette."

Jennifer volunteered no information about her private life—and Mrs. West lived up to her agreement. But in order to add some substance to Jennifer's vapid statement, West editorialized, "Jennifer is lovely to look at and fits the requirements [for Bernadette] superbly. In real life she is indeed an exemplary character, refraining from all stimulants, including even tea and coffee, and plays the role of mother to her two small sons, Bobby and Michael, in a most sincere and modest manner."

Mrs. West was obviously perplexed and annoyed that she couldn't secure a photograph of the Walkers together to illustrate her long and flattering story. When she returned to her desk in Ogden, she arranged for portraits of Bob and Jennifer to be placed side by side above the interview, which she began provocatively:

"All eyes in Hollywood are focused on Bob Walker and Jennifer Jones these days . . . Mr. and Mrs. Robert Walker to Ogdenites . . . for Bob is the son of Mr. and Mrs. Horace H. Walker of 2504 Eccles.

"Which one will reach stardom first? Or will they come in neck-and-neck? In this most unusual story of real life, Bob and Jennifer are playing the original roles."

With those two brief paragraphs Mrs. West, whose readership

was confined to Ogden, managed to outscoop the Mesdames Parsons, Hooper, and Graham; sent David O. Selznick into a frenzy; and forced Horace and Zella Walker to get an unlisted phone number.

Bob Walker was relieved, however, and roared with laughter at the opening line: "All eyes in Hollywood are focused on Bob Walker and Jennifer Jones these days."

"They are?" he asked rhetorically. "No one outside the studios even knows us yet."

At MGM, the publicity department, delighted at the coverage, regretted that the story hadn't been held until June, when *Bataan* was scheduled to be rushed into release. No one at Twentieth was overwrought by the revelation, so extremely favorable toward Jennifer, but the studio still continued to veto any photograph of the two together.

The Walkers' life-style remained unchanged, although as Bob later told a friend, he noticed Jennifer seemed exceedingly tense and preoccupied.

"Anything bothering you, honey?" he asked.

"I think I just have a case of first-day jitters. I've been sitting around waiting for so long that, now that the picture is going to start in a few days, I'm scared stiff. What if I can't live up to their expectations?"

"You wouldn't be human if you weren't a little scared," Bob reassured her. "But after all those tests you've been through, you wouldn't have gotten the part if they had any doubts. You can't compare movies with the theater. If you fluff a line, or if your reading is off, the director yells 'Cut,' and they redo it. I've heard wonderful things about Henry King. They say he's a kind, patient, and tactful man, not at all like some of these tyrants out here. And a wonderful director. Just listen to him—and don't let *anyone else* confuse you."

He was referring to David Selznick, who had been inundating King and Perlberg with suggestions concerning Jennifer's walk, speech patterns, makeup, hairstyling, and had been privately passing his ideas on to Jennifer.

King, however, after studying David's suggestions, and well aware of his impulsive enthusiasms, chose to file and forget them.

"We're going to be handing the s.o.b. a star on a silver platter,

possibly an Oscar contender, but I can live without his kibitzing," he told Perlberg. "I just hope to God we can keep him away from the set."

On March 15, her first day as Bernadette, Jennifer's dressing room was filled with flowers and good wishes from the studio brass and from Bob. But the largest arrangement came from David Selznick, accompanied by the expensively bound autographed copy of *Song of Bernadette*.

When she stepped before the cameras in a simple gray home-spun skirt, dark blouse, and black stockings, she projected the illusion of an innocent fourteen-year-old. Henry King, a great believer in rehearsals, recalled, "I rehearsed with Jennifer until we both had the same understanding of a scene. Then I would film a take. Jennifer had such a complete understanding that seldom were additional takes necessary. She was a perfectionist, never completely satisfied with a sequence, and always needing reassurance. She had an almost uncanny degree of concentration: she could cease being Jennifer and become, in an instant, the character she was playing. It's a rare quality, and it goes beyond acting."

When she completed her final scene for the day, she was almost embarrassed by the round of applause she received from everyone on the set.

She was completely exhausted when she reached home, where Bob had been impatiently awaiting her return. It was an effort even to eat the light supper their newly hired cook had prepared—let alone answer Bob's barrage of questions about the day. She was totally involved with the following day's scenes, which she wanted to memorize before retiring—usually about nine-thirty, since she needed a minimum of ten hours' sleep in order to function properly the next day.

"I think it went very well," she told Bob, "but I'm awfully tired." Jennifer's supper conversation consisted mostly of monosyllables. Bob did not press for details. He had the ability to shed his screen character almost before his makeup came off, but he was sensitive to Jennifer's total absorption in her role and did not want to distract her or add to the strain.

Since *Bataan* was an action film, he could simply scan his lines, memorize them quickly, then review them between setups,

whereas *Bernadette* was talky, with long passages of dialogue designed to capture period and place.

If he caught himself growing the least bit testy, he'd remind himself, "I don't have the fate of a two-million-dollar production resting on my shoulders."

Nevertheless, he felt strangely let down and unfulfilled when she failed to share the day's experiences with him.

As shut out and disappointed as her absolute absorption in *Bernadette* made Bob feel, it was only to be the first of an endless string of disappointments that lay ahead.

Chapter

9

The time the Walkers had free to spend with one another gradually dwindled down to practically no time at all, except for Sundays—and even on Sundays, Jennifer was concerned about the next day's schedule.

When the two had identical early-morning calls, Jennifer would get behind the wheel of the Mercury, Bob would hop on his motorcycle and ride alongside her to the Pico gate of Twentieth Century-Fox, wave, and continue on down Motor Avenue to MGM. He'd usually be back home playing with his sons when she arrived home.

He'd no sooner finished *Bataan* than he was rushed into *Madame Curie*. He felt uncomfortable in the period piece, and neither Greer Garson nor Walter Pidgeon treated him like one of the family or invited him to lunch at the commissary. Nevertheless, he managed to be ingratiating in a thankless role, and director Mervyn LeRoy insists, "He did not seem troubled in those days at all."

Actress June Lockhart retains fond memories: "Bob Walker was so kind to me, a real gentleman and a splendid actor. Mervyn LeRoy wanted to add a scene where Walker's character—as an older man now—comes to see Madame Curie win an award at the end of her career. I was the daughter he brought with him to the ceremony. It was a charming scene, and seeing this excited young girl, a member of the generation which would benefit from Curie's discovery, provided just the right capper to the story. I was startled when I first saw Bob walk on the set. He was a very young man but was made up to look like a man of fifty for our scene. In those days the makeup artists thought a man of fifty ought to look like Walter

Brennan the day he died. In any case, Mr. LeRoy loved the scene. Miss Garson, who hadn't been told of the addition, obviously wasn't pleased. When *she* saw it, she said, 'What was that?' They explained it was the new ending.

"'With that young girl? Oh no,' protested Miss Garson, who always got her own way. And my whole scene ended up on the cutting-room floor.

"My father [actor Gene Lockhart] was furious, and I was heartbroken, but I received a warm and compassionate note from Bob, who must have heard how upset I was, encouraging me in my career and adding that, when he got to be fifty, he hoped he'd have a real daughter just like me. That was the kind of man he was—so sweet, so concerned about the feelings of others."

Miss Lockhart's reactions to Bob are echoed by those of publicist Ann Straus, who arrived at MGM the same time as Bob.

"I loved Bob Walker," says Miss Straus. "He was so sweet and sensitive. Like the other young people at Metro, he enjoyed lunching at the publicity table, and the loose camaraderie of the publicity people.

"Unlike many of the others, he didn't press for what is known as the big publicity buildup. When he was called into the gallery and told to bring several changes of clothing for the standard portrait sitting, he shyly admitted that his wardrobe was rather sparse and that he only owned a couple of ties, and was genuinely relieved when informed that the large MGM wardrobe department was in a position to supply anything that was lacking."

Reluctantly he was forced to turn down Miss Straus's request for a home layout with his wife and sons.

"Oh, I'm afraid that's out of the question," he said apologetically. "There's a clause in my wife's contract forbidding any photographs of the family at home—or anywhere. I can't even give you a snapshot of us together while she's working on *Bernadette*. But after the movie is released, things will be different. I hope you're not angry. I don't want to give you a hard time."

"Bob," Miss Straus continues, "had an amazing sensitivity. One day when we were at the publicity table, he looked at me and knew instantly that I had been having a hard day—oh, maybe one of the stars had been on my back or something. He asked what was wrong. I told him it was nothing, but he said, 'Have a drink with

me after work and tell me about it.' That evening he said, 'What's the worst that can happen? That you'll get fired? So you may get a better job. Good people are hard to find. I'm willing to bet that you'll be at this studio long after I'm gone.' [Miss Straus stayed at Metro until 1959.]

"By the time he had finished his pep talk, he had me practically convinced that MGM's publicity department couldn't run without my services. That's the way he was—and he never changed his attitude toward me."

During those early months at Metro, it was obvious that everyone on the lot was charmed and impressed by Bob and considered him a valuable asset to the studio—unassuming, untemperamental, serious and professional when the cameras were rolling, witty and ingratiating during the breaks. No one could fault him either as a person or as an actor. The studio knew it had a winner and intended to make the most of it.

Bob was still in production on *Madame Curie* in June when he received a summons to report to Eddie Mannix's office as soon as he had completed his scenes for the day.

Mannix picked up a document he had on his desk. Bob recognized it immediately; it was a copy of his contract, and he watched with a sinking heart as Mannix methodically ripped it apart.

"I guess that means you're not picking up my option for another six months," Bob stammered, unnerved by this unexpected turn of events. "I don't understand. Mr. Garnett and Mr. LeRoy have been so complimentary. What did I do?"

Mannix didn't have the heart to keep Bob dangling.

"What did you do? You stole the picture. And, contrary to popular belief, we don't believe in buying exceptional talent for cheap."

He picked up a fresh sheaf of papers from his desk. "You've had the standard 'unknown's' contract. This is a new one—for seven years starting today—with starring terms and a healthy four-figure salary. As you know, because of the war, we can't give regular raises, but as they keep saying, the war can't last forever.

"And speaking of the war, here's something you should have."

He handed Bob a copy of the current best-seller *See Here, Private Hargrove*, Marion Hargrove's hilarious, joyous, and outrageous account of his adventures at basic-training camp.

"Harry Kurnitz is polishing up the script now, and you'll have your copy as soon as it's completed. Wesley Ruggles will direct, and we're lining up the rest of the cast. Your role, of course, gets star billing. When you read the book—it's all Hargrove. Any questions?"

Naively Bob blurted, "Do I look like Hargrove?"

Mannix laughed. "Of course not, but you look the way Hargrove *should* look. When this picture is released, they'll think Marion is the impostor."

Bob was impatient to tell Jennifer the news. It was still early. He impulsively decided to visit her on the set. He had never done that before—she had never encouraged it—but this was a momentous occasion: a new contract, a starring role in a best-seller. He was certain she'd be delighted to see him.

In his casual clothes, his hair disheveled by the wind, he looked like a movie-struck teenager when he approached the guard at the Pico gate.

"I'd like to have a pass," he requested, "for the *Bernadette* set. Tell them it's Robert Walker, Jennifer Jones's husband. I have identification. Miss Jones will okay it."

After phoning the main office, the guard said roughly, "Sorry, bud, but that's a closed set. No outsiders, no press."

"Can't I talk to someone? I'm sure it will be okay. As I said, I'm her husband. I'll wait in her dressing room. Perhaps you can have someone meet me here," he pleaded.

Another call, another rebuff.

"Miss Jones cannot be disturbed. By *anyone*. You better leave. You're blocking traffic."

As he reversed his cycle, he noticed the expensive car behind him—and could not fail to recognize the occupant. It was David O. Selznick, and the gateman passed him through without question.

Oh well, Bob remembered thinking, his brother-in-law runs the studio. It had happened so quickly that he didn't have a chance to call out to Selznick to enlist his help. Later he'd admit that he failed to put two and two together. "I guess I didn't recognize the signals. I thought he had business on the lot. It never occurred to me that he might be visiting Jennifer."

Jennifer returned home later than usual that evening.

After tucking his sons into bed, Bob occupied his time browsing through *Hargrove*. Although he'd been depressed by his rejection at Twentieth, he found himself roaring with laughter and confident that Americans, surfeited on gloomy reports from the battlefronts and by downbeat blood-and-guts war films, would find it a delightful diversion. His only challenge would be to make the character appealing and amusing without resorting to buffoonery.

Bob was still reading when Jennifer walked into the living room, looking wearier than ever. He had decided to say nothing about his aborted attempt to see her at Twentieth unless she raised the subject. She made no reference to it, and he presumed no one had mentioned it to her. As had been the case so many times in the past few months, she seemed in no mood for any conversation, but he couldn't refrain from sharing his good news with her: the new contract, the raise, the starring *Hargrove* role.

"That we should both be starring . . . each in a picture based on a best-seller, seems almost too good to be true," he exclaimed.

She made an effort to share his excitement. "It's wonderful." She smiled, but her voice was weak, and she still seemed lost in a world of her own. A year earlier, they might have been kissing and hugging and dancing around the room, but it was obvious she was totally enervated.

She had told Alice West that "When I play Bernadette, I *am* Bernadette, but when I'm off the screen, I'm Jennifer Jones again."

Jennifer Jones, perhaps. But not quite Phylis Walker, wife and mother. She still loved her husband and her family, was still shy and unpretentious around her coworkers, but subtle alterations in her personality were playing havoc with her emotions. These changes confused and upset her at the time. They were not really changes, however, but rather a crystallization of something which had always been inside her.

Just a few months later, she revealed: "For years I had heard people say, 'Keep your eye on the ball,' but it never meant anything to me. Then one day I happened to attend a championship golf tournament, and all at once, like a bolt from the blue, it came to me. The secret of success in anything—from games to the real game of living—is just that: to keep your eye on the ball. And the ball is your ambition or goal. I happened to check back and found

I had always done just that without knowing it. As a child, I decided to become an actress, and I kept my eye on that goal right on through. While it may seem that I swerved from the path to become a wife and mother, there was always the same ambition in my mind's eye."

Ignited by opportunity, fanned by the skilled manipulations of a powerful mogul, the flame of her ambition would consume her and take a terrible toll on those closest to her.

Bob Walker, too, retained a childhood ambition: to be wanted and loved. For him acting was a lark, a pleasant way to make enough money to take care of those he loved and who loved him. Although he took pride in his professionalism, making movies was something he felt he could abandon without regret.

Bob would later admit that although he was always aware of his wife's passion for acting, he had been oblivious of the extent of her ambition. He had been certain that once the ordeal of *Bernadette* was over, their lives together would resume their normal pattern. *Bernadette* was due to be completed on July 25, about the same time as *Hargrove* with its comparatively short shooting schedule.

Since a standard studio contract called for forty weeks of pay and twelve weeks off salary per annum, Bob began planning an August vacation, a "second honeymoon." If he was able to stash away enough gas coupons, he and Jennifer could drive to Ogden for a brief visit with his family, then on to Dallas to visit Phil and Flora, and possibly even visit the charming villages that dotted Baja California; sleeping as late as they wished, enjoying a carefree holiday.

With his new contract, and their financial affairs in the hands of a business manager who invested their money wisely in insurance and war bonds, his primary dream, once the war was won, was to tour Europe with Jennifer: London, Paris, and especially Lourdes. That fantasy, however, was reserved for the peaceful future.

Within a week after he completed his last scenes on *Madame Curie*, Bob started work on *See Here, Private Hargrove*. Producer George Haight had supplied him with a strong supporting cast, including Robert Benchley, Ray Collins, Chill Wills, Donna Reed—a promising actress being groomed for stardom, as a gra-

tuitous love interest—and Keenan Wynn as Hargrove's swindler pal.

Keenan remembers, "I had first met Bob [and his wife, Phyl] when we were involved in radio work in New York, but we had not socialized then—we were merely very casual acquaintances. It wasn't until I met them again on the West Coast that I really got to know them well, when Bob and I were both in *See Here, Private Hargrove*. We discovered that we worked very well as a team, and that bound us together. Comically, I'd say we tore the screen apart in *Hargrove*: there wasn't a dull moment on the set or off. He had a great sense of fun, would guffaw at some of my antics, then would come up with something unexpected designed to break *me* up. It was a happy set, and I got to love the guy. He was a very good actor even then—and totally unpretentious."

During the filming of *Hargrove*, Bob ran into another acquaintance from his radio days.

Although he and Jennifer never went out socially on work nights, when Jennifer didn't have an early Monday call, they'd frequently spend Sunday evenings helping out at the Hollywood Canteen.

Located at 1451 Cahuenga Boulevard and officially opened on October 3, 1942, with funds donated by members of the industry's fourteen guilds and unions, the Canteen was presided over by Bette Davis. It provided lonely soldiers and sailors with free food, entertainment, and the companionship of some of Hollywood's greatest stars. Most of these young servicemen were on their final passes before embarking for duty in the South Pacific. Many would never return.

Bob would wash dishes or clean up tables, Jennifer serve sandwiches, Cokes, or coffee. Since both were still "unknown," neither was especially sought out. The big drawing cards were the major stars and the sexy young starlets. This didn't faze the two and they went about their business quietly.

Sanford Dody (who'd later ghost-write Bette Davis' autobiography, *The Lonely Life*) was in Hollywood "attempting to become an actor" when he dropped into the Canteen one night to see if they needed some extra help.

Sanford recalls, "I had known Bob casually from our Penn-Astor drugstore days, when we were both scrounging for jobs. So I walked over to say hi. I wasn't even aware of his being in Holly-

wood, but before I could ask him what he was doing out there, he asked me!

"After filling him in, I mentioned that I was set for a bit in the Hargrove picture at MGM, the next day.

"'You are!' he exclaimed. 'That's a coincidence. I'm in *Hargrove* too.' I swear—that's all he said.

"We were then joined by an apple-cheeked young girl whom he introduced as his wife. He said, 'Look, my wife has to get to bed early, but I'm going to work here for another hour or so. When I'm finished, how about joining me for a quick drink?' We stopped in at a nearby bar, reminisced about the old days at the Penn-Astor, talked about the war, and when he left the place after one drink, he said, 'See you on the set tomorrow, and we'll talk some more.'

"The sound stage was packed with extras, technicians, milling around waiting for the action to begin. I think it was Bob who spotted me first; he strode over to me and said something like, 'It looks as if they won't be ready for some time; let's go someplace quiet where we can hear each other talk.' With that, he led me into a plush private trailer dressing room and sprawled on the couch, as if he owned the place.

"I got a little nervous about invading what looked like a star's quarters. 'Isn't this a little risky? If the guy this belongs to suddenly walks in, he could be plenty annoyed at finding two strangers in his room and start a fuss, and we could both be out of a job,' I said.

"Bob just broke up. 'Oh, we have every right to be here. This is *my* room.'

"I was slow on the uptake, still under the impression he was playing a bit. I must have looked very confused, because he quickly added, 'Oh, I thought you knew. I'm Hargrove.' Up to that minute, I hadn't known. I guess for some reason I'd never bothered to find out who was starring in the film, and I swear he never said a thing about it the night before.

"He was bringing me up-to-date about his career when there was a knock on the door and he was told that shooting was about to start. It was a hectic day, as I remember—my only day on *Hargrove*, since I was leaving for somewhere in the morning. We didn't get a chance to talk much afterward, but at the end of the afternoon he came over to say how great it was seeing me again and if I got back into town and there was anything he could do,

'Just holler.' It was a brief reunion but one I never forgot and which indicated his rare lack of ego."

Filming of *Hargrove* continued to roll merrily and boisterously right on schedule. Bob thought his first screen leading lady, twenty-two-year-old Donna Reed, affable to work with, devoid of temperament, and "possessing an inborn charm and gentleness not unlike Jennifer's."

Their romantic scenes together were adorable, exuding more purity than passion, but Bob felt awkward when the script called for him to kiss her. He was all too conscious of the fact that Donna would be the only other girl he had kissed since meeting Jennifer. Although he convinced himself it was "only acting," he still experienced "a twinge of guilt."

Throughout most of the shooting, everyone connected with *Hargrove* was confident that it had the makings of a box-office hit and that MGM, which boasted of having "more stars than there are in the heavens," would be adding a new one to its galaxy.

Then a major note of discord came from the great Louis B. Mayer. Mayer was alarmed that the film's frivolous attitude toward the service "might offend the mothers and wives and sisters of our brave men in uniform." After conferences with studio yes-men, it was decided that "toward the end, Hargrove must be given significance, relevance, and importance."

Director Wesley Ruggles disagreed, predicting that the original concept of the film would be disastrously watered down. Most of the company felt the same way, but Mayer would not budge an inch, and a pall of discontent darkened what had earlier been the happiest set on the lot.

A few months after the film had been completed, it was given its ritual "sneak preview." Tay Garnett recalled that the "audience's reaction to the phony Mayer portion was nothing short of tar and feathers.

"Ruggles had a commitment with the Rank Organization in England and couldn't return to Hollywood despite a frantic call from Louis B. Mayer. However, he told Mayer that he'd like me to do the retakes."

Garnett was offered the difficult job of resuscitation and accepted the assignment "with the proviso that we stick to the original script and we weren't, dammit, going to go noble."

Between the start and completion of *Hargrove*, its initial sneak preview, and the call for retakes, David Selznick had been busily absorbed in what was to be his first movie production since the onset of World War II.

Unable to land a military job worthy of his talents, and inspired by the success and appeal of *Mrs. Miniver*, he became obsessed with filming a story that captured life on the American home front. In other words, as Selznick put it, "a war story without battles," just as *Gone with the Wind* had been a war story devoid of combat scenes. To find such a property, he had his story department reading their eyes out. An item about his search which ran in the trade paper the *Hollywood Reporter* caught the eye of Paramount story editor William Dozier. He had just read the galleys of a forthcoming book, *Since You Went Away—Letters to a Soldier from His Wife*. It consisted of a series of letters actually written by Dayton, Ohio, newspaperwoman Margaret Buell Wilder to her soldier husband, which had eventually appeared in serial form in *The Ladies' Home Journal*. Although Dozier had been personally impressed, he didn't consider it the kind of material in which Paramount would be interested. Impulsively, he sent Selznick a synopsis of the property with his observation that the letters could be the core of a "life-on-the-home-front film, though they would require considerable treatment and reconstruction."

Selznick, charmed and moved by the letters, bought the book for thirty thousand dollars and invited Mrs. Wilder to come to Hollywood during April and May to transform the letters into story form. After she completed her assignment, he began writing the screenplay himself, using the pseudonym Jeffrey Daniel, the first names of his two sons. He expanded the simple tale, which related the vicissitudes of a mother and two teenage daughters in an America in crisis. He also expanded (and would keep enhancing) the role of the older daughter, Jan, changed to Jane. From the time he had first read the letters, he had earmarked this part for Jennifer.

On the surface, it appeared to be a startling comedown from *Bernadette*, but Selznick did not wish to risk her becoming a one-picture wonder. Once she had made the transition from the French saint to the American girl-next-door, his confident gamble that she possessed the versatility to play any part assigned her would be spectacularly vindicated.

Determined that *Since You Went Away* would be remembered as one of the great World War II epics, Selznick would let out all stops when it came to casting, sets, and other production details, running the budget up to the then-astronomical sum of $2,780,000, and the length to two hours and fifty-one minutes, the longest and most expensive film to come out of Hollywood since his *Gone with the Wind.*

As always, he strove for a perfect cast. With Jennifer set as Jane, he persuaded former child star Shirley Temple to emerge from retirement to play the younger daughter, Bridget, aware that Miss Temple's return to the screen would result in an avalanche of free publicity. Contractee Joseph Cotten was assigned to the role of naval officer Tony Willett, a disarming bachelor who nurtured an unrequited love for the girls' mother.

The mother was perhaps the most difficult role to cast. Anne Hilton, the screen counterpart of Mrs. Wilder, needed to be played by an actress of great charm, compassion, believability, and box-office value. Selznick was convinced that Claudette Colbert, a close friend, fit the bill, but had doubts that Miss Colbert would consent to play the mother of two teenagers. While deciding the best way to approach her, he received a telegram from Katharine Cornell, who had loved the book and expressed her desire to play the role.

Jennifer was speechless when she learned that her girlhood idol had actually requested to play her mother—and was startled by Selznick's firm negative reaction.

"She may be the first lady of the theater, but she simply can't carry this picture at the box office. I'm going to get Colbert—one way or another."

He got Colbert with the aid of Hedda Hopper, who phoned the thirty-nine-year-old actress and went to work on her.

"You don't expect to be an ingenue all of your life, do you?" Hedda asked bluntly. "David Selznick doesn't make failures. If the part isn't right for you, it will hurt him more than it will you. He can't afford to have anything but a success—and, if so, he has to be certain that the part is right for you."

When Colbert protested that Selznick hadn't even asked her yet, Hopper replied, "He will."

A few minutes later, Hedda was on the phone to Selznick in-

forming him that Colbert was definitely interested and that he should call her immediately. Negotiations lasted a month. Miss Colbert demanded and got, in addition to her $150,000 fee and the stipulation that only the right side of her face be photographed, an extra two days a month off.

A fourth pivotal part to be cast was that of Jane's love interest, a sensitive army enlisted man who had broken family tradition by failing at West Point.

Over the years, there have been many theories regarding Selznick's casting of Robert Walker as Corporal William Smollett III. It's been said that Jennifer suggested it; that Selznick wanted to put an end to the whispers that he had more than a professional interest in Jennifer; that Selznick, aware of the smash Bob had been making at MGM and annoyed with himself for not signing him when the idea first occurred to him, was determined at least to have him in one of his pictures. There have been other theories of a darker nature—that Selznick, increasingly obsessed with Jones, wanted to show both her and Walker how much power he held over them. At least some justification for that theory appeared to come out during the filming of that movie.

Selznick's own explanation was more bland: he had seen a print of *Bataan* and the unfinished *Hargrove* and decided Walker was the ideal choice.

He anticipated no problems in securing Bob's services from Mayer. Louis B., however, was opposed to lending any of his players to another studio unless the role—or payment—warranted the risk.

The Smollett role was appealing but hardly spectacular. The best Selznick could offer was seventh star billing—certainly a comedown from the title *Hargrove* lead—but Mayer wanted something beyond a cash payment from his son-in-law: he wanted the services of Ingrid Bergman to costar with Charles Boyer in his projected production of *Gaslight*. Walker for Bergman—or no deal.

As it turned out, it was a deal that Selznick relished. Bergman wanted to work, and the role in *Gaslight*, that of a woman being driven mad by her husband, was a tour de force, one which could only enhance Ingrid's dollar value in future loan-outs. The agreement was consummated without either Bergman or Walker having

any say, though it's very unlikely that either would have objected. For Bob—at the time—to appear opposite his wife in a class production was still another dream come true. As for Ingrid, she had yearned to play the wife when she first saw *Angel Street*, the Broadway play upon which *Gaslight* was based, but MGM had outbid Selznick for the rights. Given another chance at it, Bergman was ecstatic, even though her billing would be second to Boyer's.

David Selznick planned to start *Since You Went Away* on September 8. Although the extended vacation Bob had planned was now out of the question, he still hoped he and his wife could steal away for a few weeks to relax and recapture the romance and gaiety missing from their marriage during her involvement with *Bernadette*. The film, he thought, had drained her of all her old *joie de vivre*, and he missed the easy communication which had always existed between them. Even though her reaction to the prospect of playing lovers in *Since You Went Away* had not been the spontaneous excitement he'd expected, he was still too confident of her love to be able to see the ominous signals.

His hopes for a little time off were squelched when he received word from the studio to be available for retakes on *Hargrove*. Almost simultaneously, Jennifer was informed by Twentieth to be available both for *Bernadette* retakes and for some high-toned publicity to coincide with the December pre-release of the film.

The Ladies' Home Journal wanted to feature the Walker family in their prestigious "How America Lives" series. The article (and accompanying photos), sedately titled "Meet Two Rising Stars," would run in their January 1944 issue, on the stands in early December.

In addition to material on Bob and Jennifer's beginnings and love story, they planned extensive coverage on their current lifestyles, portraying them as a comfortable, devoted couple insulated from the pain and tragedy of the war, who were idyllically raising two spirited sons while coping handsomely with individual and successful careers—careers which would mesh when they co-starred in a blockbuster film. The American dream. A fairy tale, as pure as the waters of Lourdes.

When neither Bob, nor Jennifer, nor David Selznick voiced any objections, Twentieth scheduled the joint interview and layout,

and Jennifer went shopping for striped playsuits for the boys and a matching pinafore for herself. Bob wore his usual dark T-shirt and old gray pants.

The session was a resounding success, Jennifer gay and loving throughout.

Howard Strickling was relieved that the ice had been broken: his department had been panting for photos of the Walker family together.

"That coverage in the *Journal* is a major break for us, too," he told Bob, "and I have no intention of killing their exclusive.

"However, before you get tied up at Selznick's, we want to shoot our own picture layout as a follow-up, to plant when *Hargrove's* released. Different clothing and a large variety of poses. Every newspaper and fan-mag editor in the country will be screaming for it—and timing is everything."

Neither Bob nor Mr. Strickling had any idea how *bad* the timing would be.

"Sure," agreed Bob. "I'll ask Phyl when she wants to do it."

That second session was completed before Bob started the *Hargrove* retakes. He was delighted Tay Garnett had taken the reins. By now, both men had good reason for their mutual-admiration society. *Bataan* had been released in June, and Bob Walker, as had been predicted, was singled out by all of the critics.

Bosley Crowther of the New York *Times* noted, "Robert Walker, a newcomer, is fine . . . a garrulous youngster as green and pliant as a sapling branch, whose emotions rush rapidly to the surface and send wistful signals to your heart." And Harriet Gould informed *Liberty* magazine readers that "the superbly selected all-male cast spotlights Robert Taylor, Thomas Mitchell, and Robert Walker, whose superior work has already earned him the title role in the forthcoming *See Here, Private Hargrove*."

Garnett told Bob, "I read a couple of dozen reviews. They *all* loved you. The Palace Guard helped botch this one up [*Hargrove*]—not you. I'll do my damnedest to salvage it. It's not as tough as it seems."

"As with *Bataan*," Garnett remembered, "Bob followed my instructions to the letter, but there were two incidents that stand out in my mind whenever I think of that picture.

"One took place during camera setups and provides an insight

into Bob's gentle naiveté. When our huge sound-stage doors were opened briefly, music came drifting in. Astonished, Bob asked, 'Where's it coming from?'

"I said a Judy Garland picture was shooting on the next stage.

"His eyes opened like blossoming parachutes as he asked softly, 'D'ya suppose I could meet her?'

"I said, 'Let's go!'

"As I introduced them in Judy's dressing room, Bob's gaze was frankly idolatrous.

"Judy, a prime sophisticate even at that age, caught the whole bit and was amused. She went into her act, saying in Mae West tones, 'I've been hearing a lot about you, honey. Drop around some evening and we'll have a few belts and get *real* acquainted.'

"Bob's jaw dropped as a crimson wave spread to his hairline. After a few seconds that I filled with small talk with Judy, Bob said, 'I g-guess I'd b-better get b-b-back . . .' Backing out of the dressing room and tripping over the step, he added 'N-nice to meet you.'

"While we were walking back to our set, Bob said miserably, 'Golly, I'm sorry I met her . . . I've adored her since the first time I saw *Wizard of Oz*. And you saw how she acted, and she's got to know I'm married.'

"To Bob, wholly unaware that he was, even then, being set up for a lethal blow, any deviation from absolute fidelity was totally unthinkable."

It is impossible even to venture a guess as to whether Jennifer Jones was unfaithful to Walker during the time of their marriage. She is the only participant in the drama who can ever answer that question. She never has; it's unlikely she ever will.

Although conducted with discretion to save his wife, Irene, pain and embarrassment, David Selznick's prior extramarital adventures with ambitious starlets or established stars had been a topic of gossip for a decade. These affairs meant little to him, however, and he had always been careful to end them before they threatened his domestic tranquillity.

His feelings toward Jennifer, however, were deepening into something irrational. He was determined to possess her completely, regardless of the risks involved, but, perversely, he never entertained the possibility of divorcing his wife, who had always provided him with support and an atmosphere of stability.

If Jennifer were to become a free woman, he mused, he was certain he could successfully maintain two satisfying and diverse relationships, and avoid the possibility of a scandal that would be disastrous to her career. The morality, or lack of it, did not enter into his distorted reckonings.

A few days before the cameras were to roll on *Since You Went Away*, Selznick threw a party on the set to celebrate his return to filmmaking after a four-year hiatus. Early in the afternoon he made a point of being photographed in a group shot with Shirley Temple, an immaculately groomed Bob Walker, and Jennifer. Selznick, Jennifer, and Shirley were all beaming happily at Bob as the cameras clicked. This was the first and only time the two rivals were photographed together. It galled Selznick to see the Walkers leave the party arm in arm—but that did not last for long.

Since You Went Away began production on September 8, 1943, and was allotted a lengthy 127-day shooting schedule. Since movies were rarely, if ever, shot chronologically, arrangements were made to allow Bob and Jennifer free time for the retakes on their prior films.

Once again, Jennifer seemed distant and aloof from Bob's daily activities, as well as unhappy about her forthcoming role.

"You'll be enchanting," he assured her.

"I'm too old for the part and too big and gawky. I'm all wrong for Jane. You're a perfect Bill, but I'll never be believable."

"Look, darling, Mr. Selznick knows what he's doing. He told me at the party that he's determined to turn you into the biggest star he has, that he feels there's no role you're incapable of playing, no limit to your talent. You don't think he'd risk your career after *Bernadette* and his reputation by miscasting you? And just think of how wonderful we'll be together. We always have been."

As the days went on, however, Jennifer's anxiety intensified. She became upset over everything. Bob still refused to recognize the fact that she was changing, that she had already changed. The only time she appeared to be her old self was during the weekends when she was with Bobby and Michael. Bob found it almost impossible to get through to her. Once he lost his temper and actually yelled at her and then was horrified at his behavior when she burst into tears and retreated to their room.

He remembered thinking: Things will get back to normal once we start working together. We'll have a million things to talk and laugh about. The pressure will be off her. She'll be my Phyl again.

Each had a week of retakes left before reporting back to the Selznick studios. On the Saturday night prior to that week, they accepted an invitation to a large Hollywood gathering. Just what Bob did, just what Jennifer said, wasn't recorded. But they left early.

After they had arrived home, a very somber Jennifer dropped a thunderbolt on Bob: she thought it would be better for both of them if they separated, she said. The word "divorce" wasn't mentioned.

Neither ever discussed publicly the reason for her decision—which would eventually become obvious. To Bob and to the world.

Ever since his career had begun, Bob Walker had never been known to get drunk, never been known to get violent. But now his world had ended. He'd thought he'd never be unwanted again, that the love of this beautiful young woman would always be his. But now everything that had seemed permanent and true had been suddenly destroyed.

The next morning, after breakfasting with his sons, Bob packed a small bag and a bottle of Scotch and checked into a hotel, where he proceeded to become smashed.

On Monday, a small item was buried on the back pages of a Los Angeles newspaper. It noted that Robert Walker and Jennifer Jones had decided on a trial separation.

Bob and Jennifer appeared on their respective sets that same morning.

Tay Garnett recalled, "It was apparent that something was seriously wrong with Bob. He seemed to be falling apart; his color was pasty, his eyes were bloodshot, and he couldn't remember his lines.

"Taking him aside, I asked, 'What's wrong, Bob?'

"Fighting tears, he blurted, 'Jennifer has left me.'

"That's when Bob began to drink heavily. One noon he went into the small bar just outside the MGM auto gate, belted a few— quite a few—then walked carefully to the cashier, check in hand.

"A tall gaudy cigarette machine, decorated with a rococo mir-

ror, stood next to the cashier's counter. As Bob swung away, pocketing his change, he caught sight of his reflected face. In spontaneous savagery, he drove his clenched fist through the mirror, shattering shards of glass in every direction, breaking several knuckles, and severing an artery.

"He was carried to the studio hospital, where the doctor patched him up and gave him some fatherly advice. Bob heeded it briefly."

As for Jennifer, character actress Anne Revere, who played Jennifer's mother in *Bernadette*, vividly recollects, "Jennifer announced her separation from Bob one morning. That afternoon a very long sable coat was delivered to her at the studio—a gift from David Selznick."

It's been reported that Jennifer had agonized for months before deciding on the separation, concerned about the effect it would have on her children, on her screen image, and on Bob's emotional stability. Unlike her mentor, however, she was incapable of leading a "double life."

Her timing, coming as it did, when she and Bob were due to work together as screen lovers, would prove disastrous to both. It's possible that she hoped that once she had left Bob, Selznick would replace him in the role—but he made it quite clear he had no intention of doing any such thing.

Bob neither asked nor wanted to be replaced. Optimistically, if unrealistically, he gambled on the chance that their proximity and love scenes would eventually lead to a reconciliation. He did not, *could* not, believe his wife was actually in love with such a man. Even if there had been an act of infidelity on her part—and the thought of one made him shudder with disgust—he'd be willing to forgive the aberration.

Bob didn't hear the story until many years later, but screenwriter Gavin Lambert relates that "whenever Marlene Dietrich [who appeared in Selznick's *Garden of Allah*] had a party, she'd set up a game of 'Inquisition.' One of the most provocative questions was 'Who'd be the *last* person in the world you would go to bed with— even if not doing so meant sacrificing the lives of your children?' Her female guests, with rare exceptions, would unhesitatingly name Adolf Hitler. But Marlene, who had personally rejected and vio-

lently detested the German dictator, never failed to reply, 'David O. Selznick.'"

Obviously, in ways Miss Dietrich never made public, she had herself suffered at the hands of Selznick. However, in the months ahead, Bob Walker was destined to become Selznick's most tragic victim.

Chapter

10

Bob attempted to put his life into some semblance of order before starting work on *Since You Went Away*.

He detested hotel living, and apartments were still at a premium, but with the aid of a friend at MGM, he found a small furnished rental near the studio. It filled his modest requirements, but even the studio brass couldn't get him on the priority list for a private telephone, an inconvenience he merely shrugged off.

He took very few possessions from the big house: his phonograph, some records, a small radio, and a clock. He didn't bother stocking the grocery shelves or refrigerator. In his heart, he held fast to the conviction that, in time, he would be returning *home*.

Having gone on his big binge—and the scars on his hand were still visible—he vowed to do nothing further to embarrass Jennifer during the filming and spent his evenings alone studying his lines and concentrating on his characterization.

He reported to the Selznick lot on schedule and was warmly greeted by director John Cromwell, who patiently tried to make things as easy as possible for him. Selznick, still tampering with the script, was nowhere to be seen. Bob's initial scenes with Jennifer were informal, but when Cromwell called it a "take," Jennifer discouraged conversation and headed straight for her dressing room. During lunch hour, she remained out of sight.

A reporter cornered Bob one afternoon and tactlessly asked for his reaction to working with his estranged wife. "We're professionals, and we're acting," he replied, and walked away before he was subjected to further interrogations. The tension, however, was taking a terrible toll on him.

In late October, after completing the week's work, he left the studio and was riding his motorcycle back to the apartment, trying desperately to focus on the road ahead, when from out of nowhere a car made a left turn in front of the cycle, hit it broadside, and tossed Bob headfirst onto the concrete.

It was a miracle he wasn't killed. When he came to in the hospital, he was told he had suffered substantial but not critical head injuries. "Consider yourself a very lucky young man," his doctor said. "Your cycle was destroyed by the impact, but our X rays show you've no fractures. In this kind of collision, your face and body could have been mangled.

"Barring any unforeseen complications, you should be fully recovered within a month."

Still in a state of shock, Bob protested, "But I'm due to return to work at the studio on Monday."

"Three weeks from Monday would be my optimistic guess. Whom would you like notified?"

Bob started to say, "My wife." Then he remembered. "Call John Cromwell at the Selznick studios, or call Mr. Selznick's secretary. And please, don't say anything to the newspapers." Then, recalling the nature of the accident, he inquired weakly, "What happened to the other fellow, the one who hit me?"

"Got off without a scratch. But the police have his name and license number if you need it for insurance reasons."

"It wasn't his fault. I guess I should have seen him coming. I don't want a fuss made. I just want the hammering in my head to go away."

"It will in time. Meanwhile, I've prescribed painkillers."

The accident did not make the local papers. A few days later, however, Bob called his parents in Utah to tell them what had happened. Horace Walker, still a newspaperman at heart, called a friend at the Ogden *Standard Examiner*. On October 30 the sheet ran a small piece headlined "ACTOR RECOVERING FROM INJURIES." Describing the details of the accident, it noted that Bob was "reported out of danger today. He is expected to return to active work at the studio within a month. Walker is the son of Mr. and Mrs. Horace Walker of Ogden." The rest of the piece was devoted to Bob's screen credits. There was no comment as to whether

Jennifer had rushed to his side. Her feelings, if any, were never made known.

David Selznick was in a frenzy. Bob's absence meant he had to replace scheduled scenes with sequences he hadn't planned to get to for another month.

John Cromwell recalled, "David seemed to get even more hysterical during this picture than I heard he had been during *Gone with the Wind.*" Bob's accident could have provided Selznick with a rational excuse to replace him. Again, he did not. He lived on Benzedrine to stay awake most of the night to rewrite scenes suitable for the revised schedule.

After regaining his strength, Bob resumed work. "Sorry I caused all that trouble," he told Cromwell, "but I'll try to make up for it." Physically, he appeared well. Emotionally, he was beginning to fall apart.

Keenan Wynn, also on loan from MGM, says sadly, "That's when Bob began to change, during the making of *Since You Went Away.* Close friends like me could see the difference in him. The happy-go-lucky guy I'd worked with was transformed overnight into a morose and melancholy shadow of his former self. The film was emotionally disastrous for him. Did Selznick do what he did maliciously? I don't know. But it was heartless to bring Bob together with his estranged wife for intimate love scenes. It was almost as if Selznick were saying, 'She's my girl now—not yours.' Was this deliberate? Or was the man just too insensitive to realize the damage he was inflicting? Who knows? But I could see how badly this affected Bob. He was an especially sensitive guy."

Screenwriter Dewitt Bodeen, who co-wrote the screenplays for *Cat People, The Enchanted Cottage,* and *I Remember Mama,* has been less tactful than Keenan, remembering, "I was on the Selznick lot a good deal when he was shooting *Since You Went Away.* Selznick could not stay away from the set whenever a scene between Jennifer Jones and Robert Walker was shot. He apparently loved to watch Miss Jones and Bob make love for the camera, even though they were separated. It must have satisfied a masochistic urge on his part to see the two of them kiss and embrace. I was a little surprised that Bob didn't walk out. As for Selznick, he wanted Walker for the part and no one but Walker.

"It was too damn bad, really tragic, that Selznick had to break

them up; however, I guess the stardom and loot he offered her were irresistible. But my heart went out to that boy. He was so obviously in love with the woman and she was so patently rejecting him. I think everyone connected with *Since You Went Away* was on his side, but no one dared to say a word. Jennifer was unapproachable."

She was also, as director John Cromwell would recall, "as unhappy as I've ever seen a girl to be. Jennifer was not only uncomfortable in the part. She was also uncomfortable playing the very poignant love scenes with her about-to-be-ex-husband, and on two occasions her emotional upsets caused her to flee the set in tears. Selznick had to come to her dressing room to calm her down before she could continue.

"At this stage, David was totally obsessed by Jennifer.

"Jennifer was half-repelled, half-attracted by him. They say money is sexy but power is sexier, and David was all power. I guess it got to her. Jennifer was on edge all through the picture. She was worried about her role and Selznick and her boys and her guilt about Walker and just about everything.

"And David's neurotic courtship of Jennifer kept her in a state of mild hysteria. People said she gave an overly intense performance, though I thought she was fine in the role. But with all that was going on behind the camera, it's a wonder that she got through it at all. Claudette and I had a time calming her down."

Joseph Cotten concurs: "The set tended to be a hectic one, David sending in changes, Jennifer in a highly nervous state, especially in her scenes with Bob Walker. Claudette Colbert and John Cromwell held it all together beautifully, though. I always felt Claudette . . . was an extremely tough woman. She knew how to roll with the punches."

One of the "punches" was Selznick's perpetual rewrites of the script. With each rewrite, Jennifer's role grew a little larger. He went so far as to insert a sequence at a veterans' rehabilitation center to exhibit Jennifer's skill as a nurse's aide. (She had completed her real-life training a few months earlier.) The sequence was touching but expensive and extraneous, adding little to the basic story, while dragging out the already inflated running time.

Because of the constant changes, Bob, after catching up with the time lost because of his accident, found himself with a great

many free days and nights. By prearrangement, whenever Jennifer was at the studio, he'd drive to his former home and spend his afternoons with Bobby and Michael. He'd have an early supper with his boys, watching the clock to make sure he was gone by the time Jennifer returned home from the studio. Those visits provided both a respite from and a wounding reminder of his tremendous loss. He would then spend his other evenings alone at his small apartment, listening to music or reading, having no desire to seek out the companionship of other women in fear of jeopardizing even the remotest possibility of a reconciliation.

The lack of a telephone was a blessing, insulating him from the press, unwanted invitations, or calls from his family.

The Isleys and the senior Walkers had been shocked and perplexed by the initial news of the unexpected "amicable" separation. Bob had refused to discuss any details with his parents; Jennifer's explanation to her parents was never made public.

When either MGM or the Selznick production department required Bob, a studio messenger was sent to his apartment. Occasionally he'd drop by his home studio if he felt the need for superficial companionship or a boost to his faltering ego.

On one such day, he was summoned to Benny Thau's office, where he was told that the studio had decided upon his next picture: *Meet Me in St. Louis,* a charming, sentimental musical based on Sally Benson's *New Yorker* magazine stories about a devoted Missouri family's life—set against the opening of the St. Louis World's Fair.

Judy Garland, its star, had personally requested Bob for her leading man—the shy boy next door, with whom she falls in love.

"It's another big step forward for you," Thau added. "Your first musical, and the first chance for the public to see you in Technicolor, and Judy thinks the chemistry between the two of you will be terrific. We've informed the Selznick people to finish with you no later than Christmas, or there'll be hell to pay. This is one of Arthur Freed's pet projects. He went to the mat with L.B. for permission to make it."

Bob's lack of enthusiasm puzzled Thau.

"Anything bothering you?"

My whole life, Bob thought, but aware Thau was referring to his

assignment, merely replied, "Sounds fine, but . . . a musical? I can't carry a note and I barely get by with social dancing."

"The part doesn't require the boy to do either," Thau said testily. "If a duet is added—which I doubt—we'll hire someone to dub it.

"And oh, by the way," he concluded, "it should please you to know the revised version of *Hargrove* is a knockout. Anytime you want to see it, call my secretary and she'll set up a screening."

All the good news—the great news—failed to lift Bob's spirits. There was no one with whom he could share it, no one who really mattered.

He didn't remain idle for long. A wire came from a Selznick aide to report back to the set of *Since You Went Away* the following week. There were still several pivotal scenes with Jennifer remaining to be filmed.

The most tender of these brought the characters Bill and Jane together on the last day of his leave. They drive out to the country and are caught in a sudden rainstorm. They seek shelter in a barn, and for the first time reveal their true feelings toward each other. It was a beautiful love scene and Bob let out all stops, desperately, if naively, hoping he might evoke an emotional response from his wife.

He did, but it was hardly the response Bob had longed for. Jennifer was totally unable to cope with the intimate haystack sequence, becoming more and more unstable as the shooting continued, until, in a state of hysteria, she bolted from the set to her dressing room, locking the door behind her. Morose and embarrassed, Bob headed for his dressing room, telling Cromwell he'd be available whenever Jennifer was.

David Selznick, who had been watching the scene from behind the cameras, rushed to Jennifer's room, insisting she allow him in. Eventually he managed to calm her, and after the two emerged, Bob was summoned, and they resumed the scene from the top, anxious to get it over with as quickly as possible.

Afterward, not a word passed between them as they went off in their separate directions.

There was still one final episode to be completed: a sequence in the railroad station where Ann Hilton and Jane come to see Bill

off. The sequence involved dozens of extras to simulate the bustle of a wartime station. The core of the sequence, however, was the lovers' farewell.

It proved to be one of the most memorable in the film. Jane gives Bill her class ring, and he, as the train starts moving, gives her his valued watch to keep until his return. The last words Jane calls out to Bill as his train slowly pulls away are "Good-bye, darling, I love you. Good-bye, darling." His last words to her are "Good-bye, darling." The words were written by David Selznick.

The final shot focuses on Jennifer and was photographed using long stark shadows from a single light source to induce feelings of depression, sadness, and loneliness, quietly implying that the two would never see each other again.

Bill would die in Salerno, Italy, his death reported by telegram.

Since You Went Away would not be completed until the following February 9, but Bob's services were no longer required. As Bob left the Selznick lot for the last time, whatever hopes he may have harbored for a reconciliation were finally and irrevocably shattered. The next move would be Jennifer's—orchestrated by Selznick.

Within a few days Bob would receive another blow when he was summoned to a meeting with Louis B. Mayer. Ignoring Garland's vehement protests, he unceremoniously yanked Bob from *Meet Me in St. Louis.* The studio had decided to cast a young New York actor, Tom Drake, who had scored impressively with Van Johnson and June Allyson in the musical *Two Girls and a Sailor,* as the boy next door. He and Bob shared many of the same appealing on-screen qualities, might, in fact, have been teamed convincingly as brothers.

Mayer's explanation for the switch was tactful, perhaps even truthful. Such a part would be a step forward for Drake, but a step backward for Bob, especially after *Hargrove.* MGM was due to go into production with a major war film, *Thirty Seconds Over Tokyo,* with Spencer Tracy as the real-life Lieutenant Colonel Doolittle, the man who had executed the first raid on the Japanese capital in April 1942, with Van Johnson cast as pilot Ted Lawson. Bob would appear as the actual Sergeant Dave Thatcher, the navigator of the lead bomber.

"If that's the way you want it," Bob told Mayer. "Makes no difference to me."

Mayer made no move to dismiss him from his office, however. Adopting the legendary paternal attitude which had always served him so well in delicate situations, he brought up the subject foremost in his mind: the state of Bob and Jennifer's marriage.

"It hasn't changed," Bob said sullenly. "We're separated. I don't want a divorce. If my wife does, I won't stand in her way as long as I can continue seeing my sons."

Mayer went on to explain that his son-in-law Bill Goetz was concerned that Bob might cause "problems" either before the December 27 premiere of *Bernadette* or at Oscar time. Because of the spiritual nature of the film, a divorce or any breath of scandal could result in a boycott, millions of dollars down the drain, and Jennifer's career destroyed before it had even begun.

"My son-in-law tells me your wife promised to maintain the status quo, but he asked me to speak to you, before he came down with a case of ulcers."

"I've said all there is to say," Bob replied. "I don't give a damn about that movie. But I won't talk to the press, and I won't hurt my wife."

Bob left Mayer's office flabbergasted by the nature of the conversation. Could it be possible, he wondered, that Mayer was oblivious of the underground gossip that had been rampant for months: that his *other* son-in-law was responsible for the breakup, that his beloved daughter Irene was as much a victim of Jennifer as he?

With Christmas approaching, Bob busied himself making the rounds of the Beverly Hills shops for unusual toys for his boys and obligatory presents for his family in Utah and the studio employees who had been especially kind to him during the year. He even purchased a bottle of Jennifer's favorite scent. He had unlimited money to spend but little holiday spirit. He didn't even bother with a small tree or any festive decorations for his apartment, neither wanting nor expecting any visitors.

He did, however, look forward to spending part of Christmas Day with Bobby and Michael. He arrived at the house loaded down with gifts, but Jennifer was nowhere to be seen. The nurse

informed him she was "spending the afternoon with friends." He left the perfume—as a gesture.

It was impossible for him to realize that only one year had elapsed since he and Jennifer had been reunited in time for Christmas 1942, a Christmas he had considered one of the happiest in his life, with everything going their way.

How could he have imagined that within a year they'd be going their separate ways? It made no sense.

Bernadette opened, as scheduled, on December 27. Jennifer was not in the audience. Selznick was perturbed to learn that producer Perlberg had invited her to attend with himself and his wife. Unwilling to let Twentieth Century-Fox claim his star, David instructed her to call Perlberg to say she was ill and couldn't attend.

Jennifer was relieved to be spared the pressure of an opening. She was still frightened in crowds and nervous about seeing herself on screen. She needn't have been. The Los Angeles papers and trade-journal reviews were almost unanimous raves, although the *New Yorker* magazine rather condescendingly commented: "We won't say Jennifer Jones, the young discovery who plays Bernadette, is the find of the decade . . . but she is unquestionably appealing and makes no noticeable mistakes."

If Christmas was agony for Bob, New Year's Day and January 2 were sheer hell. Again, he spent the latter, which happened also to be the fifth anniversary of his marriage, alone and brooding about his personal future. By now he was aware of Jennifer's plans: she intended to wait until after the Oscar ceremonies and then quietly initiate proceedings for a divorce.

At this stage, Jennifer was still undecided whether to take up residence in Reno for six weeks or file under California law. She had decided, however, to waive both alimony and child-support payments and set no limits to the time Bob could spend with the boys. The marriage would be dissolved with dignity and as quietly and painlessly as possible, to spare them both additional emotional turmoil—and to prevent the press from having a field day.

When Phil Isley visited Los Angeles later that month, Jennifer confided her plans to him, and Phil knew his daughter well enough to accept that once she had made up her mind, nothing could budge her. He had grown to admire and take pride in Bob's

accomplishments and had hoped the two could have found a way to patch up whatever differences had caused their separation. (Phil's affection for Bob never diminished. Many years later, the widow of Isley's former business associate, Ralph Talbot, would recall dining at the Isleys' home and noticing "many photographs of Jennifer and Bob Walker and Michael and Bobby on display. But not a single photograph of Jennifer and David Selznick in sight.")

Phil was anxious to see his daughter and grandchildren, but his trip was designed to combine business and pleasure: he wanted to arrange a hometown tribute to his daughter with simultaneous premieres of *Bernadette* at the Ritz and Orpheum theaters, both owned by Ralph Talbot: a day-long celebration attended by Tulsa dignitaries and climaxed by a gala invitation reception at the plush Mayo Hotel attended by visiting theater men, community leaders, and Jennifer's girlhood friends and teachers.

Although Jennifer had avoided both the Hollywood and New York premieres and dreaded the hoopla involved with such a junket, she could not disappoint her father by refusing to cooperate. David Selznick, not wanting to antagonize Isley, voiced no objection to the plan. Bill Goetz was all for it, since it was the first (and only) time Jennifer had agreed to help exploit the film. The only problem was timing. Jennifer still had some scenes to complete for *Since You Went Away,* and it was essential she be back in Los Angeles no later than Oscar night, which fell on March 2.

After several meetings, Phil was told to contact Twentieth's Tulsa office and to schedule the event for February 25. Private press interviews would be permitted, but reporters had to be warned: "No questions about her marriage to Robert Walker!"

It was an eventful month for her son Bobby as well. In early February his dad had a free week before leaving for Florida for a brief period of location shooting on *Thirty Seconds Over Tokyo,* and impulsively decided to take Bobby with him for a visit to Ogden.

"I had to get away for a while," he later told reporter May Mann. "I went down to the *Standard Examiner* where I used to have my paper route and talked to my old boss and to Frank Francis, the columnist who'd given me such a nice write-up. Everyone seemed so glad about my success in pictures.

"It was a good trip," he continued. "It was pretty tough on Mother, though. Every night kids from the schools would come by—twenty or thirty at a time. Our address had appeared in the paper, so they'd come in, and we'd all sit around and talk.

"Then I made an appearance on a war-bond drive at the Orpheum Theater. Ron Glassman, the manager, remembered me as a kid standing out front, wondering how I could get in for free. And there were the boys and girls I'd gone to school with. So many married, so many at war.

"And Bobby had a wonderful time. I had told him about getting on a sled and coasting down Marilyn Drive. It's a very steep hill. After several rides with me, that little four-year-old tyke went sledding down alone. Gosh, was I proud."

Bob was putting on a brave front, however, and his sentimental journey wasn't quite as idyllic as he made it sound.

Zella Walker was as aloof as ever. Horace was pleasant as always, but Bob's attempts to communicate with either of them on an adult level were rebuffed. In their presence he was made to feel more like an adolescent than the celebrity he was, although his favorite cousin, Barbara Rabe, insists that "Zella and Horace were really so thrilled with his success in pictures. Still, neither parent was able to spread a great deal of love. At least I never saw it."

Desperate to confide in someone, Bob sought solace at Barbara Rabe's home. She was the only member of the family with whom he could talk freely about the divorce. "I remember him telling me," says Mrs. Rabe, 'There's nothing I can do about it. Hollywood blew it. She'd have been fine if she'd never gone to Hollywood. I was powerless against a giant like Selznick.' Bob had always been a very emotional boy, but I'd never seen him so totally crushed."

Other than that brief revelation in front of his cousin, Bob kept a stiff upper lip in Ogden, aware that he could control his emotions—as long as he wasn't drinking. It was only when he drank that his smoldering violence flared up. But not always. Drinking, more often than not, simply brought him blessed sleep.

The location jaunt to Pensacola, Florida, where Doolittle's men had trained for their historic mission, was uneventful though exhausting, and involved difficult shots which could just as easily have been filmed on the studio lot.

Bob was disappointed in his role in *Thirty Seconds Over Tokyo*.

Mayer had made it sound vastly superior to the one in *Meet Me in St. Louis*, whereas, in spite of third star billing, he had fewer opportunities to shine than he'd had in *Bataan*—and no blockbuster scenes. The movie was, in fact, a vehicle for Van Johnson and featured at least a half-dozen handsome male hopefuls, including the then little-known Robert Mitchum. However, Spencer Tracy as Doolittle had even less footage than Bob.

In spite of the limitations of Bob's part, Mervyn LeRoy, who had worked with Bob briefly in *Madame Curie*, had glowing comments:

"He was really a great boy. One of the sweetest things about Bob is what he'd do for others. His stand-in was a fellow about fifty, who still carried shrapnel in his leg and elbow from World War I. He had a hard time getting enough work. Bob went to the front office and asked for a contract for him. Bob never barged in to ask for favors for himself. But the stand-in, whose wife was expecting a baby, was given a steady job. Bob had a great heart.

"During the filming the real David Thatcher, with all his medals and ribbons, was invited to the set to meet his screen counterpart, but following the initial happy-to-meet-you, Bob, who had greatly admired the man, could think of nothing adequate to say. Members of the cast and crew said it was quite a sight, these two shy young men trying to make conversation."

Bob also found it difficult to establish any real personal rapport with Van Johnson.

Looking back, Van says regretfully, "I never really got to know him during the making of *Thirty Seconds Over Tokyo*. None of us really got to know him during that film. He was often very remote. It broke your heart to see the guy. Our one major scene together took place in a Chinese hospital after the bombing, when the rest of the surviving crew were being evacuated, and I had to remain behind because my leg had been amputated. The crewman Bob played insists upon staying with me, but I force him to leave with the rest. It was a very moving scene, and he played it beautifully. But we didn't lunch together even once during the shooting, really had no social contact afterward other than at publicity parties arranged by fan magazines. We'd nod or wave to one another on the lot, but that was the extent of our relationship. I suppose we were both preoccupied with our own lives. I don't, however, recall his being difficult during the filming—just lost in a world of his own."

The only cast member of *Thirty Seconds* with whom Bob became friendly was its leading lady, Phyllis Thaxter—the actress Rose Franken had selected for the Chicago company of *Claudia* and whom Selznick had met the day he also met Jennifer back in 1941.

Miss Thaxter recalls: "My *Claudia* screen test had been floating around Hollywood and MGM producer Sam Zimbalist saw it and that's how I wound up getting a movie contract and making my film debut as Van Johnson's 'wife' in *Thirty Seconds Over Tokyo*.

"One day, when I was getting ready to make the film, Bob Walker leaned over a railing somewhere on the set and said to me, 'Oh, you know my wife, Phylis, don't you?' I knew the two were separated but he seemed eager to talk about her, though there was little I could add to the conversation other than the fact that when I was on the road with *Claudia*, Jennifer's mother and father had made a point of coming backstage to see me.

"My scenes in the picture were primarily with Van Johnson, but Bob and I struck up an off-camera friendship, and one day he surprised me by inviting me to attend a cocktail party for author Robert Nathan. I had heard talk that Bob was drinking heavily—but not at that party and not with me. Oh, a few drinks socially, but nothing more. He certainly didn't let it interfere with his work—not that I could see anyway, not on *Thirty Seconds Over Tokyo* nor on *The Sea of Grass*, which we did a couple of years later.

"Bob and I continued to date for a while. We'd go to Ciro's [the *in* nightclub] or to the Players or to someone's home for dinner.

"Wherever we went, he never stopped talking about Jennifer— never anything derogatory; he just couldn't keep her name off his lips. He was very charming, but we were never serious, just having fun."

During their brief dating period, Bob made no secret of his fondness for Miss Thaxter. "She's a sweet girl, a very nice, intelligent young lady and good company."

Phyllis also possessed an incandescent beauty, a warm and sympathetic personality, and tremendous charm. Although she took her career seriously, it didn't dominate her life. Had Bob met her at any other time, their relationship might have developed into a lasting one. He couldn't get Jennifer out of his mind or off his lips, however—a circumstance which negated any chance of his becoming romantically involved with another woman.

His dates with Phyllis Thaxter petered out, and within the year

she had met and fallen in love with James Aubrey, who later became the head of CBS and MGM.

In late February, as scheduled, Jennifer, Bobby, and Michael boarded the train for Tulsa for the gala Jennifer Jones celebration.

Her father, together with her close girlhood friend Ruth Bowers and a Twentieth Century-Fox publicity man, met the threesome in Kansas City and whisked them off to a plush hotel for breakfast and to freshen up and relax during the three-hour wait for the connection to Tulsa.

Jennifer and Ruth Bowers—now Mrs. Clyde King—hadn't seen each other for nearly four years. They had a great deal of catching up to do, but because there were others present, their conversation was limited to trivialities. A Tulsa *Tribune* reporter, Roger V. Devlin, allowed access to the suite, was totally taken by Jennifer's charm and naturalness.

"She's just like the kid next door," Devlin noted, "and when I asked how she felt about her first personal appearance, she confessed, 'I'm just a little frightened. At first I had planned to just make a trip home and see my friends. Now it looks as if I'm going to be swamped. I don't mind, understand: people are being swell to me, but I can't help being a little scared.'"

When she arrived at Tulsa's Union Station later in the day, she was completely overwhelmed by her reception. There to meet her were Mayor and Mrs. C. H. Veale, in addition to her mother, a throng of former schoolmates, a mob of curious Tulsans eager to see a movie star, and a police escort assigned to shepherd her safely to the Mayo Hotel. The Tulsa Chamber of Commerce outdid itself preparing for the event.

Banners reading "Welcome Jennifer Jones" were strung across Fourth and Main streets; two huge Norman Rockwell posters of Jennifer in her role as Bernadette were mounted on the exterior of the First National Bank. Both theaters where the film was to be shown had been sold out for weeks.

Her suite at the Mayo resembled a florist's shop; of all the floral arrangements, the most lavish was David O. Selznick's. Jennifer's desk was stacked with telegrams. The phones never seemed to stop ringing.

Jennifer had only two hours to prepare for the six-thirty reception and dinner before being rushed to the theaters to be intro-

duced to the audience. Dressed in a billowing black taffeta gown with a huge corsage on one shoulder, she endeared herself to the audience and elicited a huge ovation by saying ever so shyly, "Oh, I wanted to come back so much," and "I love Oklahoma flowers much more than Hollywood's anytime."

After the lights went down and the picture began, she quietly returned to the Mayo. There were only two more commitments she had to fulfill: a reception the following day at the Sisters of Monte Cassino school and a Chamber of Commerce luncheon.

She spent the weekend in seclusion with Phil and Flora and her sons, recouping her strength from what had proved to be an ordeal. She implored the studio to keep the day and time of her departure a secret.

The Tulsa papers, as might have been expected, were delirious in their praise both of the picture and of Jennifer's performance. George Ketchem, the theater editor of the Tulsa *World*, rhapsodized, "Jennifer Jones's performance was undoubtedly inspired."

Oddly enough, though thousands of words were written about Jennifer's appearance in Tulsa, no mention had been made of her Academy Award nomination, nor the fact that she had to rush back to Hollywood to be present at the Awards.

And, of course, no mention was made of her marriage to Robert Walker—even though the event had taken place right there in Tulsa five years earlier.

It seems unlikely that her visit to Tulsa did not revive happier memories of her marriage. But that was the past—and it was over. As the train sped through the arid Southwest, her thoughts were centered on the possibility of winning Hollywood's most coveted award.

Her competition was formidable, including two of David's other contract players—both on loan-out: Ingrid Bergman for *For Whom the Bell Tolls* and Joan Fontaine for *The Constant Nymph*. The other nominations were Jean Arthur for *The More the Merrier* and the adored Greer Garson for *Madame Curie*—Bob's film!

Jennifer was the dark horse, but she wanted to win—desperately. It would be a miracle, but after all, wasn't that what *Bernadette* was all about—faith and a miracle?

The votes had all been cast. All that remained was an excruciating week of waiting for the results.

FALLING
TO PIECES

---★

*Everyone has problems but I couldn't live with mine. I
wasn't an alcoholic but I was on the way to being
one. Liquor was an outlet—an escape. When I had a
few drinks I got to thinking about "poor me" and the
broken home and all the et ceteras. My breakup with
Jennifer gave me an excuse for amplifying my troubles.*

—ROBERT WALKER

*[Jennifer] was distraught about David's unhappiness
. . . and she blamed herself. She was bad for
him. . . . He didn't love her, he loved me. . . . She
grew hysterical and tried to throw herself out of the
car—I only just managed to pull her back. . . . It
was a dramatic episode and saddening.*

—IRENE SELZNICK, A *Private View*

Nobody likes me.

—JENNIFER JONES

Chapter

11

On March 2, 1944, Bob remained secluded in his tiny apartment, liquor bottle and radio on the table. He felt he was the most miserable man on earth.

This was a night he should have been sharing with Jennifer. Not only was it her twenty-fifth birthday, the first birthday they hadn't been together since she had turned nineteen, two months after they'd met, but it was the night of the Academy's Oscar presentations.

The Academy had always given its awards at a closed industry-only dinner, but in 1944 for the first time it opened the event to the public. The ceremonies would be held at Grauman's Chinese Theater and broadcast over two local radio stations.

Honors bestowed upon *Song of Bernadette* for cinematography, interior decoration, and musical score were of no interest to him. Only one category mattered, yet he knew that whether Jennifer won or lost the coveted prize, the following day he'd be the loser.

Morosely Bob stayed tuned to the Awards. A slight smile played over his lips as he heard Jennifer's name read out as the winner of the Best Actress award. Then he passed out.

On March 3, newspapers nationwide published photographs of Jennifer at the theater and at the party which followed. David Selznick was seated strategically and discreetly between Ingrid Bergman and Jennifer, but there was nothing discreet about the loving gaze he fixed upon Jennifer. Her eyes, however, were riveted upon the Oscar held firmly in her hand.

Later that day, according to plan, she initiated divorce proceedings.

Ironically, that same week, in connection with the March 21

opening of *See Here, Private Hargrove*, the New York *Herald Tribune* introduced a feature article on Walker and Jones with this headline: "LIGHTNING STRIKES TWICE SIMULTANEOUSLY IN SAME FAMILY." The story read in part:

"In the title role is a slim young man who a year ago was known only to a handful of his cronies . . . and was a hero only in the eyes of his wife, Jennifer Jones. The newcomer's name is Robert Walker, and today he is rated the most promising masculine discovery around the MGM diggings. Jennifer Jones, meantime, has been racing along with her husband, winning the Academy Award for her work in *The Song of Bernadette*."

No mention of the Walkers' costarring role in *Since You Went Away* or of their breakup appeared in the article.

Whatever joy Selznick may have derived from Jennifer's Oscar triumph and his certainty that Robert Walker would be permanently out of her life was overshadowed on March 23, when his brother, forty-five-year-old super-agent Myron Selznick, died suddenly of portal thrombosis, exacerbated by excessive drinking.

David plunged into an inconsolable, devastating depression which neither Irene nor Jennifer could relieve. He remained away from his studio for nearly a month, returning only to add some finishing touches to the film.

Selznick's depression was deepened by the fact that only four months before he had had a bitter argument with Myron as a result of the latter's charging that he had lost clients because of a so-called "favoritism" to David. David replied with a blast, countercharging that Myron had not only never shown him any favoritism in his life, but had, in fact, stuck him with some pretty high deals *and* been the beneficiary of several clients that David had steered his way. "I am so sick and tired of hearing this completely unfair statement," David wrote. "I think one reason why you lose so many people is because you are such an extraordinarily bad judge of who are your friends and who are not." The two of them had subsequently made up, but now David regretted his harsh words.

His mood was not helped any when he learned that Twentieth Century-Fox—eager to take advantage of its one-picture-a-year contract with Jennifer, had ordered her to report to the studio on

April 24 to commence work on the film dramatization of Vera Caspary's crime melodrama *Laura*.

He may simply have wanted her for his own projects—or he may have felt the plot, about a beautiful, ambitious young girl whose personal and professional life becomes dominated by a powerful and jealously obsessive older man, was too close for comfort—but he told Jennifer that under no circumstances was she to do the film and publicly contended that Twentieth had failed to send a script for his approval. The studio threatened to take immediate legal action if Jennifer did not report on schedule.

The studio was dead serious about its threat. On May 3 it instituted a $613,000 damage suit against her, which Selznick ultimately settled by agreeing to allow Twentieth to use her services in some other mutually agreed-upon property.

The greatest damage was probably to Jennifer's career. *Laura* (which finally starred Gene Tierney) turned out to be a smash hit, and in time reached the status of a classic.

In order to take some of the onus off her separation from Walker, Selznick encouraged her to open up a little more to the press and present a happy facade. That spring, she gave an interview to a fan magazine, *Screen Stars*, in which she cheerfully discussed Bob and their sons.

"Their daddy! Well, he's their hero." She smiled. "They went to see Bob in *See Here, Private Hargrove*, and they are still playing Private Hargrove—all dressed up in fatigue hats.

"'I'm Private Hargrove,' Bobby will say. 'All right then, I'll be Keenan Wynn,' Michael will retort. They have great respect for Keenan, who races by our house on his spectacular motorcycle.

"Their father and I decided the boys are too young to see many movies. We still discuss everything about the boys. There are many pictures which they might understand but others which might give them wrong impressions. Or they might see one of those super-horror pictures and have nightmares.

"Bob and I decided that they could see *Snow White*. 'There will be a witch in it and you must not be frightened,' we warned them. After the show Bobby said, 'The witch didn't scare me, Mom!'

"When they're not doing Hargrove, the boys' idea of a great time is to play Indian in their tent. They had a pup tent sent to

them from Chicago, and we had it around for two weeks waiting for their daddy to get over to put it up.

"They invite me to crawl in with them for a powwow. When I'm having one of my lazy days, I do. And there we sit motionless for hours.

"They are starting school now, and they have so much to tell me when they get home. Anyone who will can listen to me repeating the bright sayings of my wonderful children."

Asked about Bob Sr.'s reputation as a witty fellow, Jennifer agreed enthusiastically. "He's great. He is always saying funny things. It's the way he says things . . . the way he expresses himself and puts words together."

When she talked about Bob, it was almost as if she were in a time warp.

Even when the interview touched on David Selznick, the admiration she expressed for him was deceptively objective, betraying none of her deep personal involvement.

"With Mr. Selznick, I don't have to worry. I have no feeling of fright, because anyone can place complete confidence in his judgment. I pace around restless and anxious to get back to work. But I have the satisfaction of knowing that Mr. Selznick will wait until he has just the right role for me. I can do a bad job, mind you, but never because the part is bad. I hope I have a good picture soon. I want to work—work all the time."

No one was more acutely aware of Jennifer's impatience to return to work than David Selznick. Although he had engaged former fashion model Anita Colby to instruct Jennifer on the fine points of dressing and grooming as befits a star, and the two women had become close companions, her idleness was beginning to depress her.

Selznick was a man divided in three. He had a wife he had to return to at night. He had Jennifer. And he had production plans that needed constant attention. He was deeply preoccupied with the filming of *Spellbound*, titled, at that time, *The House of Dr. Edwardes*. The director was the mercurial Alfred Hitchcock, with Gregory Peck set for the male lead. Jennifer was not right for the female lead—a brilliant psychologist—and David had cast his other protégée, Ingrid Bergman, in the role.

In spite of a frenzy of activity, David was still without a property

suitable for Jennifer. He had become attracted to Robert Nathan's haunting novel *Portrait of Jennie*, a fragile love story about an artist who falls in love with the ghost of a girl who had died many years before. MGM had had an option on the fantasy; when they'd dropped it, Selznick had picked up on it as a vehicle for his own Jennie—but that was "for the future."

In the meantime, he mulled scripts sent to him by other studios who wanted Jennifer on loan-out. Nothing seemed satisfactory. A request from RKO bemused him. They had the rights to Niven Busch's adaptation of his own novel, *Duel in the Sun*. They wanted Jennifer for the role of Pearl Chavez, a sensual half-breed who causes bad blood between two brothers—one good, one evil, and both dangerously in love with Pearl.

Busch had written the role for his ingenue wife—Teresa Wright—as a radical departure from the goody-two-shoes roles she had been playing. Impending motherhood, however, forced her withdrawal from the film. The studio then sought the more appropriate Hedy Lamarr, but she, too, was unavailable. John Wayne had been set as the evil brother, Lewt; the production had a moderate budget and was to be filmed in black and white.

Selznick found the story very interesting, with the sexual scenes a radical departure from what audiences of "westerns" were used to, and was intrigued by the idea of Jennifer's making the transition from saint and ingenue to erotic sex goddess, but he refused the offer on several grounds.

He was bothered that she had been the third choice for the role; and he was opposed to the idea of her costarring with John Wayne, not only because he thought Wayne was miscast—not sexy enough—but because he wanted to evoke no memories of that first Wayne-Jones film, *New Frontier*, a chapter of her life he preferred to be forgotten. Besides, if anyone was going to transform Jones into a sex goddess, Selznick wanted to be the one to do it.

Unable to find the right leading lady, RKO canceled the picture. Upon hearing of this, Selznick stepped in and bought the rights both to the novel and to the script. Plans began to ferment in his mind to make Pearl Chavez as unforgettable a heroine as Scarlett O'Hara. *Duel in the Sun* would be to the West what *GWTW* had been to the South.

However, nearly a year would pass before *Duel* was ready for the

camera. Meanwhile, Jennifer worked as a nurse's aide to keep occupied. And at MGM, Bob's popularity continued to soar, and his misery deepen.

Without Jennifer to share in them, they were empty triumphs.

He wanted out of the town that he felt had destroyed his happiness. Only his sons and the increasingly fading hope of a reconciliation forced him to remain.

His self-image was at an all-time low. His loneliness underscored his desperate need for stimulating male companionship. He yearned to have a friend in whom he could confide, someone he could trust, and if necessary pour his heart out to, without fear of betrayal.

He'd shortly meet someone like that—a most unexpected type of person for him—and in the most unexpected manner.

On his houseman's night off, Bob impetuously decided to dine at LaRue's, an elegant restaurant on Sunset Strip.

He was lost in thought when he became conscious of a pleasant-looking fellow standing by his table.

"You're Robert Walker," the man said.

"Yes?"

"Jim Henaghan—of the *Hollywood Reporter.*"

As Jim later remembered, "Bob seemed to freeze."

"Yes?"

"Well," Jim continued, "I've been making the rounds to pick up some items for my columns, and when I spotted you sitting by yourself—"

"If you think that's an item, Bob interrupted hostilely, you're welcome to it. But do me a favor. Don't preface it with 'Still carrying a torch . . .'"

"I didn't allow him to finish. 'Look,' I said, 'I just wanted to say hello, so don't be so damn defensive.'

"That was the God's honest truth. When Bob first came on the screen in *Bataan*—I saw it at the Egyptian Theater—I said to myself, 'Jesus, that guy comes across—like *wow*.' I knew then that he was going to make it. But, in general, I didn't have any respect for actors; I didn't care to make any friends among them, even though I was paid to praise them to the hilt. I thought they were all a little sick—and I angrily told Bob as much.

"My attitude must have startled him, because he started laugh-

ing. 'I feel the same way,' he said. 'No one here is what they seem to be. We're all a little sick. If you have nothing better to do, join me for a drink.'

"I had intended to continue and make the rounds, but figured: What the hell? I had plenty of time. One drink led to another, and Bob insisted I have dinner with him. We didn't leave until closing time—talking about the business and all the crazies and phonies in it.

"Bob was brutally honest about his career. He told me he thought MGM was insane to pay him the kind of salary he was getting; that he, too, had no respect for acting, and also thought it childish. He didn't make any pretense about being a schooled performer, said he hated the work and didn't consider himself a talent—just a personality who could follow direction.

"Bob didn't discuss his ex-wife or his personal heartbreak during that first evening we spent together, other than that initial remark about 'still carrying a torch.' He *would* later on—once I had his complete trust. Actually, there was nothing he could have said that, as a reporter, I hadn't already known. Everyone in town was aware of the Svengali relationship between Jones and Selznick. I never touched it in my columns. One line—and three studios would have yanked their advertising. We were all subjected to pretty heavy censorship in those days. A lousy way for a writer to make a living.

"We hit it off great," Jim remembered, "but I wanted Bob to take the initiative of calling. Let him make the first call. He could have had second thoughts about becoming chummy with a gossip columnist. A couple of nights later, he rang me up. He just wanted to talk to someone, he said. It was late, and I had a column to complete. He suggested dinner the following Thursday.

"Fine, I agreed, and suggested a good restaurant that was within my means. I didn't want him to get the impression he had hitched up with a freeloader.

"That's how our friendship got started. It continued to flourish until the final second of his life."

At thirty-three, Jim Henaghan was quite a ladies' man. Married to dancer Gwen Verdon, whom he had discovered when she was in the chorus line of a Hollywood nightclub, and the father of a young son, Jim still had the proverbial "little black book" filled

with the names and phone numbers of the most beautiful girls in town.

However, Bob resisted the Henaghan attempts to play matchmaker. Gwen Verdon recalls, "Jim brought me over to Bob's apartment several times, but with the exception of a party he had for Buffy Cobb, I can't remember his being with a date. It was pathetically obvious that he was still madly in love with Jennifer. Bob was so darling but he was drinking far too much. I was—and still am—convinced that getting drunk was the only way he could obliterate Jennifer from his mind. Once, when he was still sober, he confided that if he had ever been sure of anything, it was the certainty that he and Jennifer would be together for their entire lives. If ever there was a one-woman man, it was Bob. Unrealistic, but terribly touching."

Since You Went Away was given a gala invitational preview a month before its New York opening, followed by a private party at Scandia, which Selznick attended with his wife, Irene. Cast members Joseph Cotten, Shirley Temple, and Jennifer were at the Selznick table. Understandably, Bob did not attend either event. Having Jennifer and Irene together defies explanation, although Edie Goetz, Irene's sister, provides a clue when she reveals that at a party at Claudette Colbert's house, Selznick, quite drunk, "grabbed my arm and mumbled, 'I want to tell you something. I'm going to prove to the world that I can have my cake and eat it too.' He was, of course, talking about his wife and Jennifer."

The *Since You Went Away* party proved to be too much for Selznick. He drank nonstop for hours, ruining the evening for himself and his guests. His language was gross, his behavior bizarre. At one point he broke into Joan Fontaine's conversation by shouting at her, "Joan, you're full of shit. Don't give me that fucking British accent!" His guests were thunderstruck, and a pall fell over the party. This was a side of Selznick's personality to which Jennifer had not previously been exposed: a side Irene had tolerated for fourteen years, that had in fact been one of the things that had driven her to a therapist's couch in 1943. When the party broke up, Irene drove David to their home on Summit Drive in Beverly Hills; Jennifer returned to Bel Air, shaken and confused but still compulsively bound to the man who controlled her life.

Since You Went Away opened at the New York Capitol Theater

on July 20, 1944, to mixed reviews. *Time* reviewer James Agee noted that the film had "taste, shrewdness, superiority, and life." A less favorable review felt it was "too romanticized and symbolic to be accepted as anything other than an awkward, distorted version of reality."

All the reviews noted that the picture was simply too long. "Two hours and fifty-one minutes is a lot of time to harp upon one well-known theme—lonesomeness and anxiety," said Bosley Crowther of the New York *Times.* "And that is all this picture really does."

The public, nonetheless, was touched by the story, and particularly by Bob and Jennifer's portrayals of the doomed lovers. Jennifer won her second Oscar nomination, though this time she lost.

In mid-August 1944, Bob reported to work for *The Clock* opposite Judy Garland in one of her rare nonsinging roles.

During the year that had passed since their initial meeting, when she had been so outrageously flirtatious, they had grown to know and like each other within the confines of the studio.

Judy's personal problems had rivaled Bob's during that year: there'd been the divorce from first husband David Rose; a hectic affair with a married writer, Joseph Mankiewicz; reliance on drugs such as Benzedrine; sessions with a psychoanalyst; another short-lived romance with her *Meet Me in St. Louis* director, Vincente Minnelli.

Bob felt Judy and he were kindred spirits—little boy lost, little girl lost—yet when they lunched together prior to starting *The Clock,* Judy was witty and bubbling with almost contagious ebullience. Her enthusiasm about costarring with him gave his sagging morale a boost. He promised himself he'd exorcise his personal demons and stay on the wagon while the film was in production. It was a promise he was not to keep.

The Clock was a charming wartime romance based on an original Paul and Pauline Gallico story. The subsequent advertising campaign would accurately describe the New York-based plot.

"A forty-eight-hour pass . . . a lonely soldier . . . a girl in a million! Two days were all they had to make their first date . . . to hold hands in a taxi . . . to ride home with the milkman." And to fall in love and hastily marry.

Fred Zinnemann, then a young director of great promise, was assigned to the picture, but after two weeks of production, despite a

sensitive script by Robert Nathan and poignant performances by Judy and Bob, the movie was suddenly canceled, the stars and director told, "It's just not working." Judy wouldn't give up that readily. She adored the film and persuaded executive producer Arthur Freed to give it another try, with Zinnemann out and Minnelli in as director. Since MGM had spent a small fortune building a replica of Pennsylvania Station, where the girl and boy first meet, and on second-unit exterior shots of Manhattan, the studio agreed to resume production. Drastic revisions were made in the script, the original footage scrapped, and The Clock started ticking. This time around, everything seemed to progress beautifully. In the bargain, a few weeks after Minnelli took over, he and Judy resumed their affair and fell madly in love.

George J. Folsey, the cameraman on The Clock, still remembers Bob with fondness. "Like Judy, he had problems. I don't think he ever got over his ex-wife, Jennifer Jones, but he didn't let his problems affect our relationship on the set. He seemed grateful for any kind gesture.

"When lunchtime came, those of us who had been on our feet for hours usually ate right on the set. One day Walker came by when I was eating and said laughingly, 'I see you're a hypochondriac.'

"'Why do you say that?' I asked.

"'Because everything you eat is good for you,' he answered.

"I was in the habit of eating fruit and other goodies from my garden, so I asked him if he'd like my wife to make him a similar lunch. He said 'Sure,' so the next day I brought him a very healthy meal, and he sent a lovely thank-you note to her."

Folsey was not the only member of The Clock company who was concerned about Bob's generally haphazard eating habits. He seemed totally unconcerned with food, and to observers on the set he appeared to exist on paper containers of coffee and an occasional doughnut. He was painfully thin, some days even haggard, but the cameras added weight, and the makeup department was cleverly able to obliterate the red eyes and other evidence of a bad hangover.

When he was performing, he was cold sober, remembered his lines, and followed Minnelli's direction to the letter.

After each day's shooting, Judy and Vincente left the studio

together. Bob wandered off by himself, sometimes to his apartment, more often to a local bar. He felt like an outsider, particularly when it became obvious Minnelli was favoring Judy in many of the scenes she and Bob had together.

Discussing *The Clock* some thirty years later in his autobiography, Minnelli would recall:

"The actors delivered one hundred and ten percent. I had heard that Bob Walker, suffering from the heartache of a broken marriage, was looking at life through the bottom of a liquor bottle. And yet he was always cheerful and on time. I wasn't aware of the toll the picture was taking on his nerves. But Judy knew. She believed in Bob, and she believed in the picture."

Bob's cheerful demeanor between takes was as much of a performance as the one he gave when the cameras were rolling.

Although Bob was genuinely fond of Judy, her relationship with the brilliant but unhandsome Minnelli was yet another reminder to him of Jennifer's affair with Selznick, though it was irrational of him to feel that way. Judy had been a major star long before Vincente had entered her life. No matter who might have been directing *The Clock*, she'd have received the same favored treatment, yet the deference shown her was an additional assault on Bob's battered self-image.

He didn't protest when, one morning, an appealing little speech he had, in which he told his bride not to worry and gave all the reasons he felt he would be coming back to her, was rewritten and given to Judy. Minnelli explained that it seemed nobler for her to say it, and later added that he had decided to shoot the rest of the scene in pantomime, hoping that their comfortable gestures would imply that theirs was a good marriage and would endure. The picture ends with the couple parting at Pennsylvania Station.

When *The Clock* was completed in late fall, Judy and Vincente took off for a romantic idyll in New York, planning to marry as soon as her divorce from David Rose became final.

Bob was then summoned by producer Joe Pasternak for the juvenile lead in a diverting if preposterous romantic comedy, *Her Highness and the Bellboy*. Hedy Lamarr was cast as the princess of a mythical European kingdom, Judy Allyson as a bedridden invalid who loves and temporarily loses the bellhop to the exotic

Lamarr. Once again, Bob would be able to conceal his personal torment from the all-seeing eye of the camera.

The public would find him irresistibly appealing. *Variety* summed up his performance as "terrif."

And June Allyson would always remember that "working with Robert Walker was a strange and exhilarating, a once-in-a-lifetime experience. No other actor I have worked with could make a scene so true. Bob would make you feel the scene with him as something urgent and seeping with life. Many around the studio felt sorry for Bob and knew he was caught up in a terrible love triangle.

"Whenever I look back on my career and think of Robert Walker, I almost cry. I wish I could have helped him." No one could.

Bob was only twenty-six, but he was emotionally shell-shocked, physically depleted, and, with increasing frequency, in the grip of a death wish.

Sam Marx, then an executive producer at Metro, recalls: "It was an actress friend of mine who first sounded an alarming note at me. Bob and she had gone to dinner at the beach. She said he had been extremely moody. On the way home they were driving along the Pacific Palisades when suddenly he said, 'We're both so terribly unhappy. Why don't we end it all? I can drive this car off the cliff right here.' And she knew he meant it, too.

"The fact that she knew he meant it was one of the reasons she told me about it, and of course she never went out with Bob again, since that kind of caper was something she didn't relish."

At the time, Marx could only hope the incident was just an aberration on Bob's part, and he said nothing to anyone at the studio.

Far from being a mere aberration, however, Bob's suicidal tendencies intensified when he was drinking.

Vincente Minnelli was living with Judy when they received a phone call from Bob, who drunkenly informed them he was going to kill himself.

"We both got on the phone alternately talking to him," remembers Minnelli, "trying to get him to tell us where he was. He steadfastly refused to say. After much cajoling, he agreed to come over to the house.

"He showed up a half-hour later. 'Give me a drink,' he com-

manded belligerently, 'and make it snappy.' I fixed him a drink and sat down with him and Judy. We were prepared to offer Bob all the concern and understanding he would allow, but he wasn't having any.

"He hated the town, hated the people in it . . . but most of all Bob hated himself. And then he zeroed in on Judy and me. We heard a lot of ugly things. Judy reacted with superhuman patience. She was loving; she wanted to show that somebody cared.

"Bob's mood hadn't altered. I was given more brusque orders, most of them demands for drinks. I tried watering them down, but Bob would have none of that. The resentments he must have been storing up during the filming came spilling out. I chose to endure them . . . I began to realize that the solution was not to water his drinks but to keep pouring them into him until he passed out."

Bob would remember nothing about that evening. As for Jennifer, she was unaware of his suicidal impulses. He communicated with her only when sober, and would do nothing to jeopardize his relationship with his sons.

Through all this, Jennifer was bored and restless. Reluctantly Selznick negotiated a deal with Hal Wallis at Paramount for his two big draws, Jennifer and Joseph Cotten, to costar in the romantic melodrama *Love Letters*, on the stipulation that the film, which had an October 23 starting date, would be completed before the first of the year.

In Ayn Rand's screenplay, Jennifer was cast as a naive British girl who marries a soldier as the result of the sensitive and tender letters he has sent her from the front. Actually, the letters had been composed by a buddy (Cotten). The soldier himself is a brutish lout; when he's murdered, she loses her memory and is sent to prison for a year for manslaughter. Upon her release, she meets and falls in love with Cotten. Eventually the identity of the real murderer is revealed. Jennifer gave a lovely and touching performance, and although the film received mixed reviews, she received yet a third Oscar nomination. (That year, Joan Crawford won for *Mildred Pierce*.)

On the final day of February 1945, shooting finally began on *Duel in the Sun* and would continue for nine months—a traumatic nine months for Jennifer, Bob, and David and Irene Selznick.

One can only speculate on Bob's reaction had he been told of the events transpiring at the Selznick household during this period. According to Irene Selznick in her autobiography, A Private View, she had told David in February she wanted out of their marriage. He had implored her to reconsider; even though he admitted—for the first time—that he *was* having an affair, that the girl was Jennifer Jones, and that "if he gave her up and I still walked out on him, he wouldn't have anyone. Then he did give her up and wanted my sympathy for the hard time Jennifer was giving him. That got us nowhere, because she hadn't caused our situation. If it hadn't been her, it would have been someone else."

David, still according to Irene's version, begged to stay on, at least until their fifteenth wedding anniversary on April 29. As an anniversary gift, he presented his wife with a sixty-thousand-dollar diamond bracelet, and there was a brief truce. Irene Selznick, however, was adamant in her resolve, although she agreed to hold up any public announcement until August. She writes, "I don't know if he took up with Jennifer again at the time or kept her on a back burner until we actually parted. . . ."

Jennifer was definitely not on a back burner. Both personally and professionally, Selznick was involved, especially now that the shooting of *Duel in the Sun* had finally started.

Joseph Cotten had been cast as the good brother, whom the lusty Pearl wants with her heart, and Gregory Peck as the very bad brother, to whom her all-too-weak flesh is irresistibly attracted. King Vidor was the director. On March 4 the whole company left California for the rugged, hilly site some twenty miles outside of Tucson, Arizona, which had been selected for the exterior scenes.

From the time of their arrival, cast and crew were plagued by freak weather: rain and snow and temperatures hovering below the freezing mark, which caused endless and costly delays, severe discomfort for the entire company, and agony for Jennifer.

It was bad enough that she had to get up at six in the morning to apply Indian makeup, which also took a couple of hours at night to get off, so that in effect she was working fifteen-hour days for the better part of a year. What is even more interesting is to see what Selznick was willing to put her through in this bizarre, lurid monument to his sexual obsession.

The climactic scene of the movie called for Pearl to hunt down

and shoot Lewt, the bad brother, and in turn to be shot by him. She then crawls to him up a jagged cliff to be reunited with her lover for one final embrace before their deaths—"one of those chunks of theatrics," the New York *Times* would later say, "that ranks with Liza crossing the ice."

Vidor, concerned with Jennifer's safety, wanted to protect her body and knees with insulated padding, but Selznick would have nothing of it. It would lose too much realism, he claimed. Jennifer would be inhibited, he said. Vidor should shoot the scene as it was.

The result was that by the time the sequence was finally completed to Selznick's satisfaction, Jennifer's arms and stomach were covered with blood and bruises—and Selznick was beaming at having secured such magnificent footage. Everybody thought it odd, but it wasn't the only such instance. Selznick drove Jennifer to excesses of "primitive passion," in the words of the film's foreword, as if a man possessed. King Vidor even swore that during some of the heated love scenes between Jones and Peck, he could hear David O. Selznick panting in the background.

Nor was Jennifer's performance the only area to receive such attention. Morning, noon, and night, Selznick was on the set, redirecting the actors, the cameras, and even the lighting. There were strict orders on the set that not a single scene was to be photographed, and not even a single angle of a single scene, until he was brought onto the set to check the lighting, the setup, and the actors. By his own admission, "ninety-nine times out of one hundred," he found something to change.

Finally it got too much for King Vidor. After being taken to task one too many times by Selznick for the way he was shooting a scene, Vidor just quit. Selznick was unrepentant. He simply replaced Vidor with William Dieterle (though Vidor ultimately got the screen credit) and finished the film, months behind schedule and more than a million dollars over budget. *Duel in the Sun* would finally cost a record $4,575,000 to make.

The cost overruns drove Selznick crazy, but he was certain it was all going to be worth it. This film would be a triumph, he told everybody, his second *Gone with the Wind*. He would spend a million dollars to promote it, he would make everybody in it immortal. In a way, he was right. *Duel in the Sun* would indeed

achieve immortality when it was released a year later, but of a kind very different from what Selznick had imagined.

Meanwhile, Robert Walker kept busy. *The Clock* was released on the third of May 1945 to unanimously favorable public reaction and critical huzzahs. *Time* noted that "Vincente Minnelli has helped give Robert Walker an honest, touching dignity in place of the shucks-fellows cuteness he has sometimes been doomed to."

The studio didn't take the cue, however. Dazzled by the success of the first Hargrove film, they assigned screenwriter Harry Kurnitz to prepare a sequel—*What Next, Corporal Hargrove?* To take advantage of Bob's popularity, the studio arranged a gala for *The Clock* in Ogden, Utah, the proceeds of the triumphant premiere to go to the local war-bond drive.

An industry-wide strike had shut down all production on April 18 (it would continue until June 25), and it was a relief for Bob to have a valid excuse to get away for a while.

He called his parents and asked if they would meet him at the Union Pacific Station in Salt Lake City and drive him back to Ogden. He promised to stay in town for a few days' visit.

He hardly looked like a movie star when he disembarked from the *City of Los Angeles* streamliner, wearing a tweed coat with accented shoulders, trousers in the zoot-suit fashion, clipped in at the ankle, and thick horn-rimmed glasses. *The Deseret News*'s star female reporter, Maxine Martz, had been alerted to his arrival.

Totally in control, he kept his comments safe and banal: "I didn't like Hollywood at first, but now I do. I love the climate. But I'm always thrilled to get back to Utah. You know, Salt Lake is known for its beautiful girls." Before Miss Martz could question him about Jennifer, he excused himself and left to join his parents.

Aside from seeing his favorite cousin and the satisfaction of selling a great many bonds, the Ogden trip brought him little solace. On the *City of Los Angeles* en route back to Hollywood, he felt lonelier and more depressed than ever.

The strike continued throughout May. Jennifer occupied herself with nursing at a veterans' hospital; David Selznick kept tampering with the *Duel in the Sun* script, adding some seventy-five new scenes to the massive production.

Bob didn't know what to do with himself. Although he had

finally managed to secure a telephone and had hired a houseman to tend to his domestic needs, there was no one he cared to entertain.

He stayed home most nights, but he felt the walls closing in on him. All he could think about was Jennifer and his struggle to accept the reality that he had lost her forever.

On June 20, five days before the strike ended, a very nervous Phylis Walker appeared before a Los Angeles judge to request her freedom on the all-encompassing grounds of "mental cruelty."

"What did he do that was cruel?" demanded the judge.

"He was very difficult and very sarcastic."

"You can't get a divorce on that," the judge responded sharply.

"He wanted me to go into radio work, against my wishes and the advice of my agent, and he wanted—"

"That's not cruel," the judge again interrupted.

By this time Jennifer was in tears.

Reluctantly she testified that prior to their parting, her husband had often stayed away from home at night, causing her great nervousness and worry, and wouldn't say where he had been.

"That," said the judge, "is grounds for divorce."

With her lawyer at her side, she retreated from the courthouse through a back door, dashed into a waiting car, and sped away to keep an appointment with David O. Selznick.

12

Although he was still unable to exorcise the ghost of Phylis Isley, Bob did make a concerted effort to change his life-style, drink less, and get out and around more.

Before his divorce, he had become friendly with the twenty-one-year-old London-born Peter Lawford, whom MGM was also grooming for stardom. Lawford at the time was a carefree, amusing bachelor, sophisticated beyond his years, and always good for a laugh. The two would take in a movie, attend the prizefights, or have dinner, but the relationship was, at best, superficial.

Bob couldn't relate to Peter's overwhelming ambition nor admire the manner in which he courted the press or dated "name" actresses for the sole purpose of furthering his career. When he criticized Peter's life-style, the latter just laughed.

"I don't plan to marry until I'm at least thirty," Peter blithely informed him. "So why not live it up? You're always welcome to join me. There's a big demand for an extra man."

Bob wasn't interested. "I hate big parties. I have nothing in common with your rich socialite friends. I don't even own a tux. I'm sorry, I just can't play the Hollywood game the way you do."

Peter wasn't put off by Bob's outspoken contempt of his values. He was enjoying his life, whereas it was obvious to him that Bob was merely existing from day to day.

Having lost both time and money due to the strike, MGM was reluctant to keep any of their stars idle any longer. Since the script of the *Hargrove* sequel wasn't completed, and the studio was impressed by the chemistry generated between Bob and June Allyson in *Her Highness and the Bellboy*, the two were reunited in a low-budget "quickie" based on a flop play by Chester Erskine. Audrey

Totter and Hume Cronyn were assigned second leads and Richard Whorf, actor turned director, was put in charge of the project. The domestic comedy, which went into production titled *For Better or Worse*, recounted the trials and tribulations of an ex-sailor and his bride who move into a New York apartment where the doors stick, the folding beds foul up, the fireplace won't work, and a sexy neighbor, Audrey Totter, goes on the make for the groom.

When the picture appeared under its final title, *The Sailor Takes a Wife*, Bosley Crowther of the New York *Times* noted that "In intellectual dimensions it's about the size of a one-inch cube. In fact, if it wasn't for June Allyson's attractive personality . . . and Bob Walker's boyish beam . . . it would be a fearful bore. These two do manage to give it a certain pleasant cohesiveness."

The latter was due to the off-screen rapport between Bob and June. June, wildly in love with Dick Powell, radiated sunshine and "made it my personal mission to keep Bob from retreating into his shell during the long waits between setups."

So did Whorf, who at thirty-nine was a brilliant conversationalist and an extremely talented artist. Disturbed about Bob's lack of interest in food, Whorf would invite Bob to join him for lunch, and the two would discuss theater, books, art, and other intellectual subjects. Whorf, however, had his own tight circle of artistic friends, and Bob could not summon up the courage to ask to be included among them.

When *The Sailor Takes a Wife* was completed, Whorf told Bob, "Your potential hasn't even begun to be tapped. I hope I'll have a chance to direct you in something decent someday."

Socially Bob was now spending his time almost exclusively with Jim Henaghan, whose marriage to Gwen Verdon had just ended in divorce without leaving visible scars on either. Jim wanted to stay fancy free, but he was eager to fix Bob up with a nice girl, if only to get his mind off Jennifer. "There *must* be someone you would like to meet," he insisted. "Name her and if she's free, I'll play Cupid."

Bob grinned sheepishly. "Well, when I saw Diana Lynn in *Our Hearts Were Young and Gay*, I thought her pretty nice. But I just couldn't pick up the phone and ask her out. Besides, she was *acting*. She may be a bitch personally."

"Dolly's a very sweet girl," Jim assured him. "A little too saccharine for my taste, but if you'd like to meet her, I'll ask her to

join us for dinner. After that, you're on your own. If you don't go for each other, you've lost nothing but a few hours."

Jim arranged the date, but knew when to make his exit, leaving the two alone to talk.

Bob found Diana delightful; she obviously enjoyed his company. When he asked to see her again, she quickly agreed. Within a few weeks they were, in columnese, "Hollywood's newest twosome."

Occasionally they double-dated with Diana's close friend Gail Russell and her beau of the moment; more frequently they spent their evenings alone. Diana, who had been a child pianist, invited him to her home to hear her play. Bob was smitten with her, telling Jim, "She's really terrific, so warm and adorable and such great fun; the nicest girl I've met since Phyllis Thaxter."

"Don't get serious," Jim advised. "Give the relationship time."

Jim was aware that Diana was extremely career-oriented and, at nineteen, reluctant to become emotionally involved with Bob—or any other man—and he knew from the "grapevine" that Diana was dividing her attention among Bob, novelist Richard Sale, Paramount writer Stanley Roberts, and Henry Willson, a talent scout for Selznick.

He didn't want Bob to experience another painful letdown.

Although Diana was extremely fond of Bob, she had nagging fears about a relationship with a divorced man with two young children; a man who, her friends had warned her, was still carrying a torch for his ex-wife. Nonetheless, she thought there was no harm in going out with Bob—as long as they continued to have fun—nor had she any reason to bring up the other men in her life.

Columnist Cal York, however, couldn't resist provocatively noting, "Robert Walker has some stiff competition for Diana Lynn's time. At least three other notable Hollywood bachelors are pursuing her like crazy. Diana doesn't lack for dates these balmy nights."

Despite the fact that he and Diana had no commitment, Bob irrationally felt betrayed. If she really cared about him, she'd be seeing him exclusively, as he was her.

The next time they were together, he aggressively expressed those feelings.

Diana was startled by Bob's attitude. She had never seen him in

such a savage mood—so different from the sweet, considerate gentleman she had spent time with. Not wishing to make a scene in public, she assured him that she *did* care about him but hadn't realized that he considered her his steady girl.

After denying his bitter accusation that she was a tease who had been leading him on, Diana sadly added that perhaps it would be wiser if they didn't see one another anymore.

After escorting Diana home, Bob returned to his apartment, dialed Henaghan, and morosely rehashed the disaster. "Well, it looks as if I blew it again."

Henaghan reminded Bob that he had warned him not to get serious. "You overreacted, buddy. You have no claim on the girl. Give her a few days to calm down."

Bob sent flowers and a note of apology for his rude behavior. When he summoned up enough nerve to phone her, she thanked him for the flowers and the note but gently rebuffed his efforts to make another date, saying it just couldn't be the same again for either of them. She had been too hurt by the things he had said.

Bob didn't try to contact her again.

"Of course, you know what you did," Jim told him. "You were so afraid she might prefer one of those other fellows, you forced her to reject you by the way you behaved. You'll get over it, but don't try a trick like that again—unless you're aching to be hurt again."

"It seems I'm always being rejected!"

"Goddammit, stop feeling so damn sorry for yourself. You have everything going for you. You'll get over Lynn. Now, who else do I know that you might like?"

"Forget it," Bob insisted, but Jim wouldn't be put off. Within the week he introduced him to Shirley O'Hara, an aspiring actress who was living at the Studio Club, which, like the Barbizon in New York, wouldn't permit men past the lobby. He was waiting for Shirley, when he noticed a striking willowy brunette wandering around.

Actress Marie Windsor recalls, "Bob and I were both at Metro in 1945, but our paths never crossed on the lot. It was risky business having your date meet you in the lobby at the Studio Club, for it was expected that the other unattached lovelies would make it a point to parade around to see what attractive or famous

men were in the lobby. More often than not, one of these fellows would strike up a conversation which would generally lead to a date at a later time.

"That's how I got to know Bob. When he said hello, I mentioned that I was also under contract at MGM and also born in Utah. As we talked, Shirley O'Hara appeared. But before she was in earshot Bob asked if he could call me, and I whispered, 'Yes.' Subsequently I had several dates with him. I remember that he was drinking a lot and seemed very upset about his divorce. But in spite of that, I found Bob to be a very sweet, sensitive, and gentle soul— but often very moody. And his close friend Jimmy Henaghan was *always* with us. Once the three of us ended up at Bob's apartment. I wanted to go home but Bob had passed out like a light—so Jimmy drove me back to the Club. It was then I decided that Bob's life-style didn't appeal to me. So our dating ended. We remained friends, however, and we used to talk on the phone from time to time." Bob resumed "stagging" it with Jim.

"Although Bob still had frequent sieges of melancholia," said Jim, "when they abated, he had such an immense sense of humor that he would suffer almost any inconvenience if he thought a situation funny. For instance, his houseman, Harry—who looked like the president of a bank—suddenly started serving fried liver and artichokes for dinner every night. Bob didn't say a word, but *I* did after dining on the stuff three nights in one week.

"'What's with this menu?' I asked. 'Every time I come here, it's liver and artichokes.'

"'We have it every night,' said Bob. 'It's been going on for more than two weeks.'

"'Do you like it that much?'

"'I hate it.'

"'Then why do you eat it?'

"'I think it's funny,' Bob replied. And he broke up. He laughed so hard he had to take off his glasses because they were wet with tears. 'I'm not going to say anything to Harry. I'm just going to see how long he'll keep it up. It's the funniest thing I've ever heard of.'

"'Let me know when he stops,' I told Bob. 'Until then I'll grab a hamburger and come by after dinner. It's your joke, but it's my appetite, and I've had it with liver and artichokes.'

"I have no idea why or when Harry changed the menu. For a

few months Bob and I didn't get together as much as usual, and around that time he became involved with a new girl.

"I missed his company, but I hoped that the girl would help heal his wounds. Physically, she was a Jennifer type. But for Bob's sake I counted on the resemblance stopping there."

Shortly before he was scheduled to start *What Next, Corporal Hargrove?*, Bob met twenty-five-year-old Florence Pritchett, a witty, intelligent, dark-haired divorcée who had enjoyed a successful career in New York as a model and fashion writer. A favorite of café society, sought after by many influential men, the star-struck Miss Pritchett had been seized by an urge to test her skill as a celebrity interviewer and decided to spend a few months on the West Coast.

The former head of a model agency says, "What Florence really wanted was to meet and marry a famous movie star. When she turned on the charm, she was irresistible. When she didn't get her way, she could be as vicious as a tigress, although she was very adept at concealing that side of her nature."

Florence arrived in Hollywood with letters of introduction to the publicity heads of all the major studios—and assignments from many of the leading fan-oriented magazines. She emphasized that she wanted to profile only the biggest or most inaccessible male stars at the various studios. Her list of candidates did not include any women, nor did it include Robert Walker.

She had been interviewing Van Johnson at the MGM commissary when she caught sight of Bob Walker. After completing her session with Johnson, she asked publicity woman Dorothy Blanchard to introduce her to Bob.

Miss Blanchard escorted Florence to Bob's table, where the two exchanged pleasantries. Something about the tall, soft-spoken, dark-eyed girl intrigued Bob. He invited her to join him for a cup of coffee, then asked if he could drive her home.

Although there was a studio limo at her disposal, she unhesitatingly accepted Bob's offer.

"I know you must be awfully busy," he said as they arrived at the Beverly Hills Hotel, "but perhaps we can have dinner some night."

"I'd love it," she replied.

He called the next evening. "If you don't have a date, would you care to go dancing and take in the show at Ciro's on Saturday?"

Although an expert at playing hard-to-get, Florence quickly retorted, "What time will you pick me up?"

Bob found her amusing and easy to talk to—and, as he had failed to do with Phyllis Thaxter and Marie Windsor, avoided the subject of Jennifer. Ciro's, as usual, was crowded with press photographers, but Bob seemed oblivious of them when they snapped him dancing cheek to cheek with Florence. By Monday *all* the columnists ran items about Bob and his new "heart interest."

The following Saturday night they were together again at the Strip's other plush nightclub, the Mocambo, and again Bob didn't protest when the cameras pointed in their direction. He didn't even bother to remove his glasses.

A curious press asked the inevitable:

"Has New York model Florence Pritchett managed to douse the torch Bob Walker has been carrying for ex-wife Jennifer Jones?"

Confronted directly, Bob merely grinned and evaded the question with "Honestly, we're just good friends."

Florence viewed their relationship in a different light. According to a friend, "She fell madly in love with Bob, planned relocating in California, and desperately wanted to marry him but was too clever to exert any pressure." If she was annoyed that, because his Sundays were devoted to his sons, they never spent an entire weekend together, or that he didn't suggest she meet the boys, she didn't press the issue. Florence was willing to play the waiting game as long as there was no other girl in his life.

Either she didn't recognize or she didn't accept the reality that as long as Jennifer Jones was free, there was and there'd always be another girl in his life.

If, at any time, Bob considered making Florence the second Mrs. Walker, he didn't reveal that intention to anyone, including Jim. Nor did he deny the rumors that the two were quietly engaged, rumors that exploded when the two vacationed together in New York for a week in July. Their relationship was fun, satisfied his normal sexual desires, and alleviated his loneliness. He cut down on his drinking, was eating normally again, and even managed to gain some much-needed weight.

He and Florence were together in Beverly Hills when the *Enola*

Gay dropped the first atom bomb on Hiroshima. Later they celebrated VJ Day—August 7—by getting happily high.

Bob, however, was anything but happy that, in spite of the end
of the war, MGM wouldn't shelve its plan to produce *What Next,
Corporal Hargrove?*

"The script," which recounted Hargrove's activities with his
buddies in France, "stinks," he bitched to Keenan Wynn, who was
also repeating his original role as Private Mulvehill. "It's phony,
and by the time it's released, it'll be dated."

Says Keenan in retrospect, "Bob was absolutely on target. The
Hargrove sequel was the bottom of the barrel. We were both dis-
gusted with it. But he had to do what he was told—we all did in
those days."

Bob was in his dressing room on Friday, August 24, killing
time reading the papers before being called for his last shot of
the day, when a headline on page three of the Los Angeles
Examiner hit him like a thunderbolt: "SELZNICKS, WED 15
YEARS, PART."

The story, bylined Louella Parsons, revealed:

"The breaking-up of the fifteen-year marriage of David and Irene
Selznick came as a shock to their friends, even though rumors have
been fast and furious the last few years that all was not well. . . .

Irene said, when I talked to her last night, that the decision was hard
to make but seemed the best way. "We haven't been getting along, and
under those conditions, the only thing to do was separate. . . . Neither of us plans a divorce."

Later, when I talked to David, he said, "I can't think our separation
is final. We have been married so many years, and I consider Irene the
most brilliant and beautiful woman I know. We haven't discussed
divorce, but maybe the separation will clear the air. It was all my fault.
I'm difficult. Irene has taken a lot of my temperament."

Jennifer Jones's name was mentioned casually along with the
half-dozen stars under personal contract to David O. Selznick.
Louella knew how to play the game.

Bob sleepwalked through his final scene. He changed his
clothes and headed toward his car. He didn't bother to call Florence to break their dinner date.

He just kept driving.

Four days later he was the headlined subject of another Parsons exclusive:

BOB WALKER DISAPPEARS

Robert Walker has disappeared.

The likable juvenile, recently divorced by Jennifer Jones . . . hasn't been seen or heard from in forty-eight hours. He was due on the set at MGM yesterday morning at nine o'clock . . . and when he failed to make an appearance after several hours, studio officials began to worry. Contacting the young man's home only deepened the mystery, for no one had seen or heard from Bob.

Bob, who is one of the film colony's most earnest and responsible young actors, isn't the type to disappear on a holiday or as a prank. He is far too conscious of his obligations to his studio to willfully walk out on an important production. His friends here and I are sincerely worried.

The Parsons piece was picked up and sensationalized by local radio stations, which expressed the fear that Bob had "dashed off somewhere to kill himself."

The studio notified the police and checked the hospitals in the nearby counties, but there was no trace of him living or dead.

During Bob's absence, director Richard Thorpe frantically tried to shoot around him, since the studio wouldn't shut down production until they had received definite word about Bob's fate. Miss Parsons, however, didn't overstate: everyone *was* worried sick.

Then, without any prior notice, Bob nonchalantly appeared on the *Hargrove* set early Wednesday morning to resume work.

Thorpe, almost speechless, called Mayer, who angrily ordered Bob to report to the front office.

"I think you owe us an explanation. Where have you been hiding?"

Amused by the stir he had created, Bob merely grinned. "Oh, I just decided to drive up to Santa Barbara to visit some friends for a few days."

"And your friends don't have a telephone?" Mayer asked sarcastically.

Bob just shrugged. "I didn't feel like calling. If you want, you

can dock my salary or put me on suspension." He refused to be intimidated, confident that since *Hargrove* was only half-completed, the studio would do neither.

"Well," said Benny Thau, who was also present, "try telling us in advance the next time you decide to disappear. But I wouldn't recommend there being a 'next time.'"

When Bob phoned Florence Pritchett later that evening, she was unable to maintain her charming, understanding facade.

"How dare you do this to me?" she demanded. "I've been frantic with worry. Didn't you see the papers, didn't you hear the radio? The least you could have done was call me."

"I didn't want anyone to know where I was." Bob tried to control his anger.

Then Florence made what would prove to be a fatal mistake.

"Don't lie to me!" she screamed. "You were off on a bender with another woman, weren't you?"

"No, I wasn't," Bob replied. "But even if I were, it's none of your damn business. You don't own me."

Florence slammed down the phone.

Bob called Henaghan and got the expected. "Where the hell were you? I haven't had a moment's peace for days. Everyone's been calling, convinced I was keeping some deep dark secret. Feel like talking about it?"

"Not now. The studio has been on my ass all day; Florence acted like a shrew when I phoned her; and I have a heavy schedule tomorrow. Just wanted you to know I'm okay. I hear that the radio news hinted I was dead under a rock somewhere."

"Well," chided Jim, "it was a crazy thing for you to do."

"I suppose so. But we both know I'm a little crazy. It will all be forgotten in a few days. Mayer and Thau will cool down . . . but Florence . . . she was a bitch. I don't think I'll be seeing her again. I have a knack for picking wrong women."

A few weeks later Florence returned to New York. In 1948 she would marry a man named Earl Smith, who would later become the U.S. ambassador to Cuba.

After that experience, Bob rarely if ever asked a girl for a second or third date.

"If you think I'm getting too interested in anyone," he told Jim, "toss your typewriter at my head."

He did, however, strike up a platonic friendship with Jean Porter, later Mrs. Edward Dmytryk, who played the little French girl in *Corporal Hargrove*. More than forty years later, Jean still maintains an incredible loyalty to Bob.

"Many people loved him. Count me among them. He was shy and could be called withdrawn much of the time, but he had a delightful sense of humor. I loved nothing more than seeing his sad-seeming eyes suddenly sparkle and hearing him break into a laugh. We avoided the commissary and often shared lunch breaks at the nearby Culver City Drive-In, where we could really be left alone to enjoy our conversation. Our talks were private, and I never discussed them with anyone and still won't. But Bob was great! Really great."

What Next, Corporal Hargrove? turned out to be the bomb Bob had predicted. When it was rushed into release on Christmas Day, the *Times*'s critic, Bosley Crowther, noted that Bob performed the character "in the style of the writing . . . perfunctorily. . . . Now that it's over, let's hope that Hargrove will be separated from films."

Just before the completion of *What Next?*, Bob was approached by Arthur Freed, the genius in charge of MGM's musical unit. Freed told Bob that he was his personal choice for the featured role in *Till the Clouds Roll By*, an all-star extravaganza loosely based on Jerome Kern's life and his mammoth contribution to the American musical theater.

"You must be kidding," Bob protested. "I wouldn't be believable as Kern. I'm a young American type. I can't do roles that call for me to age!"

"Stop selling yourself short," Freed chided. "But let me talk to Jerry and feel him out. I want to give him the option of approving my choice. And *you're* my choice."

At their next meeting, Fred asked Kern: "What would you say to Bob Walker playing you?"

Kern was hesitant. "I don't know. Let me call my wife, Eva, and see what she thinks."

Kern was laughing when he put down the phone.

"What did she say?" Freed asked.

"She said, 'Send Robert Walker to me and you stay there and play yourself.'"

Till the Clouds Roll By was scheduled to start in late September, and Freed had decided to shoot the lavish production numbers first, because of the staggering logistics resulting from the availability problems of the guest stars. Judy Garland, Frank Sinatra, Dinah Shore, Lena Horne, Kathryn Grayson, June Allyson, and Van Johnson were just a few of the many spotlighted in various segments.

Bob, Dorothy Patrick (as Eva), Van Heflin, and Lucille Bremer would carry the largely fictitious "book." With the exception of missing the fatal sailing of the *Lusitania* (because his clock stopped during the night), Kern's personal life had been highly undramatic. The composer, in fact, had warned Freed, "If you tell the truth, it will be the dullest picture ever made."

Shortly after being assigned to *Till the Clouds Roll By*, Bob was summoned to Howard Strickling's office.

Strickling informed him that he had just gotten the results of *Modern Screen*'s annual readers' poll. Van Johnson had run away with the number-one spot, and June Allyson, in third position, was the only female among the top ten. Bob was sixth on the list, a few votes below Peter Lawford, who came in fifth.

"I suppose Van and Pete are turning somersaults," Bob laughed. "But as far as I'm concerned, you could have phoned in the news."

Strickling informed Bob that there were some important matters involved with the poll that had to be discussed personally. The magazine planned to devote an entire issue to the Top Ten and wanted to run Bob's life story in two parts. Since he had two movies coming out which needed all the help they could get, he'd have to insist that Bob cooperate despite his aversion to publicity. Both Bob and Strickling would get the finished copy for their approval before it was sent to the typesetter.

"And one more thing," Strickling concluded. "Louella Parsons is going to have an enormous party at her home for the winners and the Delacortes [George and Albert Delacorte, respectively publisher and editor of *Modern Screen*]. Even L.B. plans to attend. You'll make an enemy of Parsons for life if you refuse."

"I'll think about it," Bob replied. "By the way, have they assigned the story to anyone yet?"

"I don't know. If you have a preference, I'll pass it along. But this is the one interview you're going to *have* to do."

At dinner that evening, Bob broached the subject to Henaghan.

"Will you do the story? You're the best writer around—plus you know practically everything there is to know about me. And it will give you a chance to pick up some quick bucks."

"Not on your life, pal," Henaghan replied. "I know *too* much about you to give a fan magazine the kind of stuff they're after, and I've knocked out enough of those stories to know what they want— pure image. I can do that kind of thing with Ladd but not with you. But you'll be nuts if you turn them down. Ask for Kirtley Baskett. He actually *likes* actors. It kills me to admit it, but Strickling is right. You damn well better make an appearance at the party, or Parsons will crucify you."

Baskett's lengthy interview went smoothly. Although it was painful for Bob to "relive" the happy years with Jennifer, the copy was tasteful and tactful, dismissing the cause of the divorce with the brief line: "It's none of our business."

There were no references to Bob's drinking or disappearance. The "boy-next-door" image remained unblemished.

The Parsons party, however, was truly an ordeal for Bob, who arrived alone and wandered aimlessly among the more than three hundred guests. Louella's garden was jammed with couples, both young and old, enjoying themselves to the hilt. This fact merely intensified his loneliness.

Bored though he was, Bob couldn't help but be amused as he watched Peter Lawford table-hopping and Louis B. Mayer doing the rumba, but his heart sank when he spotted Diana Lynn with Henry Willson. For the most part, he remained alone at the bar, observing but unable to participate in the gaiety. He posed for a few mandatory pictures, paid respects to Louella and then quietly left. Later Louella noted, "I saw Bob Walker briefly. He doesn't look very happy, and he didn't stay very long."

It was fortunate for Bob that he decided to leave early. A few hours later, David Selznick made a solo appearance at the party. He and Jennifer were still not flaunting their relationship in public. In addition, she was exhausted as a result of a strenuous exotic dance sequence that Selznick had decided to insert at the last minute into the already interminably long *Duel in the Sun*.

Although Selznick was livid that Jennifer hadn't made the list, he didn't wish to offend Louella by ignoring her invitation. By the

time he arrived, however, most of his cronies had called it a night, so he joined Anita Colby and her writer friend Noel Busch for a nightcap just minutes before the orchestra went into a rendition of "Home, Sweet Home," Louella's cutsie inspiration to inform the diehards that the bar was closed and the party was over.

Bob was relieved that he had avoided a face-to-face confrontation with Selznick. He hadn't seen him since the conclusion of *Since You Went Away* two years earlier—and even a casual reference to the man was repulsive to him. "The only thing I want to read about that bastard is that he found a new woman," he had told Jim bitterly.

Nevertheless, Bob was annoyed that he had been given no warning that Selznick was one of the invited guests. He had recently turned twenty-seven, but he felt he was being ordered around and manipulated as if he were still a child—told what he had to do and what he mustn't do. And if he was a bad boy and didn't obey, he'd be punished by Papa—in this case, the studio.

When he had been a penniless youngster, he had always rebelled against such treatment by running away. He was still the rebel, but he couldn't run too far away as long as his sons were still in California. So he fought the system in his own way.

He told Strickling that although he had no choice as to the roles assigned him, he would no longer be coerced into attending any press parties or granting interviews.

Strickling, used to dealing with truculent actors, warned, "If you don't cooperate with the press, we won't be able to protect you from the press. You're not that big."

"I'm big enough and old enough to take care of myself."

Time would prove him disastrously mistaken.

Chapter

13

Bob's costars all "loved" him; the directors for whom he worked admired and respected his talent; but by now Benny Thau and Eddie Mannix, Mayer's feared top executives, considered him a major headache. His increasingly defiant and sarcastic attitude toward the big brass galled them.

Because of Arthur Freed's determination to cast him as Kern, not to mention Eva Kern's enthusiastic endorsement, they couldn't mete out the punishment they felt he deserved. They ordered a publicity blackout on Bob—which he welcomed—then decided that once *Till the Clouds Roll By* was completed, Bob would be cut down to size. They were experts at dealing with difficult actors. Bigger stars than Bob still bore the wounds inflicted by their hatchet blows, and most of their victims came groveling to the front office begging for a reprieve.

Then a pall was cast over everyone connected with the production when Jerome Kern, who had suffered a cerebral hemorrhage in New York six days earlier, died at Doctors Hospital on November 11.

When Freed received the tragic news, he suspended production. The shooting script would require both a new beginning and a different ending. While those were in the works, however, costs kept mounting, and Freed ordered musical director Robert Alton to resume filming several of the remaining musical numbers, including the title tune, as well as "Leave It to Jane" and "How'd You Like to Spoon with Me," and to prepare an abridged version of *Show Boat*.

Bob was told that he'd be called back to work when the necessary rewrites had been completed, and so, for the third year in a row,

he faced an idle and lonely holiday season. His mood only worsened when he heard that Peter Lawford was being loaned by Metro to Twentieth Century-Fox to costar in the role of a flighty young English peer with Charles Boyer and Jennifer in Ernst Lubitsch's sparkling farce *Cluny Brown*, which was scheduled to start on December 3.

Jennifer's holidays were also far from perfect. Irene Selznick had returned from New York to put things in order and would write:

"Then came Christmas. David was no guest: he was family. Christmas Eve and Christmas Day he spent with us as promised. It was as of yore. Well, almost. There was a new avalanche of gifts, climaxed by the diamond necklace. His explanation for the jewelry, and sables as well, was that time had run out for him. These were things he had always had in mind, and I hadn't let him finish. It was something he had to do. He would be deeply obliged if I would accept them, as otherwise he would find it humiliating. . . . I could no more cure David of gifts than of gambling. . . . I don't know how Jennifer put up with this."

Actually Jennifer had little choice. She was more than David's "girl," she was his chattel. If she walked out on him and her contract, she could legally be prevented from working at any studio, and David, still obsessed with the notion that there was no role she couldn't play, dreamed of parading her versatility by starring her in *Little Women*, *Joan of Arc*, and *Portrait of Jennie*.

Although she was under a great deal of emotional stress, and often infuriated by his irrational and sometimes insensitive behavior, she managed to cope with it. Her preoccupation with proving herself an adept comedienne in *Cluny Brown* enabled her to preserve her peace of mind while David was socializing at his Summit Drive home with his estranged wife, his sons, Danny and Jeff, and his friends.

Bob was not so fortunate. Temporarily, and at the worst possible time for him, he had no job to go to, no girl he cared to see. With the exception of a few afternoons spent with his sons and several dinners with Jim at his apartment, he remained in a self-imposed exile during the holidays, even refusing Jim's entreaties to accompany him to the parties to which the latter had been invited.

With too much time for thinking on his hands, his insecurities about playing the role of Jerome Kern intensified. It was difficult

enough when the composer was still alive. Now he had to carry the additional burden of doing justice to Kern's memory. His frequent calls to Freed's office asking when the new script would be ready always elicited the same impatient response: "We'll let you know."

Then he was told that the film's director, Henry Koster, had had a run-in with Freed, leading to Koster's abrupt removal. Koster had himself previously replaced Busby Berkeley. The choice of Koster's replacement was a big question mark. The once "happy" musical now seemed jinxed by tragedy and problems.

Vincente Minnelli would have been a natural successor. Only a few months earlier, he had directed his then-pregnant wife, Judy Garland, in her musical segments of the film, but Minnelli was about to start *The Pirate*, starring Judy and Gene Kelly.

It was Kelly who suggested that Richard Whorf, a close friend of his, be entrusted with the assignment. Whorf, unlike his predecessors, had no prior musical experience, but the book section was an entity within itself, and Arthur Freed, whose instincts often seemed infallible, decided he could do the job.

On January 22, 1946, the dramatic sequences finally got under way.

Under Whorf's direction, Bob started feeling comfortable in the role. Although everyone was now working under extreme pressure, Whorf rarely made demands on Bob, just tactful "suggestions" if he felt a reading or a bit of business could be improved upon. Since Bob respected and trusted the man, he complied with those suggestions without protest.

Their social relationship was confined to the studio, until one Friday, after Whorf called it quits for the day, he invited Bob to his home for a drink, recalling that Bob had often expressed a desire to view the seascapes and landscapes Whorf painted as a hobby.

Though no connoisseur of art, Bob was awed by Whorf's work. "You're terrific," Bob exclaimed. "Have you thought of exhibiting?"

"Someday, perhaps," Whorf replied. "For now, they make nice gifts. If I can save enough money to get by on in my old age, I might turn professional. But that's up the road a piece. As you know, I have a wife and three children to support. I've always been a firm believer that there's nothing a man can't do if he's sufficiently motivated. You should try your hand at painting."

"Me? I couldn't paint the side of a barn. I have thought of trying a children's book, though."

"Then get going at it," Whorf advised. "Having a hobby is a good idea." He looked right at Bob. "It takes your mind off other things."

Till the Clouds Roll By was nearing completion early that spring when Bob received a call from his brother Walter, back from the service and awaiting his official discharge at Camp Kilmer, New Jersey. The two hadn't seen each other for three years, and Walt decided to fly to Los Angeles for a brief vacation before returning to Utah to visit their parents.

Walt had served as one of the lawyers at the Nuremberg trials and had planned to return to Germany in a civilian capacity after a brief stay in the States. This would be his only opportunity to spend some time with his family.

In an interview given to Jean Kinkead, Walter would remember "a wonderful two weeks with a lot of serious talk, but with a lot of fun too. It was exciting to spend the day on the set of *Till the Clouds Roll By* watching Bob portraying an aging Jerome Kern, complete with paunch and gray hair, and seeing him repeat the same scene over five times without getting edgy or self-conscious about it."

Walt also enjoyed the so-called quiet evenings at home with Bob when Peter Lawford would drop in and play every record Bob owned, meanwhile interrogating Walt about the war and the trials.

The one dinner Walt shared with Bob and Jim Henaghan, however, turned out dismally. "I didn't care much for the man," Henaghan remembered. "He may have been a brilliant lawyer, but his personality was zilch. I don't think Bob really cared much for him, or for anyone in his family for that matter."

Nevertheless, Bob was determined to show his brother a good time.

When the studio informed him that "Miss Photoflash of 1945," Shirley Maloan, a Chicagoan, had arrived in Hollywood for a screen test and a date with her favorite movie star, who, she insisted, was Robert Walker, Bob, surprisingly, agreed to go along with the stunt. He named only one condition: that MGM make it a foursome by providing a date for his older brother on his last night in town. When the Walkers arrived to pick up Walter's date,

the lady was not one of MGM's glamorous starlets, but, of all people, the syndicated columnist Hedda Hopper.

Miss Hopper, acutely aware of Bob's antagonism toward the press and his personal problems, extended herself to make the evening a gay and informal one. Away from her typewriter, she was a witty, charming, and knowledgeable woman, and after a strained fifteen minutes or so, Bob actually found himself *liking* her. Years later, she would say of him, "This gangling shy man carried a gentle sweetness with him that touched your heart." And she meant it. If her archrival, Louella Parsons, aiming to please *her* friend David O. Selznick, was always protective of and flattering to Jennifer, Hedda would become one of Bob's greatest boosters. Privately she felt him the victim of one of the dirtiest deals in town.

Walter left town the following afternoon. "Hate to say goodbye, kid. God knows when we'll see each other again." Bob just laughed. "For a half a buck, the price of a movie ticket, you can see me anytime."

But Bob never saw his brother again.

According to cousin Barbara Rabe, "Bob's relations with his brother ended at about this time. Walter settled in Germany, where he married a German girl and had a daughter named Dorothy. Still relatively young, he died in Germany of stomach cancer. Wayne just up and disappeared. I don't believe he ever contacted his brother after Bob became a star."

In spite of Hopper's enthusiastic endorsement of Bob and his convincing portrayal of Jerome Kern, the studio brass, still outraged by his attitude toward them, were determined to cut him down, even if to do so meant acting against their own best interests.

Spencer Tracy had taken a leave of absence from Metro the previous summer to accept Pulitzer Prize-winning playwright Robert E. Sherwood's invitation to return to Broadway in *The Rugged Path*. Katharine Hepburn, Tracy's devoted companion, had accompanied him back east to lend moral support and keep him on the wagon during the difficult weeks of rehearsals and out-of-town tryouts. The play's title was prophetic. It opened in New York in

mid-November to disappointing reviews and managed to eke out a mere eighty-one performances, due mainly to advance sales.

When a disheartened Tracy and Hepburn returned to Hollywood, they were immediately costarred in a sprawling soap-opera western called *The Sea of Grass*, produced by Pandro S. Berman and directed by Elia Kazan. The basic story line about a feud between cattlemen and farmers was drowned in a sea of domestic melodrama; the Hepburn character has an affair with, and subsequently an illegitimate son by Tracy's lawyer, played by Melvyn Douglas. The boy stays with Tracy but grows up to be a nasty ne'er-do-well. He is eventually shot down by a posse and the estranged Tracy and Hepburn reconcile.

Walker's role—that of Brock Brewton, Hepburn's illegitimate son—was decidedly a minor one. It would have been more suitable for one of MGM's stock contractees than for an actor who had just had an important role in a three-million-dollar production, but Bob Walker was ordered to report as a reminder that he was being punished.

Bob retaliated by giving a performance which Crowther of the New York *Times* later damned as consisting of "no more than an ostentatious swagger and an occasionally overstudied leer."

The Sea of Grass set was an oppressive one in other ways. Elia Kazan, who had once admired Tracy and Hepburn, felt they were both out of their element. He found Tracy a man "only able to do things a few times and then losing interest" and Hepburn "woefully miscast as a middle-class girl supposed to arrive from St. Louis to become Tracy's wife." But above all, Kazan resented the lack of a good script and that none of the picture was to be shot on location. Regarding Robert Walker, he made no comment at all.

When Bob joined the *Sea of Grass* cast, his first friend on the set was Spencer Tracy. Tracy was well aware of the reverses—both personal and professional—that the younger actor had been experiencing, and his heart went out to him, an interest that might have developed into a lasting friendship had Bob not taken it as a personal affront when on several occasions Tracy, who had been making a valiant attempt (with Hepburn's encouragement) to stay on the wagon, refused to join him for drinks after work.

When Bob became insistent, both Tracy and Hepburn began

avoiding him. Once again, he was being rejected, but it was a rejection brought on by his own odd behavior. Phyllis Thaxter, cast as Bob's half-sister, was as charming and friendly as ever, but since she was now Mrs. James Aubrey—she'd married Aubrey in 1944—Bob made it a point to keep his distance. All in all, *The Sea of Grass* was proving to be an unpleasant experience for everyone connected with it. Even Kazan commented later, "If I'd put my dignity first, I'd have quit the picture before I started it."

At the time Bob was completing *The Sea of Grass*, David Selznick announced his grand plans to remake his original *Little Women* starring Jennifer Jones as Jo, the role in which Katharine Hepburn had given such a memorable performance in RKO's 1933 classic. He signed Bambi Lynn, a Broadway dancer, for the role of Beth, and Bob's former girl, Diana Lynn, as Amy, with Anne Revere (Jennifer's mother in *Bernadette*) as Marmee, but was undecided as to whether Shirley Temple or Dorothy McGuire should play Meg. Costumes were designed and made, changes in the original script ordered, wardrobe, makeup, and hair tests completed. David felt the contrast between the erotic Pearl Chavez of *Duel in the Sun* and Louisa May Alcott's beloved and spirited heroine would prove to the world that Jennifer was indeed an actress of limitless scope. *Little Women*, however, was shelved after a few weeks of shooting. Later Selznick sold the entire project to MGM, which cast June Allyson as Jo.

During the period in which Selznick was preoccupied with the gentle past personified by *Little Women*, Louis B. Mayer was involved in a project he predicted would be the ultimate World War II saga: the development and subsequent use of the atomic bomb.

Borrowing President Harry Truman's actual words, *The Beginning or the End*, for its title, and securing Robert Considine's factual material, Mayer assigned screenwriter Frank Weed to the project, advising him to avoid the pitfall of having the finished production too documentary in nature.

To solve that problem, Weed carefully integrated real-life figures such as Major General Leslie R. Groves, Groves's secretary, Jean O'Leary, Dr. Robert J. Oppenheimer, Presidents Franklin D.

Roosevelt and Harry Truman, and Dr. Albert Einstein, with a number of fictional characters and improvised dual love stories.

Bob was costarred, with Brian Donlevy, as the fictional Colonel Jeff Nixon, in love with Miss O'Leary (played by Audrey Totter). Tom Drake received feature billing as a young scientist who questions the wisdom of building the bomb, and Beverly Tyler completed the romantic foursome as Drake's young bride.

Although *Variety* would call the film "a credit of new proportions to the motion-picture industry," many critics were offended by the romantic interludes interjected into such a historic event. Bosley Crowther of the New York *Times* noted, "In spite of its generally able reenactments, this film is so laced with sentiment of the silliest and most theatrical nature that much of its impressiveness is marred."

Producer Sam Marx recalls, "Bob Walker followed Norman Taurog's direction without protest, and delivered a capable performance, although away from the cameras he made no secret of the fact that he was less than enthusiastic about the part."

With the exception of Ann Straus, who continued to set up gallery sittings, the publicity blackout on Bob was still in effect. However, the studio did allow the one public event Bob was actually looking forward to participating in.

The Hollywood Bowl Association had suggested that Arthur Freed produce a Jerome Kern Memorial Concert during its summer season. Freed eagerly accepted the invitation and put Roger Edens in charge of coordinating the event, lining up as many of the stars of *Till the Clouds Roll By* as were available to participate in the musical numbers.

Freed approached Bob and asked if he would be the narrator for the entire program. The assignment would consist of reading a Jerome Kern eulogy which Freed would pen, and delivering prepared narration to serve as a bridge between numbers.

Without hesitation Bob replied, "I'd consider it an honor."

The concert took place on July 20, 1946, and the Bowl's eighteen-thousand-plus seats had been sold out for weeks in advance.

Bob was punctual during the rehearsals, knew his lines, and although the afternoon of the final dress rehearsal was an enervating scorcher, the weather affected neither his voice nor his enthu-

siasm. It was an old pattern repeating itself: when Bob was sufficiently motivated to be at his very best, he *was* at his very best.

The evening was not without its minor disasters, however. Twenty minutes into the concert, Freed received word that Lena Horne couldn't make it. Since her numbers were essential to the continuity, they couldn't be removed. During intermission, Judy Garland was hastily summoned to rehearse and perform "Can't Help Lovin' That Man of Mine" and "Why Was I Born?" and Bob was asked to ad-lib some explanation for the change of program.

Bob remained calm, but everyone else's nerves were at the breaking point when, during the third and final segment of the concert, Frank Sinatra hadn't shown up. Then, dramatically, during the eight-bar introduction to "Ol' Man River," Sinatra suddenly appeared, crossed to the microphone, and began to sing.

The Kern memorial was the highlight of the season and Jim Henaghan, who had been covering it, recalled: "Everyone was great, but Bob was a revelation, even to me. He provided such a beautiful, poignant touch to the program, and I was so damn proud of him. I remember thinking: Now maybe those loggerheads at Metro will stop cutting off their ugly noses to spite their friggin' faces."

Perhaps they might have, if Bob had remained on a steady course.

Exactly a month after Bob's triumph at the Hollywood Bowl, he was in trouble again—serious trouble, which savagely damaged his reputation, nearly cost him his freedom and stigmatized him as an "irresponsible drunkard."

Chapter

14

Although they rarely bored each other, Jim Henaghan couldn't devote all his time to Bob. He was on deadline the night of August 20, 1946, and unable to accept his friend's urgent plea to join him for dinner.

Restless and lonely, Bob headed for a Beverly Hills bar. After a few drinks, he left, got into his new Chrysler, and was driving erratically down Santa Monica Boulevard en route home when he sideswiped a bakery truck which was cruising along the mid-8000 block. The slashing impact ripped the right fender off the Chrysler. Because he had been drinking, Bob took off without stopping to exchange licenses.

The next day he called the Chrysler agency in Beverly Hills and ordered a new fender. Meanwhile, the driver of the bakery truck had reported the incident to the police, who in turn had alerted dealers and repair shops to notify them of anyone placing such an order.

Demanding his phone number from the agency, a police officer called Bob and suggested he turn himself in. When Bob defiantly refused to comply, the suggestion became an order and a warning that a warrant for his arrest would follow.

On August 22 Bob surrendered in Beverly Hills Justice Court and entered a plea of guilty to the charge of hit-and-run driving. Although the truck driver was uninjured and the truck merely scratched, leaving the scene of the accident was still a serious matter. Bob was released on his own cognizance, and a date for sentence and probation hearing was set for September 5.

A Los Angeles *Times* court reporter was in the building at the time, and before the studio publicity department could suppress

the incident, the paper ran a three-paragraph story boldly head-lined "WALKER, ACTOR, ADMITS HIT-RUN." There was no mention of drunk driving in the article, though Bob admitted he "had had a few drinks."

"I guess I'll just have to take my medicine," he contritely told Jim the weekend before he was due to reappear in court.

"I tried to assure him that there was no danger of his being locked up; that the worst that could happen would be a fine, a warning, a few lines in the paper, and a stern lecture from the MGM brass," Henaghan said.

"But Bob was highly agitated during those two weeks prior to his hearing. He could hardly touch food, got very little sleep. He was worried about neither MGM nor the fine, but he was seriously concerned about Jennifer's reaction and possible punitive action where Bobby and Michael were concerned. When he was with his boys, Bob never drank anything stronger than milk or coffee. 'But,' he told me, 'who knows how this will affect her thinking?'

"His worries about Jennifer proved unfounded—he continued to see his sons, as always. But I underestimated the judge. He had a prize catch—a movie star—at his mercy, and he decided to make the most of it."

On September 5, after reading the charges, Judge Cecil B. Holland pronounced his verdict:

"I hereby sentence you to 180 days in jail."

Bob turned white; he clenched his fists and stood motionless for what seemed an eternity.

Then Holland, having achieved the desired effect, added:

"Suspended on conditions."

The conditions were that Bob pay a five-hundred-dollar fine, make restitution for fifty dollars' damage done to the bakery truck, refrain from liquor and install a device on his car limiting his speed to thirty-five miles an hour. Then, after another long pause, he added that he might modify the unusual order to install the governor, but warned him that if he touched liquor during his probationary period, the jail sentence would be carried out.

Before releasing Bob from the courtroom, Holland commented: "You have a bright future as an actor, but you are getting some bad habits. You owe it to your public to straighten yourself out."

Bob nodded his head and was dismissed. But when he saw Jim

the following day, he expressed his rage over the remark "You owe it to your public."

"That's all that concerned him. What I owe to my public! Not to my sons, not even to myself, but to the public. That's all they think about out here . . . the goddamn public! When that bastard [Selznick] stole my wife, he didn't give a damn what it would do to me, how it would affect my sons. As long as 'the public' didn't know the story, it didn't matter."

"I remember," said Jim, "that I let Bob vent his rage until he was hoarse and exhausted. Of course there was validity in everything he was saying. But that was the climate in Hollywood at the time. When Selznick had been filming *Gone with the Wind*, his Scarlett, Vivien Leigh, had been carrying on a clandestine affair with Laurence Olivier. David was scared to death that the public would get wind of it, and the lovers had been forced to indulge in all kinds of subterfuge to be together.

"A star could be a drunk, a wife-beater, a rapist; he could father illegitimate children. All that was unimportant, despite the morality clause in every contract, just as long as no headlines resulted and the 'image' remained unblemished. Total hypocrisy—but part of the system. Selznick was not unique in this attitude. *All* the studio heads—including some of the first-class degenerates—and the Hollywood press, myself included, played by these warped rules.

"No one knew what went on behind closed doors at the studio, which had several million invested in Walker pictures. But MGM's publicity department used all its clout to keep Bob's day in court from receiving national coverage and turning into a full-blown scandal. Within a week, the incident had blown over. Forgotten and forgiven by everyone—except Bob himself.

"I have no idea what Jennifer's reaction was. Bob never told me. I never asked. Throughout the years of our friendship, I never initiated any conversation about Jennifer. When Bob mentioned her, I listened, keeping my feelings to myself. And, believe me, I had very definite feelings about that girl! None of them charitable. Although Bob's hostility was directed solely toward Selznick, I personally felt that, as they say, 'it takes two to tango.' And in my opinion, Jennifer was a greedy, self-centered bitch.

"To the best of my recollection, Bob obeyed the rules of his

probation almost to the letter. He stayed close to home, and if he had a few drinks, he did not get into a car—anybody's. He stuck to cabs when he went out. I dropped by frequently to see him, as I was extremely concerned about his increasing melancholy. I had reason to be. He was brooding constantly.

"During one of my visits, in the middle of a conversation about a book he had been reading, he abruptly announced, 'I've had it!'

"'With the book?' I asked.

"'No, with this goddamn business, with this blasted town.'"

It was a familiar threat, but this time Bob was deadly serious.

He picked up the phone and began dialing furiously, then demanded to speak to MGM executive Benny Thau. When Thau got on the line, Bob got straight to the point.

"Tear up my contract. I'm quitting."

The startled Thau said that wasn't possible. The studio had no intention of releasing him; his contract was ironclad—and he would be banned from working for anyone else.

Bob said he had no desire to work for anyone else in the picture business and would get a job in a gas station. "I'm just fed up with acting. No more movies for me. Good-bye. I'm going to New York."

He wound up back with his family in Ogden. He said he'd stay there for the rest of his life. A week later he was back in Hollywood.

"My sons are here," he explained simply.

"He did not elaborate about the week spent in Utah," said Henaghan. "He didn't have to. It was obvious that it had provided little contentment or peace. None of his trips home ever did.

"I derived no small satisfaction from the gossip I heard as a newspaperman that there was little joy in Jennifer Jones's life during this period either; that, in fact, her life with Selznick was far from idyllic; that she had taken up yoga to attain some peace of mind.

"But my concern was centered solely on my friend . . . and how I could help him."

Jennifer's life in the fall of 1946 *was* far from idyllic.

Selznick's obsession with her had not diminished. As his life,

both public and private, threatened to unravel, his need to hold Jennifer physically and emotionally captive grew.

Two years after its initial shooting date, he was still tampering with *Duel in the Sun:* changing bits and pieces of the supposedly finished print, agonizing over every detail from its advertising campaign to its distribution, suing United Artists for its last-minute refusal to release the film under the UA banner, and finally setting up the Selznick Releasing Organization in order to have total control of *Duel's* fate.

Simultaneously, he was involved with getting his next film, *The Paradine Case,* the story of an English barrister who falls in love with the murderess he's been hired to defend, into production. Alfred Hitchcock, who was less than enthusiastic about the project, was set to direct, but after both Garbo and Ingrid Bergman rejected the role of Mrs. Paradine, Selznick and Hitchcock settled for Italian star Alida Valli. Gregory Peck was miscast as the British lawyer, with Ann Todd as his wife and Louis Jourdan as Mrs. Paradine's lover. The entire project seemed doomed from the beginning; Selznick knew the script was unsatisfactory, but he simply couldn't find the time to tinker with it as he usually did. Business problems—vast cost overruns, wastefulness, and inflated overhead—were mounting daily, and without a reliable general manager to lean on, Selznick found he was spending so much time on management and deskwork that he was quite unable to function as a producer. "I am on the verge of collapse," he confessed at one point, "and have neither the time nor the energy nor the clarity of mind to improve the situation."

He worked eighteen- and twenty-hour days; his time with Jennifer was catch-as-catch-can.

Irene Selznick had returned from New York for a few months to settle some personal matters, and according to her, David showed no inclination to relinquish his relationship with her either; he still showered her with gifts and advice. It's little wonder that David would describe himself as "in despair."

Jennifer's feelings were discussed with no one. She was never seen in public, avoided parties, and occasionally dined with Joseph Cotten and his wife, Lenore Kip, the two of them a stable, loving couple. She was pleased that Cotten was set as her leading

man in her next picture, *Portrait of Jennie*. It would be their fourth appearance together. As an actor, he was professional and comfortable to work with, and both she and David were extremely fond of him.

It may never have crossed her mind that David was meticulous choosing devoted husbands as her leading men—men who would present no risk to his relationship with Jennifer. Even such idols as Boyer and Peck (at the time) were noted for their fidelity.

Jennie was besieged with script problems, however, and its starting date was tenuous—although Jennifer, who had not acted since the completion of *Cluny Brown*, was desperate to return to work.

Bob Walker, as noted, still didn't give a damn if he never saw a camera again. Although MGM had refused to give him his freedom, the studio had no film scheduled for him in the immediate future. Bob went on his annual twelve-week break and was told to stay out of trouble.

Since Jim Henaghan had a vacation due, he suggested that Bob and he take off for New York for a spree on the town, and Bob's mood picked up considerably. He booked a suite at the Waldorf Astoria and told Jim he was going to "do all the things I couldn't afford to do when I was living in New York—or was too busy to do."

Although he had three films being prepared for release (*Till the Clouds Roll By*, *The Beginning or the End*, and *The Sea of Grass*), he made it clear to the studio that he'd be "unavailable" for promotion or publicity. "I just want to have some fun," he said firmly.

"We had a hell of a good time in the big city for the most part," remembered Jim. "But he still couldn't erase Jennifer from his mind. I went to the Stork Club with him one night. He was recognized at the door, and we were ushered into the Cub Room without delay. Waiters flocked around us, making sure we had service fit for a potentate.

"As we were having a brandy, compliments of Sherman Billingsly, the owner, Bob wryly commented:

"'This is very ironic. When we were living in New York, and I got an especially good job, we decided to celebrate. So we came here. We were lucky to get past the velvet rope. Certainly we

couldn't gain entrance to this room. But I bet five bucks that tonight we don't even get a check.' We didn't."

"One night Bob had the impulse to bum about Greenwich Village. He had a chauffeured limo drive us downtown, then instructed the driver to pick us up a couple hours later on Mac-Dougal Street at the Champagne Room.

"He just felt like strolling around. It was pretty safe in those days. After a while we found ourselves in front of a run-down building on West Tenth Street, a real dive.

"'Hardly the Waldorf,' Bob remarked, 'but I think I was happier when we lived here than I've ever been in my life.'

"He was silent as we walked the few blocks to MacDougal Street and during the ride back to the Waldorf. I was disturbed by his compulsion to put himself through unnecessary torture. After all, we were in town for laughs. I tried to think up some pranks to lighten his mood, to get that confounded woman out of his mind.

"A day or two later, I hit on something—maybe childish in retrospect but at the time highly amusing. We were going to dinner and the theater—*Born Yesterday*, as I recall, which was playing at the Lyceum Theater on West Forty-fifth Street.

"I told him I had some shopping to do—suggested we join up at the Astor Hotel just down the street from the theater on Broadway. 'Just meet me inside the door by the clock. I should be there no later than five P.M.' He had made *The Clock* with the scene at the Astor—but he didn't catch on to what I was up to. So I ran over to the hotel and I got up in a little balcony, and I sat there and watched him—and here was Bob Walker standing under the clock exactly as he had done in the picture. He stood there for nearly an hour as I watched the reactions of the people passing by, the double takes, the looks of total disbelief . . . as they stared at the real Walker reliving the scene. But without the cameras. Life imitating art.

"When I came down, I confessed the whole thing, explaining, 'I just wanted to give these people a bit of a thrill,' and he screamed '*You sonofabitch*,' but he was shaking with laughter and was in a rare mood throughout the dinner.

"I think he enjoyed the gag more than the play, which, though one of the funniest comedies of the year, had a kind of sobering

effect on him. Remember the plot? The girl, the mistress of a domineering big shot, walks out on him at the end for the love of a poor bespectacled reporter. Nothing for him to identify with, you'd think. Bob identified. It was his own situation in reverse.

"He could find a connection with Jennifer in just about everything. That was part of his sickness."

Despite his vacillating moods, the reminders of the past, and the uncertainties about his future, Bob didn't regret the trip east. It was a break in the monotony, a reprieve from the prison MGM and his apartment represented to him.

He managed to sleep throughout most of the long flight back to Los Angeles, but once the plane hit the ground, he was engulfed by another siege of depression.

The holidays were again approaching, now the roughest time for him. He had picked up some gifts for Bobby and Michael in New York, but he had little desire to send out cards or to attend any of the parties to which he had been invited.

On Christmas Day he managed a cheerful demeanor during the few hours he spent with his sons. On Christmas night he got quietly smashed with Jim.

Chapter

15

Jennifer's attention that holiday season was focused on the opening of *Duel in the Sun,* finally scheduled for pre-release at Hollywood's Egyptian Theater on December 30 in order to qualify for the 1946 Academy Awards. (For the fourth consecutive year, Jennifer won a nomination—though her performance would ultimately be passed by in favor of Olivia de Havilland in *To Each His Own.*)

Although Jennifer had reluctantly agreed to attend the premiere, Selznick spared her the agony of facing the press to hype the film. That unenviable task was assigned to the amiable Gregory Peck, who by now had reached matinee-idol status.

In an interview granted to—of all people—Walker's exgirlfriend Florence Pritchett for *Silver Screen* magazine, which she coyly titled *Pecking Away at Greg,* Peck insisted that *Duel in the Sun* was his favorite movie, and rhapsodized:

"Jennifer Jones was one of the main reasons I loved this part. I had never worked with her before, but had admired her work on screen. She, in my mind, has discovered the great secret of giving herself both as a person and as an actress. It shows in her face and is a great part of her beauty. Besides, she is clever, smart, simple, and good. We used to laugh together, when we were on location in Arizona, about just how the public would take Father Chisholm (of *The Keys of the Kingdom*) as a rotten-to-the-core cowboy making love to Bernadette as a half-breed Indian girl."

Peck's enthusiasm for *Duel* was not shared by the critics.

The five-and-a-quarter-million-dollar epic received almost unanimous pans. *Life* magazine noted that "When a single movie offers murder, rape, attempted fratricide, train-wrecking, fisticuffs,

singing, dancing, drunkenness, religion, range wars, prostitution, sacred and profane love, all in 135 minutes, the fact that it has neither taste nor art is not likely to deter the unsqueamish." It didn't. Although comedians referred to the film sarcastically as *Lust in the Dust*, and most of the other critics were merciless, the public flocked to see it.

A few weeks later, when the critic of the Catholic publication *Tidings* condemned both the film and Jennifer, Selznick furiously wrote a letter to the editor defending "the wicked and wanton slur upon Miss Jennifer Jones . . . a Catholic who received her education in a convent." He demanded an apology.

The fact that he himself was directly responsible for the most lurid scenes in the film, had no compunctions about violating Jennifer's Catholic attitudes toward divorce and adultery, and took no notice of the effect the movie could have on her children, seemed blocked from Selznick's mind. Savagely he fought the Catholic Legion of Decency to protect both his beloved's reputation and the fate of his film at the box office. By May, when *Duel* was sent out for a saturated national release, Selznick had reedited and made several cuts, eliminating the most offensive sequences and securing a B rating from the Catholic Legion of Decency. There was nothing, however, that Selznick could do to still the devastating critical barbs showered on him from all directions— barbs so savage that they undermined *his* cherished image of himself as a filmmaker of impeccable taste.

Shortly after the general opening, he wrote in despair to Paul MacNamara, his director of advertising and publicity, that they should prepare to spend a lot of money on the regaining of his personal position as it was before *Duel*, in view of what he perceived to be a "great loss of prestige" with the press and public alike. "I think the campaign on me is needed very badly, if only from the standpoint of my own morale and my own thinking, for . . . there is the matter of my family to think of . . . and I don't think I am exaggerating."

Jim Henaghan accompanied Bob Walker to a showing of *Duel* on its opening day at the Egyptian Theater. As always, Bob couldn't resist an overwhelming compulsion to see one of Jennifer's films, no matter how painful the experience. But Jim re-

membered that after the rape sequence, Bob got up from his seat and said, "Let's get the hell out of here."

"I had warned Bob that I had heard through the trade that *Duel* was damn lurid and that Jennifer's role was steamy, but he was stunned by what he saw. Sickened. After leaving the theater, we went up the street to Musso and Franks, but Bob couldn't eat a thing. I can recall him saying bitterly, 'That bastard, that goddamn bastard,' but not an unkind word about Jennifer. Never an unkind word about Jennifer."

Bob consumed far too much wine at an Italian restaurant. Mindful that his friend was still on probation and certainly in no shape to drive, Jim decided to take him to his house, since they had no plans to celebrate New Year's Eve together.

Bob, however, was in no mood to celebrate anything the following morning. "What's there to celebrate?" he asked.

"I remember," said Jim, "our sitting at the table having coffee, when Bob clutched his hands to his head and let out a piercing shriek: '*David Selznick!*' I think that eventually he'd have been able to accept Jennifer's leaving him for another man—a handsome man, say, like Gregory Peck—because of his own deep-rooted inferiority about his physical appearance, but what he couldn't accept was that a girl he had worshiped, the mother of his children, could have left him solely to gratify her own blind ambition. In his heart she was still the ethereal Elizabeth Barrett Browning."

Bob's hysterical outburst, according to Jim, would recur again and again, without warning. They'd be sitting on the beach or on Jim's lawn discussing subjects totally unrelated to Jennifer—world affairs, a new book, whatever—when Bob would clench his head and scream out, "*David Selznick!*" Then, a quiet apology, a chagrined look, and an attempt at a normal conversation.

On January 2 Bob was back at his own apartment—alone again, obsessing about the past. The day marked the eighth anniversary of his marriage to Jennifer, the ninth anniversary of their meeting. Choosing that day to marry had seemed like such a wonderfully romantic idea at the time; now it was a torturous irony. Despite his lack of enthusiasm about his career, work kept him busy and diverted his mind, but after the frantic activity of the previous few years, there was only one film scheduled for him in 1947: *Song of*

Love—a highly fictionalized musical bio-pic focusing on the romance of Robert and Clara Schumann and their relationship with the young Johannes Brahms. Casting Bob, the quintessential G.I. Yank, as the German Brahms was almost as ludicrous as placing Katharine Hepburn in the role of Robert Schumann's Polish wife, Clara. Only Viennese Paul Henreid as Schumann was at all credible.

Bob read the hopeless script and was appalled. His protests to the front office that he was woefully wrong for the role, that he was uncomfortable in costume parts, that he'd be detrimental to the movie, left MGM unmoved.

"If you have nothing suitable for me, let me go," he pleaded. "You don't need me. You have Van [Johnson] and Tom [Drake] and Pete [Lawford], and all those other juveniles back from the service."

The studio, eyeing the bags of fan mail that continued to pour in and Bob's position on the popularity polls, refused to release him from either the picture or their payroll.

He complained bitterly to Keenan Wynn about the role. Keenan recalls:

"It was the constant shit he was cast in, besides his divorce, that contributed to his erratic behavior. It damn near drove him crazy. Almost without exception, the films he was thrust into were beneath his abilities as an actor. There was a total lack at MGM of appreciation of what Bob could do as an actor. Hell! That lack seemed to extend to damn near all of us. Fortunately, I escaped to do stock work—which I regret Bob never did. It might have helped him a lot. But who knows?"

It seems unlikely, however, that at this point in his life "stock" would have worked wonders. Losing himself in a worthwhile role might have relieved his symptoms temporarily, but it could not have produced anything like a cure. The damage to his psyche cut too deep.

It also seemed unlikely that, had he been aware of Jennifer's own instability and doubts about her relationship with Selznick, he'd have found even a modicum of satisfaction or contentment. He was not a vengeful man.

Although Jennifer may not have been reliving the past that January 2, 1947, her concerns about the future were playing havoc

with her moods, as she prepared to leave for New York to finally begin filming *Portrait of Jennie*. Selznick, still preoccupied with trying to salvage *The Paradine Case*, couldn't be with her when shooting commenced.

Irene Selznick, in New York for rehearsals of her first production effort on the stage, Arthur Laurents' *Heartsong*, related in her memoirs an episode that captured Jennifer's agonized state of mind. According to Mrs. Selznick, she phoned the theater insisting Irene meet with her, claiming it was a matter of life and death.

"Then," wrote Mrs. Selznick, "she waited for hours for me outside the theater. I told my driver to take us through Central Park. She was distraught about David's unhappiness—he claimed his life was ruined, and Jennifer blamed herself. She was bad for him. His career was over. He didn't love her, he loved me. He didn't want her sons, he wanted his. If only I would take him back, I could restore him. . . . She grew hysterical and tried to throw herself out of the car—I just managed to pull her back. . . . As I quieted her down, I told her David was bad for himself, and nothing she did or didn't do could change that. It was a dramatic episode, and saddening."

Jennifer's outburst may have been triggered by Selznick's anguish over her movie. Having seen the results of the two weeks' shooting on *Jennie*, he was in a frenzy over the way the script played, the way Jennifer was photographed, the direction, the location sites, and the costs. He decided to shut down production for five weeks while he frantically tried to salvage the project by hiring a new screenwriter, Paul Osborn, and starting almost from scratch.

Work on *Jennie* was due to resume in April. In mid-March Selznick came east to take charge personally. Since several of the scenes were due to be shot around Boston harbor, he flew north to examine the site.

His trip to Boston, however, was also motivated by a strong need to see Irene, attend the out-of-town tryout of her play, and offer his suggestions to improve the show, which had been plagued by script and casting problems. The story needed revisions. Original stars Lloyd Bridges and Nancy Coleman had been replaced by Barry Nelson and, ironically, Phyllis Thaxter, both courtesy of MGM.

David had convinced himself he'd be able to contribute sage advice.

However, according to Irene, after discussing *Heartsong* and making a few perfunctory suggestions, David spent the rest of the night in her suite rehashing their relationship and breakup. Despite her protests that she was exhausted and badly needed sleep, he refused to depart until room service opened for breakfast.

On the bright side, writes Mrs. Selznick with relief, "At least there was no mention of Jennifer."

Heartsong went on to Philadelphia, where it closed on March 29—an expensive casualty—but neither as expensive nor as gigantic a casualty as *Jennie* would prove to be.

For seven months Selznick and Jennifer remained in New York struggling with the fragile story, which, had it been produced by MGM or Twentieth Century-Fox, could have been wrapped in ninety days. (Actually, *Jennie* would be before the cameras on and off for a year and a half before its first preview. It would then be withdrawn when Selznick decided to add a spectacular hurricane finale, complete with Cycloramic sound effects. It did not reach the theaters until early 1949—and lost most of its four-million-dollar-plus investment. Jennifer was praised for her performance, but she did not receive the Oscar nomination Selznick had hoped for—although her portrayal of Jennie was both brilliant and beautiful and worthy of an award.)

During the seven months Jennifer was in the East, Bob Walker's mental state continued to deteriorate. He reported to work on *Song of Love* on time, followed Clarence Brown's direction, retired to his dressing room when not needed, and hated every minute of the experience. His attitude showed in his work. When the film was released the following October, Bosley Crowther would comment, "As for Robert Walker's solemn posturing as Brahms, well, it's good for a guffaw." The majority of his other reviews were also cruel and deprecatory, with the critics, of course, all unaware of Bob's own losing battle against the miscasting.

After *Song of Love* Bob was left with a void in his professional and personal life. There was no discussion about "your next film" at the studio; in truth, the roles he might have been suitable for went to Van Johnson and Peter Lawford.

With Miss Photoflash of 1945. Behind him is his brother, Walter, talking to Hedda Hopper (unseen). (Author)

Below: Jennifer with Selznick and Orson Welles. Selznick was in the midst of handcrafting two pictures for Jennifer: *Portrait of Jennie*, (above, left) the story of an artist obsessed with the ghost of a woman, and the lurid, sex-driven *Duel in the Sun* (above right). *Duel* director King Vidor swore he could hear Selznick panting in the background. (Author/McClelland/Museum of Modern Art)

With Ava Gardner in *One Touch of Venus*. Gardner made a conquest of Bob—while involved with another man. (McClelland)

"I'd like a girl so unglamorous no man would think of trying to take her away from me," Bob confided to a friend. In 1948 he married Barbara Ford—for all of five weeks. (Museum of Modern Art)

October 22, 1948: booked on drunk-and-disorderly. Metro head Dore Schary gave him a choice—quit films or undergo psychiatric treatment at the Menninger Clinic. (Author)

Seven months later, stepping off the plane from Menninger's—"able to work, eager to live." (Western Airlines)

With Bobby, nine, and Michael, eight. (Author)

Jennifer and Selznick in Paris, July 18, 1949—five days after their marriage. (Tom Johnson Collection)

Her next released film was *Madame Bovary* (with Van Heflin). "Nobody likes me," she cried. Meanwhile financial difficulties had put Selznick's studio on the auction block. (McClelland)

His most memorable movie, *Strangers on a Train*—here with Alfred Hitchcock and Farley Granger on location, and in a scene with Granger. (Author/Jim Meyer)

His last movie, *My Son John* (with Helen Hayes). Just prior to completion, Bob was injected with a sedative and died. "I held him down," says a friend, "and he stopped breathing. For years I felt like a murderer." (McClelland)

With Laurence Olivier in *Carrie*. A month after the filming, she suffered a miscarriage. (McClelland)

With Rock Hudson in A *Farewell to Arms* in 1957. The critics were harsh, both to her and the film. *Farewell's* title was prophetic: it was Selznick's swan song. "Maybe I'm an anachronism," he said. (Goodman)

Robert Walker Jr. with Diane Varsi in *Killers Three* (1968). A haunting image of his father. (McClelland)

Robert Walker.
(Academy)

Jennifer Jones.
(Author)

His idleness and boredom became oppressive. He continued to spend a great deal of time with James Henaghan, talking, playing records, bar-hopping.

"He didn't make friends very easily," said Jim. "He didn't trust people in this town. He thought it was a crock. He had learned that, in Hollywood, the movie star is king, and he could act pretty much as he pleased, and it amused him. He would take advantage of this fact to get away with a rudeness that would have earned most guys a kick in the pants. He'd invite people to his apartment, would become morose and suddenly order his guests from his house. They'd start to go. Then he would beg them to come back. As soon as they were seated, he'd order them out again. It was a kind of game with him to see how many times he could get them out and in again in one evening. He knew they were catering to the 'star' and their humility in the face of his insolence amused him and, at the same time, revolted him. It was after an evening of this sort that he would call me on the telephone and tell me how unhappy he was."

Bob's distrust of people in general paled beside his distrust of women and especially of actresses. He lost interest in dating, though he still had occasional sex urges. Most of the girls whom he saw were nonprofessional. He'd take them to little-known restaurants and relish their disappointment at not being seen and photographed with "the movie star." Almost all were willing to return to his apartment with him. More often than not, he'd take the girl home, say good night, and write her off his list. "If I wasn't Robert Walker," he'd tell Jim, "I wonder if any of them would even kiss me good night."

Occasionally, however, motivated by liquor or a need to seek oblivion through joyless sex, he'd invite a date to his place.

Jim Henaghan chuckled as he recalled the time he decided to pay an impromptu visit to Bob late one night.

"He didn't answer his doorbell, but there was a faint light coming from his bedroom. So I found a ladder and put it up against the house and climbed up. He had a dame in bed with him, and I started rapping on the window. I heard Bob exclaim, 'What the hell is that?' and he approached the window stark naked. When he saw me, I waved and yelled out, 'Hi!'

"'You *sonovabitch*,' Bob roared, convulsed with laughter—and

he was still laughing as I scurried down the ladder and beat a hasty retreat back to my car.

"But when we spoke the next day, he didn't say a word about my prank—knowing how his silence would bug me. Consequently, I never learned how the girl reacted or who she was—or any of the events following my big moment in the window. Perhaps, of course, his silence was simply in character. I wouldn't be surprised. Those one- or two-night flings were meaningless to him.

"Although Bob insisted to reporters, on the rare occasions when he granted interviews, that the rumors about his 'carrying a torch for Jennifer' were unfounded, it was the actor acting. He was still madly in love with the woman—or more precisely, the girl—who was his 'Phyl,' even though that girl no longer existed."

Jim continued playing "court jester" to Bob, going out on wild binges with him, refusing to accept the possibility that he was, in fact, doing his buddy considerably more harm than good.

His antics provided Bob with relief from his deep-rooted melancholy, but they were only a temporary and dangerous panacea.

Remembering those days—and nights—Jim recalled, "I guess I loved the guy too much either to recognize or to accept the fact that he was seriously mentally ill, that it would take a great deal more than a few laughs, some drunken sprees, or a romp in the hay with a broad—or even a sympathetic listener—to help him save himself. He was hell-bent for self-destruction. I don't think anyone realized that. Then."

16

Bob struggled to lift himself from his doldrums that summer of 1947. He rented a cottage within walking distance of Jim's house in Malibu to provide Michael and Bobby with a healthy atmosphere during the months they were due to spend with him.

Whatever stability and peace of mind he enjoyed that summer, he attributed to the loving companionship of his sons. He taught the boys to swim, and Van Johnson remembers "how happy the three seemed" when he spotted them clowning around on the sandy white shores of Malibu.

Jim Henaghan, who had a home-movie camera, took roll after roll of film of the three, later lost, which captured Bob at his very best. "But," said Jim, "I always felt he loved his sons with such intensity because they were Jennifer's boys. I remember his telling me that although he had been powerless to keep Selznick from stealing his wife, he would stop at nothing short of murder to prevent that man from taking control of his sons."

That, of course, was a needless worry, since, as noted, Jennifer had told Irene earlier in the year, "David doesn't want *my* sons. He wants his."

MGM's refusal to commit itself about Bob's next movie failed to disturb him. Except for the mandatory twelve-week hiatus, his paycheck continued to be sent to his business manager, Charles Trezona. Aside from the rent due for the Malibu cottage and the salary for the housekeeper who had replaced Harry, his expenses were minimal. He was no gourmet or clothes horse and was a collector of nothing. And when he had custody of the boys, he abstained from alcohol and kept his distance from women.

On June 15, shortly after he had been reunited with his sons, he had asked for and received MGM's permission to portray the title role of *Clarence* in a CBS radio condensation of the Booth Tarkington novel, and acquitted himself admirably in the role, happy to be back in radio—the medium which had launched his career.

(Jennifer, after sending her sons back to California, had taken off for a brief vacation in Bermuda with Anita Colby, now her closest friend and confidante. She craved sanctuary from David's torturous indecision and endless script changes on *Portrait of Jennie*. He, in turn, was threatening to scrap the entire project, just as he had closed down *Little Women* the year before. The whole *Jennie* venture, he felt, was "doomed to be one of the most awful experiences any studio ever had.")

Bob rarely left his sons' side for the remainder of the summer, and the boys thrived under his care and guidance. In the evenings after dinner, when it came time for bed, he'd read passages to them from Antoine de St. Exupéry's *The Little Prince*, and although the meaning of the words may have escaped the young minds, Bob believed that "the melody entered and remained."

Comic books were forbidden in the Walker household, and Bob would haunt the local bookshops to find some honest works of children's literature capable of holding his sons' interest.

After Michael and Bobby were asleep, Bob would wander down the beach for a cup of coffee or a glass of sherry and conversation with Jim.

"Then," Jim recalled, "there was this woman, the wife of an executive at MGM—I forget which one—who was a psychologist, and probably at her husband's suggestion, she called Bob to ask if she could try to help him. He had agreed, although, remembering the experience of his youth, he didn't have much faith in such things. She came to see him, maybe once a week. Though Bob's skepticism remained undiminished, the lady liked to brag about how she'd 'straightened' him out. So one summer day she brought Benny Thau and about a half-dozen other executives from MGM to the house to show him off.

"I sat there, and she talked to him, and he talked to the others, and he was very sane all during the whole thing. And then there was a lag in the conversation, and he suddenly turned to her and shouted, '*You gave me the crabs!*'

"Caught completely off balance, she loudly protested, '*I did not!*'

"'Oh, yes you did!' he insisted. 'Do you want to see them?' This grotesque exchange shook up the whole group. Bob did it as a gag, but she went nuts, she went goofy and started yelling, 'You're crazy, you're crazy.'

"She had brought the guests to the house to show how normal Bob had become, and she didn't have the wit to realize he was baiting her. Nor did Bob—infuriated by being put on exhibition— have the control to check his imaginative but gross accusation."

The incident was reported to Louis B. Mayer, who, in spite of his reputation for firing rebellious and troublesome actors, still insisted upon holding on to Bob.

Mayer, at the time, was having emotional difficulties of his own. After a three-year separation, he was in the process of divorcing Margaret Shenberg Mayer, his wife of forty-three years, who had become a victim of involutional melancholia and had been in and out of psychiatric hospitals since the mid-1930's.

However, not even Mayer was spared from Bob's irreverence toward studio moguls. According to Jim, "Bob did the craziest things where Mayer was concerned.

"He'd call Mayer up and try to talk him into spending a weekend at his house. He knew damn well Mayer wouldn't come, but he'd insist, 'Come on down, I have a nice room for you. Sorry it's in the back of the house, but what do you like to eat, L.B.?' and he wouldn't let him hang up. He'd do all sorts of crazy things like that. He had no regard for any of those executives, just contempt for this industry which he felt had taken his wife away from him.

"Bob didn't give a damn if he ever faced a camera again. The only satisfaction he derived from being what he derisively termed 'a movie star' was his conviction that he was ripping the studio off for thousands of dollars by remaining idle. He considered that an enormous joke."

Aside from the aforesaid "craziness" with his lady psychologist and Mayer, Bob behaved quite normally throughout the summer of 1947.

"He wasn't interested in dating while the boys were with him," remembered Jim, "and he kept his temper in check. He never talked about the future, since the future he had once envisioned

had been so unmercifully destroyed, but I never saw him in a suicidal mood. Never. Bob was living—'existing' would be a more accurate description—one day at a time. He'd do nothing—and then act on some spur-of-the-moment, offbeat whim."

When Michael and Bobby were invited to spend a weekend at the home of one of their pals, Bob impulsively decided to drive down to La Jolla, a charming beach community a few minutes north of San Diego, to see the Playhouse's stock production of Noël Coward's *Tonight at 8:30*, with Dorothy McGuire, Ann Richards, and John Hoyt.

Several months earlier, while costarring in *Gentleman's Agreement*, Miss McGuire and Gregory Peck had discussed their mutual desire to do live theater again and had bemoaned the fact that their film contracts did not allow them time to return to Broadway.

Together they formulated the idea for what would be known as the Actors' Company, which would enlist the services of well-known stars in revivals of hit shows, the same format that had been so successful at Santa Barbara's Lobero Theater six years before. Since David Selznick still controlled McGuire's and Peck's contracts, they approached him for permission to go ahead with their project and for whatever artistic and financial aid he'd care to contribute. Selznick was enthusiastic. Peck then suggested La Jolla, his birthplace, as the company's home base.

The town's leading hotel, the Valencia, a huge and venerable Spanish-style building, contained suites luxurious enough to satisfy the demands of the cream of California society, as well as movie stars, and its small single rooms were moderately enough priced to solve the featured players' housing problems. The "playhouse" itself was the large and comfortable high-school auditorium.

The Actors' Company opened in June to a celebrity-filled house. Throughout that and subsequent summers, its audience, a mix of Hollywood luminaries and San Diego locals, remained at capacity. Success was guaranteed from the start.

Even Bob Walker was curious, although seeing Dorothy McGuire brought back painful memories of the *Claudia* days. If there had been no *Claudia*, Selznick's and Bob's wife's paths might never have crossed. During the past six years there had been

so many "ifs," but of course there was no way to wipe the slate clean and rewrite the script. When the final curtain fell, acting in his usual impulsive manner, Bob went back to congratulate second lead Ann Richards. She was the same Australian actress who had left Metro to sign with Hal Wallis just when Bob had started working there.

Miss Richards had appeared as Dilly Carson, Jennifer's best friend in *Love Letters*, and Bob had admired her performance in that film and in *Tonight at 8:30*. What he was not aware of, however, was that Ann Richards had originally been set to play the Jones part opposite Barry Sullivan, but that Selznick, in one of his manipulative deals, had persuaded Wallis to cast Jennifer and Cotten in the leads. Sullivan was out completely and the heartbroken Miss Richards demoted to a featured role.

Without malice, Miss Richards comments, "Perhaps things worked out for the best, because I think Dilly was a more human, sympathetic character and remained my late husband's favorite of my screen performances.

"Mr. Selznick was not in evidence during the shooting, nor were Jennifer's two boys. She never mentioned Robert Walker. She seemed a nice person, though I can't say I got to know her well. But she was very professional. We didn't lunch together, and I don't think I ever saw her again.

"I first met Robert Walker when he came to see the play at La Jolla, and he was very complimentary about the performance and said he hoped to do a play there sometime. He also invited my mother and me for dinner. I was very impressed with Robert because he was a very different kind of person—shy, gentle and quite reticent. He did not have the aggressive preoccupation with self that so many actors have.

"My mother was even more impressed. She had quite a long talk with him, and he was very interested in her stories about her arrival in the United States a few months earlier in the only available berth on a 'brides' ship.' Mother thought Robert was charming, interested in others, self-effacing, and altogether disarmingly winning."

He could be and *was* all that, when he was with people he respected. It was the hypocrites and ass-kissers who became the victims of his wrath.

Miss Richards doesn't recall having seen Bob again, but after four decades still retains glowing memories.

Back in Hollywood, struggling to find a solution to the problems plaguing *Portrait of Jennie*, David was forced into the showdown with Irene Selznick that he had been putting off for two years.

Mrs. Selznick, due to go into rehearsal with her production of *A Streetcar Named Desire*, had flown west to be with her son Danny while he underwent surgery. Irate at what she considered David's indifference to the boy's condition and disturbed by a blind item which had appeared in a column about "a wife standing in the way of her husband's remarriage," she told David that she intended to file for a California divorce before returning to New York and her play. She would not, however, be available for the hearing.

Jennifer should have been delighted by the news, but according to her friend Anita Colby, she still had ambivalent feelings about becoming Mrs. David O. Selznick. The traits that had disturbed Irene, disturbed Jennifer even more: his drinking, his reckless gambling, his dependence on pills, and his erratic working hours. Jennifer was still young and strong-willed. But she didn't fool herself into believing she could alter his habits of a lifetime. Her only consolations were her unshakable conviction that David wasn't cheating on her and his passionate assurances that he'd stop at nothing to make her the biggest star in the world.

Furthermore, Jennifer had indicated clearly that she didn't see a second marriage in the immediate future, when, just prior to leaving for location shooting for *Jennie*, she had bought a beautiful pink stucco French Riviera house in Brentwood and hired a team of decorators to redo the whole upstairs to serve as private living quarters for Bobby and Michael and their governess, a middle-aged lady named Kermit.

Although the house included a guest room, there was nothing about it which reflected David Selznick's needs or tastes.

After their summer with their father, the boys joined their mother at the Brentwood house. She had returned there because Selznick had decided to reshoot most of the exteriors and complete *Jennie* at his Culver City studios, a ten-minute drive from her home.

Discussing the boys, Jennifer noted that she had developed what she called "a deaf ear in their direction," and that she "could study

her lines, entertain guests, paint, or take a nap, unruffled and undisturbed even if they're chopping the rafters in two." Kermit took care of their goings-on and kept them out of trouble.

Even though Jim Henaghan lived nearby, Bob, reluctant to spend the fall and winter months in foggy, damp Malibu, looked for and found a house in town. It was about this time that he met Lee Russell Marshall, whose divorce from actor Herbert Marshall had just become final. They'd dine together frequently at quiet, out-of-the-way places either alone or with Jim, who recalled that "Bob loved Lee, and, with me, she witnessed much of his misery." It wasn't, however, the kind of love that would culminate in marriage, but rather the love of two dear friends, each of whom had experienced heartbreak and now sought solace in the other's company. The two were never photographed together, and few were even aware of their relationship. Mrs. Marshall made no demands on Bob, nor he on her. Instinctively he knew that she was interested in him as a human being, not as a movie star.

Bob had read about Irene Selznick's petition for a divorce in the local papers, but according to Jim, "he accepted the news stoically. By now it was anticlimactic."

The executives at MGM continued to subject Bob to the silent treatment; he wasn't given the slightest inclination if and when he'd *ever* be called back to work. And still he didn't care.

In early October, Horace Walker called, suggesting Bob come home to celebrate his twenty-ninth birthday on the thirteenth. The family hadn't seen him in two years, missed him, and wanted a get-together in his honor. Bob didn't have the heart to refuse his father's invitation.

Bob was on his best behavior during the family reunion, acting as if he hadn't a care in the world, concealing his annoyance when well-meaning relatives asked him what his next movie would be and expressing his delight when they complimented him for past performances. (*Song of Love*, uncompromisingly panned after its New York opening, hadn't yet been seen in Ogden.)

He talked freely about Bobby and Michael, and to his great relief, no one asked about Jennifer. It's possible Zella or Horace had warned them to avoid the subject. Nevertheless, he was relieved to see the last guest depart. It wasn't the happiest of birthdays.

He remained in Ogden for a couple of days, then took off for nearby Draper for a visit with a favorite aunt, Maude Walker, who taught grade school in that rural town.

Mrs. Walker tentatively asked if Bob would consent to make a surprise visit to Draper Junior High School and give the kids a treat.

"Sure," Bob agreed, "it might be fun. But keep it a secret."

On October 16, during the assembly period, Bob was introduced by a pretty teenage student, Delores Day, and given a "cheering screaming ovation." When the furor subsided, he was peppered with juvenile questions about Hollywood. Bob observed the sea of eager faces and had no desire to disillusion the kids. He said all the positive things he was certain they wanted to hear.

When the question-and-answer session was over, he spent an hour signing autographs—over 450 of them—then promised to get the names of the students present from his aunt and send the requested photographs to them as soon as he returned to Hollywood.

It was a promise he diligently kept.

The *Deseret News*, which reported the event, concluded that "the kids were marking down October 16 as one of the momentous days of their school life." However, when the paper requested an exclusive story, he replied, "You know all there is to know about me. Sorry, I no longer give interviews," and before leaving Ogden, he asked Zella and Horace to refrain from giving any interviews either. "My private life is my own business."

Jennifer was also off-limits to the press, which now considered her the most uncooperative star in Hollywood and rarely, if ever, had a kind word to say about her.

Her only ally was Louella Parsons, David's longtime friend, and even with Louella she watched her words carefully when the two met for "a cup of coffee" at the latter's home.

"You know, I'm sure," she told Louella, "how I've been criticized for not talking to the press and not answering every question they see fit to ask me. Well, that's not because I want to be difficult or make it hard on the reporters whose job it is to get stories about me. Once a girl has decided to become an actress or a public figure, she has no right to object to questions . . . but there are many things in my life I'm not free to discuss. They involve other

people. I'll gladly answer any questions so long as they are limited solely to myself, my work, my individual plans. But it is neither fair nor decent to talk about situations involving other people's lives. And that alone is the reason I've always fought for privacy, even though I know I've antagonized many people."

Pinned down about her relationship with David Selznick, she'd admit only that "He is so instinctively right about everything. His mind is so brilliant, so searching. He is the most wonderful man I have ever known."

Jennifer did not use the word "love" in the course of the conversation, but Miss Parsons editorialized: "In the long time they have been in love, it has not always been happy for her. It never is for women who give their hearts to brilliant and erratic men. But I think she had rather be miserable with David than happy with any other man."

David continued to act in a manner designed to lend truth to Louella's summation.

Immediately after the major *Portrait of Jennie* scenes were supposedly completed, David flew off to New York to attend the December 3 opening of Irene's *A Streetcar Named Desire,* in spite of the fact that Irene had made it clear that she did not want him in the audience and that there were no tickets available. "I'll sit anywhere," David insisted, adding that he'd make himself so inconspicuous that no one would know he was there. Worn down by his pleas, Irene managed to come up with a single ticket. David kept his promise about being inconspicuous at the theater; he didn't even remain for the cheering curtain calls.

Instead, uninvited, he appeared at George Cukor's opening party at the 21 Club, where he greeted the other celebrants and jubilantly behaved as if *he* were both the show's producer and the host of the festivities. David remained at 21 until the last guest departed, then escorted Irene back to her Fifth Avenue apartment, undressed her, and tenderly put her to bed before departing for his suite at the Waldorf.

A few days later, Selznick was back in Culver City viewing the *Jennie* footage and dictating more of his interminable memos suggesting retakes and sketching his ideas for additional scenes. The following Sunday, he was visibly elated by the rave review *Streetcar* received in the New York *Times.* It was yet another

indication that he was emotionally unable to break the ties that bound him to Irene. Jennifer had to be furious, but there was nothing she could do about it. So she held her tongue and continued to dance to his tune.

Toward the end of December, Bob received word that he was being loaned to Universal International, together with another MGM contractee, Ava Gardner. They would costar in the screen adaptation of Kurt Weill's 1943 Broadway musical *One Touch of Venus*. The basic story line—the romance of a department-store statue of Venus, which comes to life when kissed by a young window dresser—was retained, but only three songs from the lilting Weill score remained in the bastardized screenplay, and the musical's stunning ballet, "Venus in Ozone Heights," had been scrapped. Bob's role of Eddie Hatch was of the "oh gosh, oh golly" genre which he had come to despise, but he docilely accepted the assignment.

Once again the long arm of coincidence reached out to touch him.

William Goetz, who had selected Jennifer for *Bernadette* when he was filling in for Darryl Zanuck, had left Twentieth Century-Fox in 1943 and had formed a new company, International Pictures, capitalized, in part, by a million-dollar loan from Mayer. In 1946 Universal merged with International, and Goetz was appointed vice-president in charge of production.

When he requested the services of Gardner and Walker for *Venus*, Mayer quickly complied. He felt the title role could bring his rising starlet to major stardom, and, additionally, he'd be recompensed for the thousands paid to the idle Bob Walker. To Mayer it was a no-lose deal.

And for Bob—no-win. Whether he knew it or not, stepping onto the set of *Venus* was as reckless as stepping in front of a loaded gun.

And whether *she* knew it or not, Ava Gardner was about to pull the trigger.

17

Ava Gardner, a raw but strikingly gorgeous brunette from Boon Hill, North Carolina, arrived in Los Angeles on August 23, 1941, under contract to MGM.

Her fellow passengers on the streamliner *Super Chief* included Metro's reigning queen, Hedy Lamarr—and David and Irene Selznick. David had timed his trip back to California to coincide with Phylis Walker's appearance at the Lobero Theater and to arrange the *Claudia* screen test.

Ava and her sister, Mrs. Bappi Tarr, were accompanied west by MGM publicist Milton Weiss, who may have pointed out Irene Selznick as the daughter of Ava's new boss, but because of the Hollywood caste system, it seems unlikely that he would have been bold enough to introduce her.

Ava's life was in ascendancy by the time Bob Walker arrived in Culver City, though it was due more to her January 1942 marriage to Mickey Rooney, the studio's most popular young star, than to the unbilled bit roles in which she was cast. Her fantastic face and figure were also in evidence, as the studio flooded newspapers and magazines with cheesecake art. She was an undeniable asset to the publicity department, a real bargain at her $150-a-week salary plus acting, speech, and grooming lessons.

Her chaotic marriage to Rooney guaranteed a lion's share of column space; their May 21, 1943, divorce made headlines, and the public, through their fan mail, indicated that they wanted to see more of the sensual young woman on the screen. MGM complied by casting her in roles which didn't tax her still minuscule acting talent but amply displayed her charms.

Bob Walker had little more than a nodding acquaintance with

Ava at MGM. Even after his breakup with Jennifer, he made no attempt even to establish a casual association. By now Ava had acquired a reputation as a fast-living party girl, out with Peter Lawford one night, attorney Greg Bautzer the next.

In late 1943 she became involved in a tempestuous romance with Howard Hughes, who hired bodyguards to monitor her every movement. When Ava cursed the billionaire for his "possessiveness," he slapped her so violently he dislocated her jaw. Ava, in turn, hit him with a heavy brass bell, which knocked Hughes unconscious. The two eventually patched things up and resumed dating, but Ava couldn't tolerate their oppressive relationship and started going her separate and carefree way.

She didn't remain unattached for long. In 1945 Ava met the erratically brilliant bandleader and clarinetist Artie Shaw. To Louis B. Mayer's shocked displeasure, she moved into Shaw's home on Bedford Drive, in flagrant violation of the morals clause in her contract.

The two became victims of such malicious gossip that on October 15, 1945, with great trepidation, they took their vows in Beverly Hills.

After her marriage to Shaw, Ava's career took off when she was loaned out to Universal to appear in the riveting role of Kitty Collins in Mark Hellinger's production of Ernest Hemingway's short story "The Killers." She made such a stunning impact as the sensual, deceitful gangster's moll that Mayer forgave her past indiscretions and cast her as the other woman in *The Hucksters*, a scathing indictment of the advertising world, with Clark Gable and Deborah Kerr. As her career picked up momentum, her marriage to Shaw began to deteriorate.

Artie had fallen in love with a glamour girl, but he wanted the fourth Mrs. Shaw to become a homebody and made demands Ava was incapable of fulfilling. Later Shaw would tell Ava, "You were one of the great sexual things in my life. If everything else had been on a par with that, we would have been together for an eternity."

Unfortunately, very little else was on a par. That didn't stop Artie from shrewdly managing to wangle Mayer into giving Ava a new three-year contract paying $1,250 a week, with the promise of

a ten-thousand-dollar bonus at the end of the third year, contingent on her appeal at the box office at that time.

That was Artie's farewell present. On October 24, six days after their first wedding anniversary, the Shaws were divorced, but remained friends in the years that followed.

Ava licked her wounds for a few months, then drifted into an affair with Howard Duff. Howard was an affable young bachelor who'd made it to the top in radio as Dashiell Hammett's fictional detective Sam Spade, and was now being groomed for stardom at Universal.

Marriage-shy after two divorces within a period of two and a half years, Ava was characteristically unfaithful to Howard in her fashion, deriving pleasure from his discomfort whenever she dated another man.

Shortly after starting work on *Venus*, Ava capriciously decided to add Bob Walker to her string of conquests. Their mutual disdain for MGM formed the initial basis for their friendship. Their propensity for alcohol led to frequent dates and eventually to what Ava considered a casual affair. Although charmed by his wit and sensitivity, Ava was more interested in Bob's availability as a willing drinking companion. At age twenty-four, Ava had a fondness for liquor, and, remarkably, her heavy consumption marred neither her looks nor her "morning-after" performance on the set.

During this period, Bob was living in his studio dressing room, having turned his house over to his parents, who had decided to vacation in California.

When he appeared on the set in the morning, he was able to remember his simple lines, but his right foot and left hand twitched almost constantly, his face was puffy, and he was in no condition for close-ups. As a result Ava was favored in many of their scenes together.

Nevertheless, whenever she suggested a night on the town, he complied.

By now Bob had become sexually infatuated with his leading lady and was perhaps the only person at Universal unaware of her simultaneous dalliance with Duff. He shrugged off Jim Henaghan's warning, "Don't get too involved with that dame; she's dynamite." Bob insisted, "She's the most unambitious actress I've

ever met. She doesn't give a damn about movies, and she likes me for myself. When I told her I thought she deserved first billing in the picture, she just laughed and replied, 'Who wants it?'" This was true enough.

According to a Universal publicist, Bob first became aware of Ava's duplicity one lunch break, when, after he'd knocked at her dressing-room door, a deep baritone voice (Duff's) replied, "This is Ava here," which was followed by the sound of male and female laughter. And, of course, the door remained unopened.

Bob lingered in the background until Duff emerged, then stormed into Ava's quarters in a jealous rage. A violent argument ensued. Bob, losing all control, smashed Ava across the face, but she escaped from the room before further damage was inflicted.

He was sobered by his action. He had never struck a woman before, and Henaghan would say, "When Bob turned violent as a result of his emotional problems, he would put his fist through windows and punch at walls. I was with him at times like this, but he never hurt anyone else—just himself."

Howard Duff didn't take Bob's behavior lightly, recalling, "He was a tragic alcoholic. When he tried to beat Ava up, I would have liked to cream him—only he was so helpless."

About the same time, Sam Marx recalls, "I was at the Sportsman Lodge, a restaurant on Ventura Boulevard, not far from the Universal studios, and I saw Bob with a group of young people. They were apparently having a good time, and I paid them very little attention. But when I looked over later, Bob's head had flopped over, and he had literally passed out in an empty bowl of soup. The shocking thing to me was that none of the kids at the table were paying the slightest bit of attention to him. So I got up and went over and introduced myself as a friend of Bob's, and, as they were not terribly concerned about his condition, I called a waiter, and we got him into my car. On the way out, I was trying to find out where he was living, because I didn't know, and he mumbled something about getting him to Universal. So I drove him there, and the guard suggested I take him back to the gym, where the trainer had been looking after Bob. Bob was barely conscious; the trainer came out, and between the two of us we dragged and carried him to his dressing room and put him to bed.

"I never discussed it with Bob afterward; I didn't think it the thing to do. I did mention it the next day to Ben Thau, because I felt that maybe we could suggest things to Bob in case he was getting alcoholic—which it turned out he was. But Thau told me that he'd like me to just forget the incident, and he would sort of take care of it. As far as I know, that was the end of it."

Out of camera range, Ava now ignored him completely, which only triggered his fury. On one occasion, he tacked an unprintable sign onto her dressing-room door. Contrite, he tried to phone her at home. When she recognized his voice, she hung up. When he persisted, she changed her number. By the time she had departed Universal, Ava's now-torrid affair with Howard Duff was the talk of the studio and the town. In less than a year she'd dump Duff and resume her relationship with Howard Hughes.

During his final days at Universal, Bob found a close friend and ally in the person of Shelley Winters, who was heading for stardom after *A Double Life*, in which Ronald Colman had given his Oscar-winning performance as a schizophrenic actor.

Ignoring Bob's abortive affair with Ava and the additional damage it had inflicted on Bob's battered psyche, Miss Winters, who had initially met and danced with Bob at the opening of the Copacabana Club in 1946 but never dated him, related only wonderful things about him:

"It was at UI that I got to know Robert Walker rather well. We used to meet in the commissary for lunch a couple of times a week.

"In my opinion Bob was a consummate actor and had that same extraordinary quality that Spencer Tracy had: his eyes were truly a mirror of his soul. He never needed words to let you know what he was thinking or feeling. I saw *The Clock*, the film he did with Judy Garland, at least ten times. Watching him was a profound lesson in film acting. He had a special sense of humor that would make the audience laugh immediately after his most poignant moments. He never took himself or his problems seriously. It was a very difficult period of his life. When he was working on *Venus*, I believe he was avoiding MGM, his home studio, and used to hang around my set sometimes, because he was lonely and had nowhere to go. He used to tease me gently about my Blond Bombshell image. I casually mentioned once that I liked clowns and stuffed

animals, and so whenever he came over to my dressing room, he would bring one.

"He took me all over Southern California to strange out-of-the-way places I didn't even know existed. Somewhere in L.A. there is a Japanese garden teahouse that you can get to only by climbing a mountain. We also went to what surely must have been the first commune somewhere down the beach toward Laguna, where lots of kids, married and unmarried, lived in Quonset huts.

"Once we drove up to Big Sur, and he talked of buying a house and raising his children up there. I never raised any objections to these daydreams, because he was so obviously trying to put his life together again.

"He was a quiet, gentle, lovely young man."

Walker's relationship with Winters might have been friendly, but the episode with Gardner still rankled in his soul. One evening at Henaghan's, Bob blurted out, "I'll never get mixed up with another actress as long as I live! They're able to put on too good an act. You can't trust any of them. And I'll steer clear of beautiful women too. I'd like to meet a girl who's so unglamorous that no man would think of trying to take her away from me."

Trust Jim to know just the girl to fit the bill: Barbara Ford, the twenty-five-year-old daughter of legendary director John Ford.

When Ford, a longtime friend, invited Jim to attend a small party on his yacht, the *Araner*, berthed in Newport Bay, Jim persuaded Bob to go along. "You'll have a great time—just don't let the old man intimidate you. His bark is worse than his bite."

After introducing Bob to John and Mary Ford, he steered him toward Barbara, with an offhand "You two should get to know one another." Then he left them to their own devices.

In a conversation held shortly before her death from cancer on June 27, 1985, Barbara Ford recalled, "I fell in love with him instantly, the very same day Jim introduced us—and I'm probably still in love with him. The thing that first impressed me was his lack of ego. He wanted to talk about what interested *me*—which was film editing. He was curious about my background, about my growing up in a show-business atmosphere."

The Fords, however, had protected both their daughter and their son, Patrick, from the usual Hollywood pitfalls. After the Lindbergh kidnapping in 1932, John and Mary had agreed that

their children would be safer away from Hollywood and sent them to the Punahoe School in Honolulu, where they thrived, despite their separation from their parents.

Barbara, who had inherited Ford's wit and energy, was clearly her father's favorite, but he was usually too absorbed in his work to show her the love and attention she craved.

Ever since her late-teen years, Barbara had wanted to marry and have her own family, but she was choosy, and she had never met a man who had held her interest for any length of time—or of whom her conservative parents approved—until she met Robert Walker.

Barbara wistfully remembered:

"Bob had fabulous humor, great compassion. He was a gentleman and probably too sensitive for his own good.

"They tell me I have a good sense of humor too, so that is one of the things that attracted us to each other. We were together all the time after we met . . . mostly in Catalina on Daddy's yacht. We spent the time with Duke Wayne, Ward Bond, and, of course, with my father and the rest of my family. They were all crazy about Bob. His two boys, Michael and Bob Jr., were with us a lot too. They were marvelous youngsters and enjoyed themselves hugely: Catalina is great for kids. We fished, swam, and water-skied (though I wasn't very good at the skiing).

"Funny, the foolish little things you notice—and become so important in memory. I remember that Bob and Daddy could switch glasses. Both had bad eyes, and occasionally I'd hear Daddy say, 'Hey, Bobby, you've got my glasses on,' which he did. Daddy adored Bob, and vice versa."

Nevertheless, both John and Mary Ford were astounded when, after knowing each other for less than six weeks, Bob and Barbara revealed their decision to marry. Staunch Catholics, the Fords were disturbed that their daughter had chosen to marry a divorced man of a different faith. However, they realized that any opposition would be futile and they gave the couple their blessing and suggested that the wedding take place July 3 at the Ford mansion at 6860 Odin Street, Barbara's birthplace. It was the senior Fords' own twenty-eighth wedding anniversary.

Racing against time, Bob and Barbara secured a marriage license and phoned Hedda Hopper to give her the scoop on the

engagement. Just four days later, Bob called Hedda again, saying there had been a slight change. The marriage would take place on schedule, but to avoid the usual fuss, the two decided to wed on the *Araner*, which would be anchored in a tranquil cove at Santa Catalina Island. Aside from the judge, only Barbara's parents would be present. Barbara planned to wear a simple white suit, and after the ceremony she and Bob would board another yacht for a private honeymoon cruise.

But there was still another change of plans—this time due to Jim Henaghan's violent opposition to the marriage: "I knew he wasn't in love with her—and I went over to her house and said, 'Let me see the license!' I took it and pocketed it and told Bob, 'You can't have it. You can't marry her.' The reason I did this was not for him, but for Jack Ford, and because Barbara was Jack's daughter, I didn't want to see her hurt. I just took the damn license and said, 'No way, not until you both have enough time to know what the hell you are doing.'

"Then one day—July 8, I believe, just before the license was due to expire—I received a call from Bob asking to see me. He demanded I bring the license over immediately. 'Barbara is here and we want to get married today.'

"'Are you drinking? Has she been drinking?'

"'No,' he replied. So I went over to his apartment and again asked, 'Are you sure you want to get married?' And he replied, 'Yes, I'm positive. I want to be married, and Barbara wants to be married.' And he added, 'Since you helped screw up our original plans, you can damn well set it up for us—today!'

"So I called Harry Brand, a publicity man I knew, and asked if his brother, Eddie, who was a Superior Court judge, could perform a wedding ceremony that same evening. Harry said he'd see to it. I went down to the Beverly Hills Club and said I wanted to rent a room there for a wedding, then I called Nancy Guild, who was a friend of Barbara's, and asked her if she would be the maid of honor. I returned to the club with Judge Brand, then phoned Barbara and Bob and said, 'Come on over. It's all set up for six P.M.'

"He was cold sober and really wanted to marry her, and asked me to be best man. The other person in the wedding party was Nancy's husband, Charles Russell, a young actor under contract to

Twentieth Century-Fox. I never learned why neither Bob nor Barbara contacted her parents. Perhaps she tried and couldn't locate them.

"Someone at the club, however, contacted the press, and the place was swarming with photographers. Bob said, 'Let them in,' and we posed for pictures. The story made the front page of the Los Angeles *Times* the next morning, together with a four-column-wide photograph. Bob's wedding attire consisted of a pair of gray slacks and a sports jacket; Barbara looked like a high-school student in a peasant blouse and a flowered cotton skirt. The entire thing had been so hastily arranged that no one had bothered to supply a wedding bouquet, a wedding cake, or even a bottle of champagne."

The fivesome had a token wedding dinner at the Tropics, a nearby Polynesian restaurant, and Bob returned to his apartment with his bride.

The next morning he realized he had made one of the greatest mistakes of his life.

Chapter

18

Bob and Barbara married on a Thursday. Before the weekend was over, Barbara's anticipation of an intimate cruise was shattered. Bob abruptly informed her that their honeymoon would be put off and that he wanted to spend two weeks in Ogden so she could meet his family.

Zella and Horace Walker had been shocked by their son's unexpected marriage, hurt not only because they hadn't been invited but also because the first they had known about it was when they saw the story and pictures in the Ogden *Standard Examiner*.

Barbara recalled, "When they telephoned Bob, neither of them asked to speak to me. It was a short conversation, but Bob promised to bring me to Utah, which seemed to appease them.

"Bob said that his mother's only comment about me was 'Well, she may be a nice girl, but she sure looks like a female Barry Fitzgerald.'

"I didn't take that slur seriously, dismissing it as Bob's wicked sense of humor.

"I wanted to turn Bob's new place into a real home for us, and I became occupied with the decorating phase, hanging wallpaper and curtains, buying kitchen appliances, all of that stuff. I guess I expected that our marriage would last forever.

"Then Jennifer Jones started phoning. But constantly. Just to hound him, in my opinion. I think she was very evil to Bob.

"She'd call to say that the boys needed new shoelaces or a couple of pillowcases, whatever. I was mystified. After all, she had a maid and a houseman to run those kinds of errands.

"Nevertheless, Bob and I would dash down to J. C. Penney's

and get the shoelaces and the pillowcases and drive to Jennifer's house.

"She was always out, however, or instructed the help to say that she was out, and we dropped the packages off with her maid, Veda.

"Bob would be in a terrible mood after those shopping trips, humiliated by being treated like a delivery boy. He became an entirely different man from the one with whom I had spent those idyllic days in Catalina. Nothing I did seemed to please him, and I desperately wanted to make him happy. I was insanely in love with him."

The marriage was deteriorating—fast—but Barbara rationalized that Bob and she were merely going through "a normal period of adjustment, to be expected after such a short courtship."

In early August Bob inexplicably locked himself into his room for four days and refused to come out. "I'd leave a tray at his door," she said, "and then spend the day with my parents or friends. I never told them we were having difficulties. After all, I was positive that there was nothing we couldn't solve." (Later she would say, "I knew there was talk that our marriage had never been consummated. But it *was*." She wouldn't elaborate.)

Meanwhile, the situation simply worsened, for there was no way Barbara could appease her difficult and emotionally bankrupt groom.

On August 14, a few days before their scheduled trip to Ogden, without provocation Bob went berserk. He manhandled Barbara with such fury that she could barely struggle to the phone to call her father.

Henaghan remembered, "I got a frantic call from John Ford, who said, 'Jim, someone has to save her from Walker. He's been beating the hell out of her.' So I rushed to his apartment, where I found her sobbing on the sofa. Bob was in the bedroom. I confronted him and demanded, 'Have you been beating her?' He replied, 'Yeah, I can't stand her.'

"'You son of a bitch,' I yelled, 'assaulting the daughter of a friend of mine!' I returned to the living room and grabbed her and said we were leaving the place immediately. Bob tried to stop me, but I shoved him away, and Barbara and I left. I took her home

with me, and she stayed overnight. The next morning the Fords came by and drove her to their house on Odin Street.

"Bob called Mary Ford that afternoon, not to apologize, but to angrily proclaim, 'You can keep her. I don't want her. Take her back to where you got her.'

"I had known, when they married, that the two were headed for disaster, because it was so obvious that Jennifer Jones was the only woman he loved. I anticipated that he and Barbara would never make it. But I thought the marriage would last maybe six months. I didn't expect a breakup in less than six *weeks*. In retrospect, I'd say Bob was taking his frustrations out on his bride because she wasn't Jennifer; punishing her because she wasn't Jennifer."

The following day, when Barbara regained some semblance of composure, she phoned both Hedda Hopper and Louella Parsons and informed them that she and Bob had separated and that she planned to file for divorce.

In a carefully worded statement, she told Louella, "I have tried very hard, since we were married, to work out our problems and adjust our differences, but I know now that it's impossible. I'm going to Catalina to get myself together."

She left for that island with her mother and two girlfriends, Mrs. Dick Haymes (actress Joanne Dru) and Mrs. Mark Stevens. By then Bob had left town.

After his call to Mrs. Ford, he had gotten into his car and driven to Ogden alone, keeping his whereabouts a secret not only from the press but also from Henaghan and MGM.

Although the elder Walkers had been shaken by his sudden marriage, they were totally unprepared for the breakup. Other than revealing that he had made a mistake, Bob did not elaborate on the circumstances that led to the parting, and the Walkers were wise enough not to hound him for details. He even refused to discuss his estrangement with his cousin Barbara Rabe. When his parents had visitors, he remained in his room, shamed and resigned to agree to any financial compensation Barbara might demand in court.

Jennifer Jones was "unavailable for comment" about Bob's abortive marital escapade. She was too preoccupied with her own problems.

As a result of David's wild extravagance, his film company was falling apart. In debt to the banks for some twelve million dollars, he had no plans for future productions of his own. Instead, he made a deal with Columbia Pictures to provide Jennifer's services for John Huston's production of *We Were Strangers*, based on *Rough Sketch*, Robert Sylvester's novel dealing with a phase of the 1933 Cuban Revolution. Jennifer cared neither for the script nor for the part of China Valdez and the Cuban accent it required, but Selznick desperately needed the funds her loan-out fee would bring.

We Were Strangers wasn't due to start production until August 31. To placate Jennifer, Selznick, aware of her desire to return to the stage, permitted her to do a week of stock at the La Jolla Playhouse. The play they chose was an obscure, sophisticated 1929 comedy called *Serena Blandish*, which had originally starred Ruth Gordon.

Aside from a normal case of opening-night nerves, she sailed through the week, bolstered nightly by an enthusiastic audience reception, and gaily told a local reporter that "hearing real applause volleying my way was as great a thrill as winning my Oscar." She added, "I definitely plan to make my Broadway debut as soon as I'm free of movie commitments." She was, however, vague as to just when that would be.

Jennifer was less jubilant during the filming of *We Were Strangers*. Her beautiful long hair was chopped into a boyish bob, her wardrobe was dowdy, the exhausting climactic scenes were filmed in a claustrophobic, mud-filled tunnel, and she had a tendency to depend upon grimaces to convey emotion.

John Huston recalls that "Jennifer Jones looked for direction in every move she made. I would say, 'Sit over there, Jennifer.' She would say, 'How?' At first I was confounded, but I discovered she wanted to be told when or how to sit, stand, or walk across a room. She put herself completely in the hands of the director . . . more than any other actress I ever worked with. And she was not an automaton. Jennifer took what you gave her and made it distinctly her own.

"David's love for her was very real and touching, but in it lay the seeds of failure. . . . Everything he did was for Jennifer. His whole life centered upon her, to the detriment of his good judgment."

Physically and mentally spent after *We Were Strangers*, Jennifer decided to take a brief trip abroad alone with her sons. Selznick wasn't overjoyed by her plans. He had wanted to be the one to show her Europe for the first time, but in a rare burst of defiance, Jennifer insisted she needed a vacation. Her main motivation for leaving, however, may have been to attempt to see the noted psychoanalyst Carl Jung in Switzerland. She had read him and wondered if he could resolve her ambivalence about marrying David once his divorce became final. She hired a tutor for Michael and Bobby in Switzerland, but, to her great disappointment, was unable to arrange the meeting with the ailing Jung. In order that the trip not be a total waste, she went on a shopping spree in Paris. She purchased the most elegant Dior gowns and the most chic sports attire—purchases far in excess of her needs, since she rarely attended glittering premieres or lavish parties, but confined her social activities to small gatherings at either her home or David's.

An incident which occurred at the latter's indicated both Selznick's frame of mind and his all-but-irrational obsession with Jennifer.

David's most cherished possession at the time was the Robert Brackman rendition of the portrait of Jennie that was used in the movie. Prior to a dinner party which the producer was hosting in honor of Clare and Henry Luce of the Time-Life empire, Daniel O'Shea, in collusion with Joseph Cotten, ordered a large photocopy of the painting. The two men then mischievously defaced it with a large black mustache, then replaced the Brackman which David had on display in his dining room with the doctored copy.

Joseph Cotten says, "In retrospect, it was a foolish prank, but we thought David, who had always enjoyed our practical jokes before, would be highly amused."

Cotten and his wife, Lenore, who were escorting the Luces to the party, let the couple in on the gag before they arrived at Selznick's home.

When the guests entered the dining room, Mrs. Luce "innocently" remarked, "What an unusual painting!" It was at this point that David noticed the sacrilege. According to Cotten, "He became so enraged that he failed to realize the picture was only a copy." Even after Cotten confessed that the original painting had

been temporarily removed, David would not be placated. "I don't think it's funny," he roared. His seething anger lasted throughout the evening, turning what was to have been a festive dinner party into an embarrassing disaster. His guests, including Jennifer, departed shortly after coffee was served.

In addition to his dwindling fortunes, or perhaps because of them, Selznick's affection for laughter became a thing of the past. By contrast, in spite of his emotional problems, Bob Walker had regained his sense of humor, although Henaghan admitted, "It was a very sorry sense of humor."

Bob returned from Utah and was delighted when Jim gave no indication that the Barbara Ford debacle had affected their friendship. "In fact," Jim recalled, "we never discussed that stormy afternoon. I never asked him to explain why he beat her up, and he didn't offer to. It was never an issue at any time. I understood."

Although Barbara's day in court wasn't scheduled until December 16, by now Bob had dismissed his second marriage as "just a bad dream," vowing: "Next time, if there *is* a next time, I'll insist on a long engagement, a *very* long engagement."

His spirits seemed to take a turn for the better when, during a weekend with Michael and Bobby, the boys informed him that they were being sent to the exclusive Black Fox Military Academy, where they'd be dressed in "real soldier suits and caps—just like Private Hargrove." Bob had wanted his sons to have the best education money could buy. The academy's scholastic and disciplinary reputation was flawless, and within a few weeks the boys adjusted to their new world, making friends and concentrating on their studies.

Bob told Jim, "They're still too young to decide on careers, but I just hope to God neither of them will want to become an actor."

His own career at MGM was still in limbo. If, after *Venus*, there had been any further requests for his services by another studio, he wasn't told about them.

He found solace in his friendship with actress Ida Lupino, whom he had met before his marriage to Barbara Ford. Theirs was strictly an intellectual relationship with no romantic overtones. Nevertheless, she was always there to lend support when he needed it. Ironically, in 1951 Lupino became the wife of Howard Duff, Bob's erstwhile rival for the favors of Ava Gardner.

For the most part, however, Bob continued to spend his spare time with Jim whenever the latter was available.

"I know," said Jim, "that a lot of people in this town thought we were a couple of fags, but neither of us gave a damn *what* they thought. If there is such a thing as love, I loved Bobby, just as I later loved John Wayne, but there were a lot of perverted minds that couldn't accept the fact that two men could love each other without being sexual deviates."

Jim remembered an evening about this time "when Bob became so smashed that I wouldn't allow him to drive home by himself. So I took him back to my place and let him sleep it off. The next morning he came down waving an empty wallet in my face. 'You son of a bitch,' he said, 'you stole all my money!'

"'You *spent* all your money last night. You gave the waiter your last twenty bucks as a tip,' I told him.

"'I did not . . . you stole it,' he shouted. 'I bet if you ever found me dead, the first thing you'd do is empty my pockets.' We both roared at that last ludicrous image.

"It became, in fact, an outrageous running gag between us. I would look through his record collection and scream that the records were mine and he was looting me of my possessions. Or he would see me with a new pair of cufflinks and yell, 'Those are mine. You lifted them from me.' It was the one private joke I'd have reason never to forget."

Bob was by now completely estranged from the Hollywood scene, but he kept up with local news through the daily copies of the *Hollywood Reporter* Jim had at his house.

Bob derived no small satisfaction from reading about the collapse of the Selznick empire. The man's fortune was gone, his power diminished. Nevertheless, he possessed the only asset Bob wanted: he still had Jennifer.

Changes were also taking place at Metro-Goldwyn-Mayer. In 1944 Selznick had hired the brilliant forty-year-old screenwriter Dore Schary as head producer for his Vanguard unit, which was created to make moderate-budget "program pictures." Within a short time Schary and Selznick had become antagonists, prompting David to hand Schary over to RKO in a co-production deal which included the services of some of his stars. Schary then served as vice-president of production at that studio during 1947

and 1948. Ultimately he resigned to assume a similar post at MGM.

At the time he left RKO it was rumored that Nicholas M. Schenk, president of both Loew's and MGM, was grooming Schary as the successor to Louis B. Mayer, who seemed more absorbed in his new marriage to Lorena Danker and his passion for breeding racehorses than he was in the fate of the studio he had created. Mayer was still head man, but his position was in jeopardy, and Schary neither feared nor respected Eddie Mannix, Benny Thau, or any of Mayer's other yes-men. Schary was his *own* man with his own ideas, secure in the knowledge that he had Schenk in his corner.

After reviewing the MGM contract list, Schary summoned Bob Walker to his office for an important conference.

Schary's attitude toward him was warm, sympathetic, and understanding. He had deplored Selznick's disregard of Bob, admired the latter's talent, and was horrified by the manner in which it had been abused by the studio. Although he was aware of Bob's drinking problem and the fracas with Ava, he was still convinced Bob could remain an important asset to the studio.

"You're only thirty. You have your whole life ahead of you," Schary told him.

After their meeting, Bob told reporter Harrison Carroll, "I had a talk with MGM's new production boss, Dore Schary. He's an understanding man. He promised to find me suitable roles. I believe in him, and I trust him. With this worry removed and with the lessons I have learned, I'm sure that I'll be able to run my life on an even keel."

Bob had every intention of doing just that. However, a few days later, on October 22, he was in serious trouble again. A chance meeting with starlet Patricia Dane (the former Mrs. Tommy Dorsey, dropped by Metro after appearing in a half-dozen minor roles) led to their stopping off at a small bar near his home for a few drinks.

After leaving the bar, Miss Dane persuaded Bob to permit her to drive his new Cadillac sedan back to her place. Neither noticed the patrol car lurking in the shadows of the parking lot.

The two hadn't gone more than a couple of blocks on the nearly deserted West Pico Boulevard when the police ordered them to

pull over to the curb. They ordered Miss Dane to step out of the car and give them her driver's license.

"Don't pick on her," Bob protested. "I'm to blame for this. She doesn't know what she's doing." Then, as an afterthought, he belligerently threatened radio patrolmen E. L. Trinkletter and L. L. Brown: "I can whip you both."

Bob was forcibly removed from his side of the car by the officers, who insisted upon giving *him* a sobriety test.

Later he'd tell Jim, "It was the silliest thing I ever experienced. The damn cops just stand there and give you about a twenty-foot start. They seem to encourage you to make a break for it. I couldn't resist. I started to run and stumbled a few times. Naturally, they caught me, but their indignation was ridiculous."

Bob and Miss Dane were forced into the patrol car and driven to the Lincoln Heights jail, where they were booked as drunk and disorderly.

Asked to admit to the drunk charge for the records, Bob defiantly replied, "Why, I've been drunk for twenty-five years." Resentful that the police were treating him like a common criminal, he took a poke at one of the officers. When five of them threatened him, he took them all on—a no-win situation.

At the time of his arrest, the Associated Press reported that "in a dazed condition, he pleaded with the detective in charge to telephone his wife, Jennifer Jones, to ask if she would help him get out of jail."

When the detective offered to call his lawyer instead, Bob's violence redoubled. The police threw him into a chair, and a photographer snapped three quick pictures destined to make Walker's name notorious as they were splashed across front pages coast to coast. Bob, totally disheveled, his shirttail out, was frozen in the act of snapping his fingers angrily at the photographer . . . then thrusting his fist at the police. His face was contorted with defiance, rage, and despair.

The pictures were far more devastating than the "punishment." Bob gained his liberty after posting a fifty-dollar bond; Miss Dane, after pleading guilty to drunk-and-disorderly charges under her legal name of Thelma Patricia Byrnes, paid a $150 fine and was released by Municipal Court Justice David Colman.

According to Louella Parsons, Jennifer was horrified and interrupted a holiday at Del Mar to return to Hollywood. "I heard," Miss Parsons later reported, "that she had a long talk with him and begged him, for the sake of their children, to take hold of himself." Miss Parsons also revealed that David Selznick had called on his ex-father-in-law, imploring Mayer not to exercise the morals clause in Bob's contract.

That gesture seems hard to believe. However, Selznick *was* at the time negotiating with MGM about something else. The studio wanted Jennifer for the title role in Pandro Berman's production of Gustave Flaubert's *Madame Bovary*, the classic French novel of small-town ennui and sexual obsession. Vincente Minnelli would direct.

Lana Turner had been the original choice for the role, but to weave Lana—the nation's sex symbol—into an already erotic plot seemed to court sudden death at the hands of the Breen Office, then Hollywood's guardian of public morality. The removal of Lana from consideration left Metro with no contract players right for the role. Jennifer was available, and the studio also agreed to cast Selznick contractees Louis Jourdan and Christopher Kent in leading roles in order to procure Jennifer in time for a projected mid-December starting date.

Assessing her own performance in the film, Jennifer later confessed that at that particular point in her career she was simply "unprepared to play a part which was so completely out of keeping with my own personality." There were some ironic comments about that statement. The *Bovary* plot centers around an avaricious woman who abandons her hardworking husband and child in order to pursue a path of romance and social climbing. In doing so, she destroys her husband's life and her own.

In the meantime, Dore Schary was deeply concerned about the furor Bob Walker had created not merely by his arrest but also by the wide circulation of the jailhouse photograph. He had been certain that after their warm and productive conversation, Bob would stay out of trouble. Schary recalled, "The simple way out, of course, would have been to fire him. With Jones due on the lot, I was told that would be to our best advantage. It's so easy to kick a guy when he's down, but I couldn't do that to him. Aside from my own instincts, I had heard too many good things about Bob to give

up on him. He was mentally and emotionally ill and needed expert psychiatric help, away from the pressures of Hollywood."

Bob remained incommunicado in his apartment, refusing to answer either the telephone or the doorbell. The jailhouse photo had panicked him. He was devastated by the certainty that it had been seen not only by his sons but also by their teachers and by the families of their classmates.

Bob later revealed, "I would rather have had a knife stuck in my side, because then I should have known what was wrong. There was terrific remorse the day after. I decided that sometime soon I was going to end up dead."

Henaghan, who had a duplicate key to Bob's place, let himself in that evening. He found Bob on his bed, cold sober, naked and unshaven, staring at the ceiling.

"Why the hell didn't you call me?" Jim asked. "I've been trying to reach you every hour on the hour. Strickling has been bugging the hell out of me. Schary is demanding to see you. They figured I'd be hearing from you."

Bob shrugged. "They could have sent a telegram saying I was canned. Why drag it out?"

"If you're canned," Jim replied, "face it like a man. You can always get a job at a filling station."

The following morning Bob called Schary. That afternoon, clean-shaven and neatly dressed, he entered the Thalberg Building, where the executive suites were located.

He had expected fireworks, but Schary never raised his voice. Bob, however, recognized his contract lying on the desk. In a businesslike manner Schary initiated the conversation. "I've decided to give you a last chance and a choice. You can tear up this contract, quit films, and eventually destroy yourself, if that's what you want. Or you can agree to undergo psychiatric treatment at the Menninger Clinic in Topeka for however long it takes to get to the root of your disturbance. We'll have to take you off salary, but we will pay all your hospital bills. I've been in touch with the clinic; your father will have to commit you. Sleep on it, and call me in the morning."

The following day Bob called Schary.

"I'll give Menninger's a try," he said. "But I don't believe in

psychiatry, and if I can't stand it there, they won't be able to keep me."

"If that is your decision, fine," Schary replied. "I'll make the preliminary arrangements. I suggest you be prepared to leave within a week."

Henaghan recalls, "The night before Bob left, he phoned me. I had not heard of his impending departure and suggested we get together for lunch the next day. He was very angry.

"'You know damn well I'm going away in the morning,' he said.

"'Where are you going?' I asked.

"'Now, don't you start lying to me,' he shouted. 'You know very well where I'm going.' And then he hung up.

"I *didn't* know until several days later that Bob and his father had boarded a plane early that next morning for Topeka. It would be months before I'd hear from him again. Nor, with one exception, which I'd read about in the papers, would I have any knowledge of his activities while he was away."

Aside from Dore Schary, no one would. It was as if Bob had vanished into thin air.

WHOM THE GODS DESTROY

---★

I thought of a mental institution like an insane asylum. Fear hit me. I thought that someday soon I was going to end up dead.

—ROBERT WALKER, 1949

Bob didn't want the shot. I held him down as the doctor injected the fluid. I forcibly held him down— and he stopped breathing. For years I felt like a murderer.

—JAMES HENAGHAN, 1981

Bob's death was such a waste. He was a talented actor and a man who simply switched onto a siding and ran into a dead end.

—DORE SCHARY, 1979

Chapter

19

"After I left Schary's office," Bob later admitted, "I hated myself and blamed myself for things for which I shouldn't have blamed myself. I felt everybody was against me, hated me, couldn't understand me. I couldn't even understand myself. I kept asking myself, 'Is there something about me that others can see and I can't?'

"When I first arrived in Topeka, I couldn't bear the thought of people looking at me. It was as if the whole world had its eyes focused on me. Actually, nobody gave a damn."

Registering at an obscure hotel, he visited the clinic for a week of tests. On the basis of these, a board of psychiatrists recommended that he be committed, and warned his father and Dore Schary that Bob would require at least one year of treatment, possibly even two.

Horace Walker sadly signed the commitment papers.

The sanitarium, considered by many the best psychiatric facility in the world, had been established by Dr. Karl Menninger, his brother, and his father in 1925 in a converted farmhouse on the western edge of Topeka, and it expanded as its reputation increased. Its services ranged from in-depth therapy to electric-shock treatments, and it treated both men and women.

Joseph Mankiewicz's wife, Rosa Stradner, a well-known actress, had been treated there, and Mankiewicz had once tried to persuade Judy Garland to commit herself to Menninger's when he'd felt she was falling apart. Judy would have none of it. "I'm not nuts," she'd screamed.

Bob was unaware of the exact nature of the clinic's physical facilities.

He said, "I got the idea that the clinic was something like a country club, so I asked for a single room and bath. First thing I noticed was that all the doors were locked. Then everything sharp, including my razor, was taken away from me—you could only shave with an attendant watching. The room I was taken to had bars on its window. When I was told: 'You're rooming with so-an-so,' I said I was leaving. That first night, a patient who understood how a newcomer felt gave up his room and bath without my knowing it, so it would be easier on me."

For the first four weeks he was under observation only, no analysis. "You have to have a recreational therapist with you even on walks over the grounds."

He lived in one of several "lodges," with fifteen patients to each floor.

During that first month at Menninger's, he wrote to his sons, who, used to their parents going away to make movies, thought their daddy was off on location.

He sent brief notes to his parents. Dore Schary telephoned frequently. But Bob wasn't aware that Schary was also in touch with the clinic's administrator to keep himself apprised of Bob's progress, or rather, at that time, the lack of it.

After nearly a month of getting nowhere, Bob was intent on leaving.

Schary begged him to stick it out a little longer.

Desperate to be released from the claustrophobic confines of the hospital, Bob pleaded with his keepers to allow him to spend just one day in town to pick up some books and records. "I'm perfectly capable of taking care of myself, and I'll be back before supper," he promised.

On December 5 he received permission to go to Topeka by himself.

Sometime during the late afternoon he became acquainted with a man and two young girls, whose identities were never disclosed, and the four headed for a quiet bar. The man suggested they continue the party at a local hotel a short distance away. Upon arriving at their destination, they got into an argument with their cabdriver, who, they claimed, had overcharged them.

The hotel doorman called the police, who hauled the four rowdy passengers to headquarters. Upon learning that Bob was a

patient at Menninger's, Police Sargeant Russell Purdie called the clinic and was advised to hold Bob until one of their representatives arrived to pick him up.

The quartet was sitting peacefully at the station when Bob suddenly jumped to his feet and smashed his fist through the plate glass covering the bulletin board. Before he could be stopped by Officer Purdie, he had shattered two other glass panes.

Officer Purdie, who suffered a shoulder injury in the melee, recalled: "He was a wild one. His leather coat and tweed slacks were spattered with blood from his badly lacerated hands. He was in deep shock."

By this time Dr. Fred M. Tatzlaff of the clinic had arrived at the scene and had rushed Bob to a nearby hospital. He held Bob down while Dr. James Bowden attended to his wounds. Nearly a hundred stitches were required to repair the self-inflicted damage to his hands. Then Dr. Tatzlaff drove the dazed actor back to Menninger's.

The drunk-and-disorderly charges against Bob were dropped by City Attorney Frank Eresch, who declared the actor "a very sick man."

Despite the injuries to his hands and the evidence of his blood-stained clothes, Bob didn't remember any of this, and the clinic carefully kept newspaper and radio reports of the incident away from him. A week later, however, he read about his escapade in a newsmagazine.

He raged. He wasn't crazy, but he would be if he stuck around any longer. "I was more determined than ever to get away, because I was sure the clinic had driven me to my display of violence," Bob would later tell Hedda Hopper.

He contacted his father and begged him to come and take him away. It was suggested Bob should see one of Menninger's analysts. "I told them I didn't want to. Why spend more money on an analyst when he couldn't do me any good? Even then, I was making excuses to keep from facing facts."

Soon afterward, a psychoanalyst who had been assigned to Bob anyway came to his room, said he knew the actor was leaving, but had just stopped by to say hello. "The analyst," said Bob, "stretched himself out on the bed and let me do the arguing. At the end of about an hour I thanked him for coming but told him I was

still going to leave. The next day I found some excuse to ask him to visit me again. I still argued that I was leaving. It was some time before I realized I was doing all the talking—not him. I made up my mind to stay."

He had one hour of analysis a day, six days a week. "For three weeks I spoke to nobody but this doctor, keeping myself shut up in my room, eating scarcely anything, sleeping very little, drinking cup after cup of coffee. When I started to get some insight on the cure, I began to work constantly at it. Pouring out your thoughts and mind is an emotionally exhausting experience."

It all came out, the old wounds, the anger for the wounds, and the guilt for the anger. He talked about his life—way back to his baby days. He realized that his problems went back to his childhood, when he had felt unwanted. "By emotionally reliving your life," he'd later say, "you find your problems yourself and come to your own conclusions. The analyst doesn't tell you."

He grew thin and felt shaken. He felt he was making no progress at just the time, of course, when he was progressing fastest.

He was beginning to know his deepest self, and the understanding that comes out of that kind of introspection, he said, brought freedom and relief as he had never known before.

"But you could never know the thrill it was when I realized that hate was leaving my heart.

"Everybody has problems, but I couldn't live with mine. I wasn't an alcoholic but I was on the way to being one. The way I reacted to reality—such as my divorce from Jennifer—reflected my immaturity. I played it like everybody should pity me. I unconsciously was trying to get attention and pity, which is not realistic and mature.

"Being psychoanalyzed was like getting rid of a ton of bricks I'd been carrying around all my life."

While Bob was still in the early stages of analysis, his name continued to make headlines in Hollywood—but, as before, newspapers, and now news and movie magazines, were kept from his sight.

On December 16, ten days following Bob's explosive behavior at the Topeka police station, Barbara Ford observed her twenty-sixth birthday by obtaining her divorce. In testimony, asserting "extreme cruelty," she reluctantly admitted that Bob struck her on

occasion, called her vile and profane names, and once, after a movie premiere, wouldn't let her in the car with him and drove off alone. She asked for no alimony, just twenty-five hundred dollars for her attorney, George Stahman, and the restoration of her maiden name.

"My attorney," Barbara later said, "wanted more sensationalism. He was trying to make a name for himself, but I wanted the marriage to end with dignity. I didn't want Bob's money. I married him because I loved him. I was able to support myself. And I didn't want his commitment to Menninger's to be brought up, but naturally some of the papers had to add that!

"I was heartbroken and guilt-ridden, convinced that in some way I failed Bob miserably, though I had tried my best to be patient and understanding during the brief time we were together."

Coincidentally, on the exact day Barbara received her divorce, Jennifer started filming *Madame Bovary*.

Vincente Minnelli tells a story that reflects her state of mind at this period.

"Jennifer was getting deeper into her character . . . I felt she was a perfect Madame Bovary.

"I felt this even more strongly after Emma sweeps in after her first adultery, and, as a means of atoning for her sins, smothers her little girl with attention. But the child, sensing something different in her mother, wants nothing to do with her.

"To get the reaction from the little girl (Dawn Kinney), she was not permitted to meet Jennifer before the scene. I instructed Jennifer, when it came time to film, to take away the little girl's favorite pair of red shoes. That came as a complete surprise to the child and we got the right reaction.

"The little girl, however, hadn't distinguished between the real and the make-believe and continued turning her back on Jennifer.

"This wouldn't do in Emma's death scene, after her taking poison. The child was supposed to extend her arms to Emma. Now Jennifer had to court the little girl. She had her to lunch in her dressing room; she brought her little presents. Came time for rehearsal. The little girl still refused to have anything to do with Jennifer. 'She took my red shoes.' She glared accusingly. It was more than Jennifer could bear. She fled the set in tears. I set out in pursuit.

"'She doesn't like me,' Jennifer cried. 'She thinks I'm terrible. Nobody likes me.'"

Jennifer's cry from the heart was not paranoid. She was aware of the press's antagonism toward her. David's friends shared Huston's attitude that "his love for Jennifer had planted the seeds of his destruction." Irene Selznick's friends wanted no part of her. And she was (with the exception of Parsons) damned for what had been her calculated rejection of Bob, whom, with few exceptions, everyone loved in spite of his emotional problems.

David, meanwhile, in spite of his professional problems, or perhaps because of them, couldn't resist his penchant for parties, and Jennifer, of course, was now his official hostess.

One night, a group of guests was invited to a party at Jennifer's house. When they arrived, no one was on hand to greet them but the maid. They waited for an hour, and no one even offered them a drink.

Finally David arrived, his arms full of bundles, his voice booming welcome. "Where's Jennifer?" he asked. One of the guests, who apparently knew more about it than the latecomers, said, "She's dressing."

David took a look around. "Has anyone had a drink?"

"No," said one guest politely, "but we don't mind."

At that moment Jennifer came down the stairs. She had been held up at the studio, she explained, until eight o'clock. But the final exasperation, insofar as the guests were concerned, was that she was holding a half-finished martini in her hand.

She was chagrined to learn that the maid hadn't offered cocktails. She was further upset because she had been unavoidably detained at the studio. Her friends knew that she had been sipping her cocktail while her hair was being dressed to bolster her courage and her spirits. But the damage had been done. Privately, those who remembered Irene were thinking: Irene was always such a wonderful hostess.

The result, of course, was that David and Jennifer battled all evening.

Jennifer's frequent quarrels with David Selznick were now taking a tremendous toll on her nervous system, although ironically the neurotic tendencies exhibited during the filming of *Madame Bovary* enhanced her performance.

In addition to her discomfort with the role, Jennifer was upset about working for Irene Mayer Selznick's father, nor was it especially easy to work for Dore Schary, still Bob's strongest ally at the studio.

At one point Minnelli was filming a complicated ballroom sequence, when, he recalls, "We were informed that *Look* magazine was going to photograph all the stars currently working at the studio, the picture to be published in commemoration of MGM's silver anniversary. Fifty-eight of their eighty players sat for the family portrait. Jennifer, still attired in her ballroom gown, reluctantly agreed to pose, insisting 'I'm not an MGM star.' In the published photo, Jennifer, a few seats away from Ava Gardner, gazes blankly into thin air.

Conspicuously missing were Lana Turner, Elizabeth Taylor, and, of course, Robert Walker, who was still undergoing extensive therapy in Topeka.

Jennifer's unhappiness was compounded when *Portrait of Jennie* finally opened in New York on March 29, a devastating financial failure.

With Irene's divorce final since the previous January, everyone in Hollywood expected David and Jennifer to marry as soon as she completed *Madame Bovary*, but when questioned by Louella Parsons about her marriage plans, Jennifer evasively replied, "I don't know, Louella, I honestly do not know."

Even Selznick was only slightly more specific. "I don't know exactly when or where we will be married, but it will be sometime before the end of the summer, probably in Europe."

On April 7, the *Hollywood Reporter* headlined: "SELZNICK STUDIOS GOES ON THE BLOCK. Two-day Auction Sale of All Production Equipment." It was perhaps the darkest moment in David Selznick's career.

Life, however, had taken a turn for the better for Bob, who was now making remarkable progress at Menninger's. Schary kept in constant contact with both Bob and the sanitarium, and early in May he received word that Bob had recovered from his breakdown and would officially be released from the hospital on Sunday, May 15. Schary was further informed that Bob was both mentally and physically capable of returning to work, preferably in a film that would not be too stressful.

Schary had a light romantic comedy, *Please Believe Me*, scheduled to roll in late summer. The film was designed to provide a change of pace for Deborah Kerr, who had recently scored as the alcoholic wife in *Edward, My Son*. Its story, sheer fluff, starred her as an English girl who, after inheriting a ranch in America, is pursued aboard ship by three eager young men. Peter Lawford was set as a flirtatious young millionaire, Mark Stevens as his protective lawyer. The role of a charming gambler/fortune-hunter remained to be filled.

Schary felt it a good choice to mark Bob's return to his home studio where he hadn't worked since *Song of Love*, and to bolster Bob's self-confidence, guaranteed him second billing.

Bob slipped quietly into Los Angeles just two days after a chastened Selznick had departed for Europe on a combined business-pleasure trip.

Louella Parsons noted that Jennifer had generously offered to turn over her home to her ex-husband so that he could be there with Michael and Bobby while she was in Europe. It was an offer Bob found easy to refuse. Although he believed himself "cured" of his obsession for her, he thought it foolhardy to risk living in her house, surrounded by her possessions. Instead, he found a house in Pacific Palisades for himself and his sons, which they whimsically named Rancho de Tres Haricots (bastard French-Spanish for "The Ranch of the Three Stringbeans").

Aside from his sons and Dore Schary, he contacted no one.

Jim Henaghan recalled: "He didn't try to get in touch with me for two months, and I didn't try to get in touch with him. I wanted him to do it his own way.

"One evening he called and said, 'I'm right near you. Can I drop by?'

"'Sure, come on,' I answered. While I waited for him to arrive, I was concerned I might not handle the situation properly. Within a few minutes he was in my doorway. I invited him to sit down, but there was a feeling of strain between us, and we sat in silence. Finally I broke it.

"'Look,' I said, 'let's get this over with. Just how nuts are you?'

"He started to laugh, and he roared for five minutes, holding his sides and doubling over, because the laughter was hurting his

stomach. But it did the trick. We hadn't seen each other for nine months; it suddenly seemed less than nine hours, and our friendship picked up exactly where it had left off. Bob never mentioned Jennifer that night."

A few days later, however, he had cause to think about her, when he picked up the morning paper and read that Jennifer had become Mrs. David Selznick aboard the chartered yacht *Manona* on July 13, off the coast of Portofino. The British captain of the vessel performed the ceremony, witnessed by Mr. and Mrs. Louis Jourdan and Mr. and Mrs. Leland Hayward.

Avoiding the press, the newlyweds boarded the yacht of Prince Pignatelli and sailed to nearby Rapallo. Then, to assure legitimacy of the ceremony, the couple returned to Genoa for a second ceremony at city hall.

All too soon, however, their romantic odyssey had to wind down, since Jennifer was due in England to make Michael Powell and Emeric Pressburger's *Gone to Earth*, on loan-out by Selznick. This legend of a superstitious half-gypsy girl who marries a local minister, commits adultery, becomes pregnant, and dies young, had little to recommend it. Once again, Selznick's "infallible judgment" let Jennifer down. *Gone to Earth*, released in 1952 under the title of *The Wild Heart*, was a disaster. For a star who could have had her pick of roles, David had chosen a turkey.

After returning to MGM, Bob was besieged by the press for a statement about Jennifer's marriage. He handled the awkward situation with poise and good taste.

"I wish her all the happiness she deserves. She is first and foremost the mother of my sons."

Questioned about his own life and future plans, Bob unhesitatingly replied, "I now have a love for life and a love for people. I have new interests. I want to become active in my community and the Screen Actors' Guild. Before, I was just running around trying to lose myself. I'll be here with my sons until Mrs. Selznick returns from Europe. Then I'm going back to the clinic for another month of analysis, just to be on the safe side.

"Ultimately I want to find the right girl and have a real and healthy marriage. But there is a lot of time for that. Above all, I

want to spend more time than I ever did before being a buddy to Bobby and Michael.

"I hope to live a long, long time and make sure my sons never suffer the torments I went through."

Bob was approaching his thirty-first birthday.

Within two years he would be dead.

20

After conquering a slight case of first-day jitters, Bob sailed through the filming of *Please Believe Me* under the direction of Norman Taurog.

He hadn't seen Peter Lawford for over a year, and Bob, who had undergone such drastic changes in his own life, was amused that Lawford's outlook and personality hadn't altered; he was as social and ambitious as ever. His career had moved steadily upward with important roles in *Good News*, *Easter Parade*, and *Little Women*, and he was still playing the fame game to the hilt.

Peter avoided any conversation about the Menninger months, but, Bob would remember, good-naturedly bitched: "I've been working my bloody ass off while you've been loafing, and now you're the one who's getting second billing to Kerr. Whose arm did you twist?"

"Nobody's. I don't give a damn about the billing. You want it—talk to Schary."

"I did."

The matter of billing became a running gag, but the offstage banter carried over onto film, and the two worked well together. (Later, writer Joel E. Siegel would comment, "Of the entire cast, Robert Walker, in a nicely stylized performance, comes off best.")

Occasionally Bob and Peter would take in a movie together, but Peter no longer tried to persuade Bob to accompany him to parties. The word had been spread discreetly by the Schary office to avoid involving Bob in any situation where he might be tempted by alcohol.

Publicist Ann Straus recalls: "It was wonderful having Bob back at the studio, and we picked up our friendship where it had left off.

"I used to have open house every Sunday, and Bob would come over once in a while, and sometimes he'd stay for a meal. After his return from Menninger's, I invited him to the house for dinner. I had several other guests coming, and I didn't know what to do. Because of Bob's problem, I wondered if I should serve liquor. He sensed my dilemma, though, and said, 'That's all right. You go ahead and serve your guests. I don't mind. I just won't drink. It doesn't bother me to see other people drinking.'

"He was so sweet and considerate. It was impossible not to love him."

At peace with himself, Bob was determined to make peace with those whom he had offended in the past.

He sought out Howard Strickling and informed him he'd be willing to grant any interviews requested, "that is, if anyone is still interested." Strickling, in fact, had received numerous calls from reporters asking to query Bob about his stay at Menninger's and his recovery. He had turned them down, certain Bob would not discuss that difficult period of his life.

When Strickling broached the subject, however, Bob just grinned. "Set them up. I have nothing to hide . . . anymore. I'd like to see Hedda, just spare me Louella. She won't know what the hell I'm talking about."

He spent an afternoon with Hedda Hopper on her patio, recounting many of his experiences while he'd been away. He apologized for not going into every detail, explaining, "I spent six and a half months of exhaustive, albeit exciting, introspective research, and there are many things I would like to say regarding that effort. In fact, I'd like to reveal my whole case history. . . . I am grateful for what I learned. In a sense, I want to share my knowledge with others. Just as I did, so many others carry around completely needless burdens of self-doubt, of shame and guilt and other destructive feelings. I'd like to, but let's face it, I can't. I'm strictly a layman. And I'm not selfless enough at this point in my life to try to become a truth-crusader. I'm too darn busy making my own mistakes and then trying to understand why I made them so I can do better next time. And, anyway, who am I to say that psychiatry will help the next fellow? I don't know. I only know that, with the help of psychiatry and psychoanalysis, I am now, to a certain extent, the driver, not the driven.

"The breakup with Jennifer gave me an excuse to proclaim my troubles. Whenever I had a few drinks, I'd get to thinking about Poor Me and the broken home and all the et ceteras. Only now can I talk about the whole situation freely.

"I wasn't an alcoholic, but I was only moments away from becoming one, which is a slow form of self-destruction."

He spoke of trying to shield his sons from the truth about himself.

They wanted to read the first newspaper interview he'd given. "Since it mentioned several unpleasant subjects like drinking, I hesitated. Then I decided to keep nothing back from them. The boys read it, and I explained the things they couldn't understand."

After assuring Hedda a scoop for her newspaper column, Bob then consented to talk with Pauline Swanson of *Photoplay* magazine, reversing his often expressed disdain for fan rags. Miss Swanson padded her story with the early details of Bob's turbulent life, then quoted Bob verbatim about his feelings toward analysis.

"I went into that clinic a beaten guy, and I was released a whole man, able to work, eager to live, but as much as I would like to help others who may be as desperately unhappy as I was, I cannot do so. What I have learned of myself is a highly personal and private knowledge that could not be communicated. Not only would I have trouble verbalizing it, but few people outside the professional would understand.

"So I can't here plead the cause for psychiatry for the other fellow, but I do plead for an understanding of emotional disturbances as mental illness. If people would only realize—and I certainly didn't before I went to the clinic—that mental illness *is* an illness, and that treatment is available, a lot of other men and women, as sick and desperate as I was, could find help before it is too late.

"We should stop setting up impossible goals. We accept other people's faults. Let's be a little more forgiving of our own.

"You can't psychoanalyze yourself. It's much better to talk to an understanding friend. Don't be ashamed to put fears into words. Spill everything.

"People are beginning to accept psychiatry. And look what happened to medicine in the early days. Time was when the study of anatomy was looked upon as tampering with God's work.

"But medicine persevered and survived.

"And psychiatry will survive and do its work.

"And then what a people we will be."

Thoughtfully he added, "And if my being a movie star will move more people to listen to my story than would otherwise listen, I thank God that I'm a movie star!"

Strickling and the lesser members of Metro's press department were astonished by Bob's frankness. It seemed impossible to believe that this was the same man who, just a few years earlier, had terminated interviews by walking away in the middle of a columnist's most innocuous question. Now the department was becoming concerned that he was talking too much about a subject that was still foreign to a large segment of the cinema audience.

"You've got it all off your chest," Strickling remarked one afternoon at lunch, "and your story and viewpoints will probably be rehashed for the next decade or so. Let's get on to other matters. After all, your next two films are light comedies."

Bob just laughed. "Anything you say. But with the way I'm living now, you'll get some awfully dull interviews."

He stopped dwelling on the miseries of the past, and although he avoided discussing Jennifer Jones Selznick, he talked incessantly about Bobby and Michael.

"It's so wonderful having them with me all the time. I still read to them every night, and right now we're going through *Swiss Family Robinson*. Once a week we take in a show, usually a drive-in.

"They work for two hours a day scraping paint off a fence and a shed and get fifty cents a day for it. When we moved into the new house, I just took along some sticks of furniture, three beds, a few chairs, and a table. I'm letting them help me furnish it their way— piece by piece—and they have pretty damn good taste for kids of eight and nine.

"I wanted to take them to South America before I met Barbara. Perhaps we'll do that next spring. And eventually I want to buy a couple of horses so they can learn to ride. I've been teaching them to fish and hunt. They go on terrific rabbit hunts from which they come home with a lot of adventures and no rabbits."

When asked when Jennifer would be back to reclaim them, he'd reply without bitterness, "I really don't know. But right now they

have their nurse watching over them when I'm tied up at the studio. They're happy kids, and that's all that matters."

. (Many years later, when the grown Robert Walker, Jr., was asked about those days in Pacific Palisades, was shown pictures and reminded of anecdotes his father had so proudly recounted, he just shook his head and said, "No, I don't remember that." When pressed about events he did remember, he remarked enigmatically, "If an experience is painful, why relive it by talking about it? And if it is a happy personal one, why share it with strangers?" Shades of his father as a young man.)

Just before the completion of *Please Believe Me*, Bob was given his next assignment, the starring role in Dorothy Kingsley's *The Skipper Surprised His Wife*, a lightweight bit of nonsense about a Navy commander who tries to run his home like a ship when his wife is temporarily incapacitated. He was deeply disappointed that the studio hadn't come up with something better, but shrugged it off, concerned only that the title was too close to his previous *The Sailor Takes a Wife*.

Director Elliott Nugent's problem, however, had little to do with the picture's title, but rather with the choice of the right girl to play the surprised wife.

MGM's three sparkling ingenues, June Allyson, Janet Leigh, and Gloria DeHaven, all had previous commitments, so in spite of its enormous list of contractees, the studio had to resort to hiring free-lance actress Joan Leslie for the lead opposite Bob. Joan reminisces:

"*The Skipper Surprised His Wife* was very important to me. It was one of the first pictures I'd done after suing to be free of my Warner Brothers contract. For a while there was an unspoken agreement in Hollywood not to hire me, but when I got *Skipper* at the prestigious MGM, opposite Robert Walker, I figured things were going to be all right.

"Bob Walker was a darling person, so sincere, so considerate. I had just begun going with the man who would become my husband, and on the first day of shooting I received a beautiful bouquet of flowers with a card signed 'Love, Bill.' Now, Bill Caldwell was the name of my 'steady,' so that night, when we went out to dinner, I told him how much I loved the flowers and thanked him.

He didn't say anything, but sent me flowers the next day. I soon found out that the first flowers were from Bob Walker, who had signed the card 'Bill' because that was the name of his character in our picture.

"I think I could have become more personally involved with Bob if I hadn't been already committed. I had no idea then that Bob had recently come back from Menninger's. He did not seem troubled around me, only very sensitive.

"My mother died during the filming of *The Skipper Surprised His Wife*. She had been ill for some time—my sisters would be with her during the day, and I would go to her directly from the set every evening. When we finally lost her, I called the studio and said I wouldn't be in for a couple of days. When I returned, I remember telling Bob, 'It's a terrible thing, but you just have to go on, and, in time, I guess you get over it.'

"'No,' Bob replied, 'it's very hard for me to understand anything like that. I've never lost anyone that close to me. I don't think I could take it.'"

At the time, Joan Leslie wasn't aware of the peculiarity of Bob's remark. He *had* lost the person closest to him, Jennifer, and during the filming of *Skipper* there had been warning signals that he might soon lose the companionship of his sons.

Although Jennifer had been frustrated both by the delays and by the direction of *Gone to Earth*, she and David had decided that it would be advantageous for them to pursue their separate careers in Europe. Postwar production was booming, and David had sizable financial reserves abroad due to various laws forbidding removal of funds from overseas.

In mid-October Jennifer, miserable and guilty about not seeing Bobby and Michael for seven months, started making plans for their future: she and David would fly to California for the Christmas holidays, then return to Europe around the first of the year, taking both boys back with them for an indefinite stay.

The fact that she'd be disrupting their education at Black Fox Academy, as well as the stability of their life with their father, did not seem to matter. Nor is there any indication that she was concerned about the effect the separation might have on Bob's still delicately balanced mental health.

On October 20, shortly after learning about Jennifer's decision,

Bob narrowly escaped injury in another traffic accident. However, this time he was not at fault. While waiting for the signal to change at the corner of Wilshire and Beverly Glen Boulevard, his sedan was struck sharply in the rear by another automobile. Although the back of his car was savaged, he received only a few bruises and persuaded the police, who had been called to the scene, to let the other fellow off without a citation.

He was grateful the accident was of such a minor nature that he was able to return to work on schedule the following day.

During this period, he and Jim Henaghan remained close friends, but they did not see each other as frequently as in the pre-Menninger years. Jim was a "night person," and while working, Bob was determined to maintain an early-to-bed, early-to-rise schedule so as to be fresh and photogenic for the cameras.

The two friends kept in contact by phone, and Jim would drop by the house occasionally for coffee and small talk, but their drinking-buddy days seemed a thing of the past.

"Bob had calmed down considerably," Jim recalled. "He was even able to accept the fact that Jennifer would be depriving him of his sons for a year or so. Nevertheless, he was apprehensive about the influence Selznick would have on them. 'I've been making them earn their allowance so they will understand the value of money; that's something that man is oblivious of. This is such a crucial time in their lives. I don't want them to return spoiled rotten. But there's no point in becoming upset over something over which I have no control.'"

Bob also tried to conceal his disappointment when, after completing *The Skipper Surprised His Wife*, MGM had nothing for him on their immediate agenda.

From past experience he knew idleness was his deadly enemy. Schary, whose position at Metro was continuing to strengthen, assured him that there was no danger of his being let go when his option expired. A year earlier, the studio had bought Ross Lockridge's 1,110-page, sprawling best-seller, *Raintree County*, and the writing department had been struggling to turn the mammoth novel into a workable screenplay. Schary wanted Bob for the role of John Shawnessy, an idealistic Yankee schoolteacher enticed into a disastrous marriage by a neurotic Southern belle, but he had no inkling when the film would be ready to roll. He promised Bob

that when the time arrived the part would be his and that Bob would be a surefire candidate for an Oscar nomination. Hollywood talk, but Schary did not make idle promises.

(As it happened, *Raintree County* did not go into production until the spring of 1956. The ill-fated Montgomery Clift played Shawnessy.)

"In the meantime," Schary advised, "be patient. If you're wanted by another studio, we'll negotiate a loan-out. I know how important it is for you to keep busy." There were, however, no outside requests for Bob's services. The other major studios were hesitant about hiring an ex-drunk who had been in a mental hospital, in spite of repeated assurances that Bob was completely well again and not drinking.

On December 16 Bob's divorce from Barbara Ford became final, and although he was now a free man, he was still gun-shy about dating, despite urgings from Jim, Pete Lawford, and Ann Straus that he seek female companionship.

By now Peter was seriously involved with Sharman Douglas, the attractive daughter of Ambassador to Great Britain Lewis Douglas, and was willing to relinquish his cherished bachelor status if Sharman's parents granted their approval. At the time, Sharman was houseguesting with Elizabeth Firestone of the ultrasocial Firestone Tire family, and Peter was eager to play matchmaker for Bob. "Elizabeth is pretty and bright, and she's a great fan of yours. I know you two will hit it off. Let's make it a foursome for dinner some night. What do you have to lose?"

"Not yet," Bob stalled. "Perhaps after the boys leave for Europe. I don't want to complicate my life at the moment."

To Bob's surprise and relief, however, he learned through the boys' nurse that Jennifer and David had totally revised their plans. Although they still intended to be back in Los Angeles by Christmas, they had abandoned the idea of returning to Europe to pursue their careers.

Initially Bob presumed Jennifer might have had a change of heart about disrupting the boys' schooling, but through Jim's sources he quickly learned the actual facts.

When Selznick viewed the completed version of *Gone to Earth* (*The Wild Heart*), he was devastated. Under no circumstances would he permit Jennifer to be seen in such an unmitigated disas-

ter. Since he controlled the American release, he vehemently
insisted on remaking the movie *his* way and filming the revised
version in Hollywood under the direction of Rouben Mamoulian.
Only thirty-five minutes of the original two-hour-long production
were salvageable. A less emotional man would have shelved the
United States release completely, but David didn't want his wife
stigmatized in the eyes of the industry as having appeared in any
film so bad it couldn't be released. He arranged to rehire most of
the British cast, bring them to America, and reshoot the movie
after the holidays, in effect throwing good money after bad.

Bob didn't waste his time gloating over Selznick's embarrassment. He was too damn happy about not having Bobby and Michael spirited away from him. For the first time since 1942, he
actually enjoyed Christmas and looked forward to the dawn of the
new decade, the half-century mark.

"My seven years of bad luck are over," he told Jim. "I have such
good feelings about the fifties, about my life and my career.

"Who knows, I might even find the right girl. But if I do, I'm
going to be damn sure it's forever. I don't want to be hurt again,
and I don't want to hurt anyone else again, physically or mentally."

Early in the year, worn down by Peter Lawford's persistence,
Bob agreed to join him, Sharman Douglas, and Elizabeth Firestone for dinner, with the stipulation that they spend the evening
at an out-of-the-way bistro frequented by neither journalists nor
photographers. Peter hadn't exaggerated Miss Firestone's charm,
and within the month they had become a regular foursome.

Bob was still either unwilling or emotionally incapable of becoming deeply involved with Elizabeth Firestone. On the surface,
at least, she seemed content to enjoy his company without pinning
him down to any definite commitment. When cornered by a
columnist from *Motion Picture* magazine, who asked point-blank
if it was serious between him and Elizabeth, Bob merely smiled
and replied, "It's serious—for the moment—but not binding. Pete
and I aren't planning a double wedding, but I'm available to be
best man if he asks me."

Lawford's wedding plans foundered when he flew to London to
very properly ask Ambassador Douglas for Sharman's hand in
marriage and was met with fierce parental opposition. Shortly after

his return, for reasons disclosed by neither, Bob and Elizabeth Firestone amiably went their separate ways.

For a brief period Bob became attracted to Nancy Davis, an unexceptional but pleasant starlet under contract to Metro. She had come to Hollywood a few years after appearing on Broadway in a minor role in *Lute Song* with Mary Martin and Yul Brynner. Nancy had a down-to-earth, gentle charm which Bob found appealing, and it appeared that they had found something like romance, although Nancy was also dating the elusive, divorced Ronald Reagan. After his painful breakup with Jane Wyman, Reagan seemed more interested in playing the field than in being tied down to any special woman.

Ann Straus remembers that "Bob and Nancy had several dates." They, too, avoided being photographed, and both insisted that these dates were "purely professional." Whatever its status, the relationship also dissolved within a few months, long before her romance with Ronald Reagan became serious. Nancy and Bob liked each other a great deal, but their pleasant interlude didn't seem to generate any sparks. Nevertheless, Nancy was a stabilizing influence on Bob during the weeks they spent together.

Bob began to despair of regaining the emotional capacity to fall deeply in love again.

Now that Jennifer had charge of the boys, he began considering once more the month's return to Menninger's which he had spoken about earlier. There were still problems to be ironed out, and he felt the need for additional therapy.

He was advised, however, that it would be foolish to return to the Topeka clinic when there were so many excellent psychiatrists in the Beverly Hills area. Any one of them could help him through difficult periods or bouts of depression.

Louis B. Mayer, who had enlisted the services of the Vienna-born psychoanalyst Dr. Frederick Hacker to provide support to Judy Garland while she filmed *The Pirate* three years earlier, suggested Bob contact Hacker if he was really determined to resume analysis, although there was no guarantee that the busy therapist would be able to fit him in. Hacker was not the typical couch-and-yellow-pad analyst. In Garland's case, he actually visited the studio and watched the "dailies" with her to bolster her confidence. Hacker had many celebrities among his clientele, and, evidently

intrigued by Bob's case history, managed to find the time to treat him.

Other than to tell Jim Henaghan that he was under Hacker's care, Bob didn't discuss the details with anyone, except to admit that he "found them useful" and Dr. Hacker "extremely simpático."

Publicly Bob maintained a low profile throughout the spring of 1950. By now requests for interviews were almost nonexistent, his name noticeably absent from the gossip columns. He had not been seen on the screen for nearly a year and a half, and privately told Jim, "I wonder if I'll be able to draw a fly."

"Do you care?"

"I want to justify Schary's faith in me."

Schary, eager to make the public Walker-conscious again, scheduled June releases of *Please Believe Me* and *Skipper* within three weeks of each other. Both films were considered diverting summer fare, calculated to draw a healthy if not hefty audience.

Almost simultaneously, Bob was given his next assignment: as the conscienceless young bastard in Metro's adaptation of Luke Short's adult western novel *Vengeance Valley*, which was due to start shooting just outside of Canyon City, Colorado, in July. The story of the no-account son of a cattle baron, who impregnates a naive waitress and shifts the blame to his upstanding and patient foster brother, was ahead of its time. Although the character of Lee Strobie was similar to the part Bob had played in *The Sea of Grass*, it was a far more important—though not the starring—role. That went to Burt Lancaster, and to secure his services the studio had to guarantee him above-the-title billing, with the other leads relegated to costarring status below.

Bob didn't give a damn. "For a role like this, I wouldn't care if my name came last. I think I can act the hell out of it."

He was also pleased by the picture's projected schedule, which would provide a wonderful vacation for Bobby and Michael in the great outdoors and enable the boys to ride, rope, and hunt to their hearts' content while he was involved with some of the less palatable sequences.

With one notable exception, Bob had little off-the-set contact with the members of the cast or with the director, Richard Thorpe. Joanne Dru, who played his abused wife, was now married in real

life to John Ireland, the featured heavy in the film, but she was still close to Barbara Ford and was not inclined to socialize with Bob once the cameras stopped rolling.

The bulk of *Vengeance Valley* was shot during the month of August, the traditional month taken by psychiatrists for vacation, leaving their patients to cope with their own problems. However, Bob felt he hadn't a problem in the world that August of 1950. The chemistry between him and the rugged Lancaster was remarkable, both off camera and on, and the two became fast friends. (When the movie was released the following February, the New York *Times* noted that "Robert Walker plays the wastrel with almost as much authority as Lancaster does his protector.")

Jennifer voiced no objection to Bob's taking the boys to Colorado for the summer. Her plans to work exclusively in Europe were postponed yet a second time, when William Wyler, failing to obtain the services of Jeanne Crain from Darryl Zanuck, offered her the title role in *Carrie*, which was based on the Theodore Dreiser novel *Sister Carrie*.

Although Wyler had accepted David Selznick's advice to obtain Laurence Olivier for the male lead, the intimidating director told Selznick he wanted no further interference from him during the filming—and none of his memos.

The social comment of the classic novel was almost totally ignored in the screenplay. Instead, the plot focused exclusively on the story of an ambitious young woman and the aristocratic older man (Olivier) whose life is eventually destroyed because of his consuming passion for her.

By now Jennifer was desperately in need of a good picture, the services of an expert director, and the prestige of costarring with the newly knighted actor. Olivier told the press that the sole reason he had accepted the role of Hurstwood was to be with his wife, Vivien Leigh, who'd be working concurrently on *A Streetcar Named Desire*.

To Jennifer's dismay, just prior to starting *Carrie*, she recognized symptoms she hadn't experienced for a decade. A discreet visit to her private physician confirmed her suspicions. At age thirty-one she was pregnant again.

Although David, forty-eight, was bursting at the seams, positive

he'd be blessed with a little girl as beautiful as his wife, the event couldn't have come at a worse time for Jennifer. If she revealed her secret to William Wyler, it was possible she'd be replaced as Carrie. Abortion was out of the question. So she kept the news quiet, confident that the Edith Head turn-of-the-century costumes and heavy corsets would disguise her condition during the two and a half months required to complete the picture.

She might have pulled off the deception if it hadn't been for an anonymous tip received by Louella Parsons in late August. Parsons immediately reported Jennifer had absented herself from the set one day to see her doctor because she was "expecting a baby early the following year."

Jennifer issued a heated denial: "I wasn't needed in the scene being made that day, so I received permission to see my husband off to Europe."

When Wyler confronted her with the Parsons column, Jennifer confessed the rumors were true and admitted that she had been worried her pregnancy might cost her the role.

"Nonsense," he replied. "Camerawork can solve any problems that come up during the next month or so. But no picture, not even one of mine, is worth risking your health for."

However, it was impossible for her to relax—and she continued to wear the heavy corsets.

Although he never discussed her off-screen personality, Wyler would later laud her as an actress. "She was always a joy to direct, completely professional in her approach to her work . . . a perfectionist . . . always a little tense on the set and extremely conscientious, [yet] never quite satisfied with her work."

In spite of Wyler's patience and consideration, *Carrie* undermined Jennifer's physical well-being. The picture was completed in early November. On December 16, stricken with excruciating pain, Jennifer was rushed to Cedars of Lebanon Hospital in Los Angeles, where she suffered a miscarriage.

With the exception of her brokenhearted husband and her physician, who assured them both that Jennifer could bear other children in time, she discussed the bitter experience with no one.

As soon as she felt well enough to travel, she and David made plans to spend a relaxing holiday season abroad with Michael and Bobby. For the first time since embarking on her career, she felt no

compulsion to work, and David tried to spare her from the reality that there had been no requests for her services, especially after word had spread that both *The Wild Heart* and *Carrie* had been indefinitely shelved. Neither picture would be released for two years.

The year 1950 may have been a disastrous one for the Selznicks, but it was a triumphant year for Robert Walker. Just prior to the Christmas holidays he had completed the most challenging and rewarding role of his career. For the first time since arriving in Hollywood, he was able to look upon himself as an actor, not merely a movie star or personality kid.

In the fall of 1950, Alfred Hitchcock, whom Selznick had imported to Hollywood a decade earlier for *Rebecca*, was the man who performed the miracle.

Chapter

21

Bob, home from the Colorado location of *Vengeance Valley*, was astonished to learn that Alfred Hitchcock had requested his services for *Strangers on a Train*, a bizarre and soon-to-be-classic murder melodrama he was about to produce and direct for Warner Brothers. The role was that of a psychopathic playboy killer named Bruno Anthony, and, Dore Schary told him, Bob had been Hitchcock's only choice.

Excited though Bob was at the prospect of working with a director of such stature, he yet found Hitchcock's use of the term "casting against type" a little unflattering. Hadn't he just given a most convincing performance as an unmitigated bastard in *Vengeance Valley*?

A copy of the original work, Patricia Highsmith's 1950 novel, was sent to Bob with the message: "To help you get under the skin of the weirdo you'll be playing!" Reading the fascinating Highsmith book, Bob would soon discover that, in comparison with the absolute evil of Bruno, the Lee Strobie of *Vengeance Valley* was merely a disagreeable youth . . . and not at all a role to convince the hard-nosed Hitchcock that Bob had the potential to play his own opposite.

What, then, *had* enabled Hitchcock to see in Walker an actor capable of a performance that would so stridently negate his well-established "little-boy-lost" image? One can only speculate. Had Hitchcock seen the grotesque jailhouse picture (and who *hadn't* seen it)? Was Hitchcock cognizant of Bob's six-month confinement at Menninger's (and who wasn't), where not only had he been a mental patient himself but had had ample opportunity to observe a gamut of others?

Whatever the reason, it is an established fact that the duality of man's nature, his own included, had always fascinated Hitchcock. "Two people in each person," as Patricia Highsmith had written. The trick would be not so much "casting against type"—and thus forcing the actor to be what he wasn't—as stimulating Bob's access to his own darker side. If Hitchcock could manage to capture that darker side on film, he knew he would attain the definitive portrait of Bruno Anthony.

There could have been yet another reason for Hitchcock's determination to obtain Bob's services. Notorious for his strange and often cruel sense of humor, the director, still seething with antagonism toward David O. Selznick since their 1947 *Paradine Case* debacle, had to be aware of the delicious irony of casting the ex-husband of David's bride in a role guaranteed to send Bob's career soaring—a role which might even win him an Oscar nomination.

Famed detective novelist Raymond Chandler had been recruited the previous July to write the script. Chandler was still working on what was only a first draft, but the character, if not the fate, of Bruno Anthony was already perfectly crafted and just waiting for Bob's uncanny feel for the part to breathe life into it.

Although Jack Warner was bending to Hitchcock's will by arranging for MGM to loan Walker out—Warner had wanted the part to go to one of his own contract players—he refused to allow the director free rein in casting the other pivotal roles.

For example, Hitchcock wanted William Holden for Guy Haines, the romantic lead, but he was curtly informed that Holden would not be available—Warner instead choosing to use Holden for *Force of Arms*, an updated but watered-down and non-credited version of Ernest Hemingway's *A Farewell to Arms*. Warner also demanded that Ruth Roman be cast as the film's female lead, although Hitchcock felt that the earthy, brunette Miss Roman would be very much out of her element. In his mind's eye he saw a cool and classy "Hitchcock blond" in the part of socialite Anne Morton. Jack Warner got his way, though. In a final compromise, Farley Granger, whom Hitchcock had directed in *Rope* two years earlier, was signed to appear as Guy Haines.

Warner did not, however, interfere with Hitchcock's numerous alterations. In Highsmith's original novel, the drama was set in locales all over the USA. By limiting the exteriors to Washington,

D.C., Arlington, VA, western Connecticut, and Long Island, Hitchcock cut his location budget in half. He also changed Haines (Farley Granger) from an architect into a tennis pro. This switch enabled Hitchcock to stage a tennis match toward the end of the thriller that would provide an element of excruciating suspense, building then to a shockingly violent climax at an amusement park.

Despite these considerable manipulations, the basic theme of the story remained intact.

Two young men meet in the bar car of a train, have a few drinks, lunch together, and discuss their mutual problems. The clean-cut tennis player is having difficulties trying to convince his estranged, trampy wife to give him a divorce to free him to marry the girl he loves.

The outwardly good-natured rich boy (Bruno) is filled with paranoid hatred for his father, who he feels is interfering with his life. Bruno then seriously suggests that the two swap murders: Bruno to kill Guy's wife, and Guy in turn to kill Bruno's despised father. Neither would be caught, since there would then be no motive to link either murderer to his victim.

Horrified, Guy dismisses Bruno as a lunatic. Obsessed with the scheme, however, Bruno stalks and strangles Guy's wife, then tries to threaten Guy into fulfilling his part of the "bargain." When Guy fails to do so, Bruno devises a fiendish plot to provide the necessary proof that Guy murdered his wife.

Jim Henaghan recalled that, "During all the time I knew him, Bob had never shown any excitement about a part or a picture. But he was damned excited about *Strangers* and about the prospect of working with Alfred Hitchcock, and vastly flattered that Hitchcock had wanted only him. As I've said, Bob was the last person to be impressed by his own career—he considered acting a crock. Suddenly there was a radical change in his attitude. Now, for the first time, he wanted to be accepted as a *real* actor.

"One weekend, on the spur of the moment, we drove down to the Army and Navy Academy at Carlsbad and made the rounds of the school property, unnoticed, while he pointed out familiar buildings and landmarks. He told me many things about his time there and of his best-actor awards. He wanted to visit his former

drama teacher, a Mrs. Atkinson, but because it was a weekend, she couldn't be located, and he said wistfully, 'I'd like to win one more award for her.'

"I don't know if Bob was aware Jennifer was expecting Selznick's child. Neither of us ever discussed the subject. He was still making regular visits to Dr. Hacker 'to keep on an even keel,' he explained, adding, 'and I'm pumping him about psychopaths . . . research for the role.'

"As for his drinking at this time, he'd have a glass or two of sherry every so often, but it didn't affect his behavior. With or without the sherry, his conversation was single-track. All he wanted to talk about was *Strangers on a Train*. In the past he rarely, if ever, discussed his films except to deprecate them. But *Strangers* was different, and he couldn't wait to get his hands on the finished script."

Neither could Alfred Hitchcock!

In late September, after returning to Hollywood from location-scouting in the East, Hitchcock read Chandler's second draft and was appalled by what had happened to the screenplay.

In Hitchcock's estimation, it was barely coherent. In a desperate effort to salvage the production, which Jack Warner was even threatening to cancel, Hitchcock dismissed the renowned Chandler and hired Czenzi Ormonde, one of Ben Hecht's assistants, to pull the story together and, with Barbara Keon, to sharpen the dialogue. Working around the clock at home, Hitchcock enlisted his wife Alma's aid to clarify scene divisions and sequence specifications. On October 17 Hitchcock, convinced that he now had a workable script, returned to New York, together with Bob, Farley Granger, and several key members of the crew, to commence filming on location.

During the week of October 20, scenes were shot at New York's Pennsylvania Station, the Danbury, Connecticut, railroad depot, and the Jefferson Memorial and various other Washington, D.C., sites. By the end of the month the company returned to Burbank for interior filming.

Reminiscing about the two months that followed, Farley Granger says, "I thought the world of Robert Walker from the very beginning.

"He was *such* a nice man, so wonderful, and such a fine actor.

Very professional . . . totally in control . . . always on time . . . never temperamental. No problem at all. He was great in the film; his potential was limitless. His career was just beginning to take wings.

"Bob never discussed his past troubles, and there was no indication of the troubles to come."

Farley also remembers "dining with Bob at the Hitchcocks' home. You might expect the man to unbend. But the conversation was invariably limited to the amenities—and the picture. Always the picture. Mr. Hitchcock would bring up a topic for discussion, listen to our comments, then add his own. He was every bit as much the director at dinner as he was on the set. Full of ideas, animated, gesturing. But socially detached."

Farley also recalls that of all the cast, "Hitchcock outspokenly singled out Ruth Roman for harsh criticism. He had to have one player in each film he could harass.

"But Bob was very happy working with Hitchcock, and it was evident that Hitch was happy working with him."

Everyone connected with *Strangers on a Train* adored Bob. "A very sweet guy," Ruth Roman told a visiting reporter, Erskine Johnson, and Hitchcock was overheard to chide him with wry but affectionate amusement, "You and your quiet dignity!"

When the unit publicist told the reporter, with whom he'd been chatting between takes, "You don't hear much about Bob after working hours. He doesn't expose himself the way a lot of actors do," Bob, with no little amusement, responded, "Brother, I've *done* my exposing. Now I'm concentrating on my lines." When Johnson reminded Bob about earlier reports of his temperament, Bob scoffed: "Temperament. That's a lot of horsefeathers. Years ago I worried about the things that were written about me. Now I don't care. I'm a darn good father. I mind my own business. My last few pictures at MGM couldn't have gone more beautifully, and this loan-out to Alfred Hitchcock is fine too. Do you know the only thing that would get a rise out of me? If someone wrote that I was a lousy actor. Otherwise, I don't care."

Queried about his reputation for moodiness, Bob retorted, "Who isn't moody? Anybody going round happy all day is nuts."

He did more than just concentrate on what was in the script. According to film historian Donald Spoto, during sessions with

Hitchcock, "The two worked out a series of subtle gestures with which they hoped to bypass the censors' rumblings about the sub-theme of a homosexual courtship." These not only got by the eagle eyes of the censors but escaped the notice of critics and audiences of the period as well. Decades later, after *Strangers* became a cult classic, the issue of Bruno's homosexuality would be discussed and written about extensively, the subject of heated de-bates.

Though everyone connected with the production—including Jack Warner, cameraman Robert Burks, and even Hitchcock's own daughter, Patricia (who played Ruth Roman's kid sister)—was aware of the unusual favoritism Hitch lavished on Bob, no one resented it or him. It was that obvious that his dazzling perfor-mance would be the major ingredient in the film's success. And it was.

Except for a few finishing touches, filming was completed by Christmas, and although Bob was not in the audience to view the first sneak preview at the Huntington Park Theater on March 5, it didn't take him long to feel the delicious warmth of the audience "comment cards." One and all, they abounded with such words as "a revelation," "chilling," "remarkable."

Modestly Bob told Jim, "It's all due to Alfred Hitchcock's ge-nius." Jim reacted angrily, "Don't be so goddamn humble. The fat slob had four flops in a row before *you* came into his life, and Jack Warner's gnashing his teeth that he hasn't a piece of your contract. I just hope those bastards at Metro will appreciate you now. You're a shoo-in for an Oscar nomination."

"Don't bet on it," Bob replied. "But I'd like one. Who knows if I'll ever get another crack at it."

Although his reviews were every bit as effusive as the preview cards had been, Bob was *not* nominated for a 1951 Oscar, how-ever. Warner Brothers couldn't be expected to push a rival studio's player when Marlon Brando was in contention for *A Streetcar Named Desire*. (Brando was narrowly defeated by Humphrey Bogart, who won for *The African Queen*.)

Nevertheless, Bob's Bruno Anthony left an indelible impression on the minds of audiences young and old.

David Newman, a writer-director whose screenplays include *Bonnie and Clyde*, *What's Up, Doc?*, and *Superman*, would later

write, "On the simplest level, the choice of Walker as Bruno, the sinister, charming, psychotic, Oedipal maniac, was the quintessence of 'casting against type.'

". . . It took a Hitchcock . . . to cast Bob in a role that was a revelation for everyone concerned, not least for Walker himself. And what a perfect performance for its [our] time. In a culture that was beginning to pride itself on neurotic self-awareness, here was our symbol—that edgy, psyched-out, psyched-up, fey, genuinely violent personality who appealed to old ladies. The homosexual thing, barely disguised, was the wild card there, and why hadn't we noticed it before, hey? It was a case of a director defining for the first time precisely that unexpected quality in an actor which would determine his 'persona' from that day forward. Bob had found the role of his lifetime—which he must have known."

And the ever-so-hard-to-please Pauline Kael would be equally enthusiastic in her *5001 Nights at the Movies*. She wrote ". . . Robert Walker brought sportive originality to the role of the chilling wit, dear degenerate Bruno. . . . Technically the climax of the film is the celebrated runaway merry-go-round . . . [but] even this high point isn't what we remember best—which is Robert Walker. It isn't often that people think about a performance in a Hitchcock movie; usually what we recall are bits of 'business' . . . Walker's performance is what gives this movie much of its character and its peculiar charm."

Shakespeare wrote, "There is a tide in the affairs of men, which, taken at the flood, leads on to fortune." Bob was riding that tide— eager to keep working—in an up mood in those early months of 1951. Ida Lupino recalls his telling her, "I'm thrilled about *Strangers on a Train*. My career has never been more stimulating. This is going to be my best year."

But the tide was running out for Robert Hudson Walker, and his "best year" was going to be his last year.

Chapter

22

During the months following her miscarriage, Jennifer Jones suffered a depression. Nervous and listless, she rarely left the Selznick dwelling, and David encouraged a prolonged rest.

Occasionally she'd invite a few of her and David's close friends—the Cottens, the Jourdans, Charles Bickford and his wife, Beatrice—to dine with them. More often, she'd shut out the world, listening to music with her husband or embroidering. When Bobby and Michael returned to Black Fox after the family's brief Christmas abroad, time lay even more heavily on her hands.

She was still very much into yoga, which provided some little peace of mind, but as she approached thirty-two, there was no way to escape the sinking awareness that her career stood at its lowest ebb in eight years. Both *The Wild Heart* and *Carrie* were gathering dust in their studio vaults, and she had no clue to when either might be released—or to when she'd be offered another role.

David Selznick, still deeply in debt, had vowed he wouldn't produce another picture until he was once more completely solvent. To maintain his extravagant life-style, he continued to sell off his remaining properties. Whether—or how much—Jennifer contributed to running the household is not known. It is, however, most unlikely that she paid the bills for the gifts Selznick continued to shower upon Irene—gifts which she claimed were often accompanied by a card signed "Bigamist."

Although their professional lives were in decline, the Selznicks continued to receive numerous invitations to large parties, charity and industry functions. Mostly, Jennifer refused. Her preference for seclusion became a subject of contention between the couple. When an invitation proved too irresistible for David, he'd show up

stag, inventing plausible excuses for his wife's absence. Still a gregarious man, he missed the life that he had once lived to the hilt, the shop talk, the camaraderie with his friends and rivals. And he was always on the alert for news of a property that might prove suitable for Jennifer: a blockbuster that would boost her faltering career and revive her flagging spirit.

He dismissed the slump in his own fortunes with a flippant "I'm enjoying the freedom and relish having the time to do things I never managed to do before." In truth, the dimming of his creative vigor, the loss of his apparent infallibility, were corroding his exalted vision of himself. He somehow still managed a cheerful front—and indeed he still controlled the one possession closest to his heart. He still possessed Jennifer.

Ironically, during the period when Jennifer was merely existing from day to day, Bob Walker was outwardly enjoying life to the fullest.

Dore Schary, gaining ground in the power struggle for control of MGM, assured Bob that although there was nothing important enough for him on the studio's 1951 production schedule, the other studios had been put on alert that he was available for loan-out—but only for a role that would add luster to his stunning comeback.

Bob's desire to keep working was at its peak, and once again he was in a mood to play. He began opening up to friends, old and new, of both sexes.

Sharlee Hudson, who'd marry Keenan Wynn in 1954, recalls, "I was born and raised in the Los Angeles area, but I was not in show business. I met Bob on the beach through Peter Lawford, not long after Bob completed *Strangers on a Train*, and we dated a number of times. He had many friends, including Burt Lancaster, whom I used to see at his house quite often. But usually we'd go off in a group to Ciro's or the Mocambo. Peter was often with us, as were Gary Cooper and his wife, Rocky, who were also friends of Bob. He was drinking on and off, but not bad, and we all had a wonderful time. Our relationship wasn't serious, just fun, and I remember his teasing me that I had the same last name as his middle name—Hudson. At that time, he had a wonderful Filipino houseman named Pete, who took care of him and the boys when they stayed over on weekends. Jennifer's elderly Swedish

housekeeper would come along, too, and help out. He had such a lovely relationship with his sons, but I never heard him mention their mother at all, not even in passing.

"To me, Bob was a divine, marvelous man with a most attractive quality about him. He didn't have a mean bone in his body."

Sharlee Hudson Wynn didn't mention why the two stopped dating, but there was a very definite reason. Bob had met a new girl: a quiet, gentle divorcée named Kay Scott Nearny.

Not surprisingly, it was Jim Henaghan, by now emotionally involved with a woman of his own, who again played matchmaker.

Jim recalled: "I met Kay, a former starlet, through her mother, who was the switchboard operator at Paramount. She was a pretty young thing, quite affable and soft-spoken. I thought Bob might like her, so I set up an introduction. The two were suddenly inseparable. I know Kay wanted to marry him and that Bob wanted to remarry eventually. But before committing himself, he needed to be convinced of the wisdom of his choice. On the surface, Kay seemed happy with the relationship the way it was going." Coincidentally, producer Sam Marx, who also knew Kay very well, says, "Kay was a rather delicate girl, charming too; they made a very lovely couple. She was devoted to Bob and I know he must have been to her. According to Kay, however, Bob was still in need of psychiatric help, and certainly she was in a position to know.

"Kay was a talented writer, and she also wanted to try her hand at composing. I got her a job at Universal scoring a movie, but, unfortunately, the film never went into production.

"She was very knowledgeable about composers, and damned intelligent. She reminded me and others of a young Margaret Sullavan type: she had a mop of brownish blond hair, pert looks, and was a tiny five feet tall. I don't think any man she knew failed to think highly of her. Everything about her slim figure and bearing reflected class. Bobby Walker's feelings toward her were very, very strong.

"Bob and Kay avoided nightclubs. He preferred spending intimate evenings at her house, listening as she played Chopin and Debussy on her piano. I'm surprised in a way that, when she and Bob came together, it wasn't enough to set his life straight. I could

tell how strongly she felt for him, and I can only believe that he shared those feelings."

Bob was already dating Kay exclusively when he received word that Paramount wanted him to play John Jefferson, the male lead in Oscar-winner Leo McCarey's production of the controversial anti-Communist melodrama *My Son John*. America's "first lady of the theater," Helen Hayes, who had been absent from the screen for seventeen years (except for a cameo in *Stage Door Canteen*), was signed to play John's tormented mother.

Apolitical, Bob was immune to the "better-dead-than-Red" hysteria then sweeping Hollywood, and although he considered the script an overemotional dose of propaganda, he was excited at the prospect of working opposite Miss Hayes.

McCarey had chosen his cast with an eye for credentials. In addition to Helen Hayes, who'd won the 1931 Best Actress Oscar, Dean Jagger, cast as Bob's father, and Van Heflin, the FBI man, had each earned supporting Oscars. McCarey's opinion was that Bob's performance in *My Son John* would raise the cast's trophy total to four.

The script set up a series of opposing views: Americanism versus Communism, Catholicism versus atheism, anti-intellectualism versus intellectualism, and came down firmly on the side of the former in each case.

The Jefferson family (bearing the same name as the author of the Declaration of Independence) enshrine all that is best in Americanism. They live in a small town. Father, Dan Jefferson, is a staunch member of the American Legion and superintendent of the local school. Mother, Lucille, is revered by the rest of the family as the classic All-American Mom. Her entire world and outlook are summed up by the Bible and the cookbook. The two younger sons, Chuck and Ben, are just off to serve their country, fighting Communism in Korea.

However, the family nurses a viper in its bosom, the eldest son, brilliant young government official John, who is in fact a Communist. When his mother learns this, she is prepared to hand him over to the authorities for treason but persuades him to give himself up. Before he can do so, he is gunned down in the street by a carload of Communists.

Before he dies, John records a speech to be delivered at his old university. In this speech he declares that he had always prided himself on being an intellectual and had thus gone astray. He denounces intellectuals as being at the root of the country's troubles and actually refers to the Communists in true nonintellectual fashion as "scummies."

My Son John began production in late spring and initially everything progressed smoothly. Kay Scott visited the set whenever she could, and one Saturday afternoon, when he was filming a sympathetic scene, Bob brought Bobby and Michael, decked out in their spiffy academy uniforms, to Paramount. They had been dying to watch their dad making a movie, and he was so pleased by their approval that he encouraged the picture's still photographer to take some shots of the three of them together as a memento of the afternoon.

As spring drew to a close, he looked forward to having Bobby and Michael with him for the entire summer. When he wasn't on call for the picture, Kay and he would drive north in search of a suitable vacation retreat. To be suitable, such a retreat could be nothing less than a full-fledged ranch with ample stables. Ever since their stay in Colorado, the boys had talked endlessly about having their own horses.

In the meantime, frustrated by her inactivity and lack of job offers and anxious to do something positive with her life, Jennifer volunteered to tour American military hospitals in Tokyo and Korea. In mid-May she left for the Far East in an unpublicized mission to help cheer thousands of wounded Americans. For her untiring efforts she received a gold medal from General James Van Fleet, field commander of the United Nations forces, as well as a citation from the American Red Cross.

When Selznick was invited to attend the Venice Film Festival, scheduled for late August, Jennifer agreed to accompany him abroad, despite her undiminished distaste for such circuses. She simply had to do something, *anything*, to muffle her fears that her career was over. David constantly assured her those fears would prove to be unfounded; that once *Carrie* was released she'd be in demand again. (*Carrie*, however, wasn't released until June 1952.)

By now Bob was becoming increasingly disenchanted with *My Son John*. Especially abrasive was his director's maniacal pursuit of his "message." So obsessed was McCarey with hammering fear of Godless Communism into the public's psyche that he seemed to abandon all proper concern for the vulnerable psyches of his own often bewildered cast.

Having worked with Hitchcock, who had every detail of every scene letter perfect before the cameras started rolling, Bob found it difficult and often confusing to be confronted by McCarey's well-known passion for improvisation. From day to day the cast never knew which lines would be revised on the spot, what bits of business would be radically changed.

Typically, McCarey offered no explanations for his sudden brainstorms and turned a deaf ear to protests—a mannerism that rattled even the ultraprofessional Miss Hayes.

Van Heflin, who in *Till the Clouds Roll By* had portrayed Bob's mentor, was now cast as his bitter and ultimately triumphant adversary. He had also played Jennifer's cuckolded husband in *Madame Bovary*, his final appearance on the Metro lot. Understandably, Jennifer's name never came up in their conversations, but they didn't lack for other subjects to hash over, such as their gripes about their current movie—or the expected but unnecessarily brutal ouster of Louis B. Mayer in July from the company which he had co-founded. Bob found it difficult to shed tears over Mayer's fate, remarking coldly, "Nothing lasts forever!"

Although the two men admired one another, Bob's and Heflin's relationship didn't extend beyond the studio gates. For reasons he was unable to explain, Bob found himself uncomfortable—the proverbial fifth wheel—in the company of happily married couples.

Since Bob was still in production when Michael and Bobby returned to his home in Pacific Palisades, he hired Emily Buck, who had previously worked as governess to Margaret Sullavan and Leland Hayward's children, Brooke, Bridget, and Bill. She would be his housekeeper, replacing his houseman, Pete, but would also keep a sharp eye on the boys while he was at the studio. As soon as

he was dismissed from the set, he'd go home to have supper and romp in the pool with them.

Speaking of those relatively untroubled days, Bob's friend Keenan Wynn remembers that "Although I hadn't seen much of him after his return from Menninger's, he called me often during the summer of 1951. I had my boys, Ed and Tracy, with me at the time, too, and since Bob had a pool at his place, and I didn't, he suggested we all get together as much as possible. However, it never happened. I was working on *Phone Call from a Stranger* opposite Bette Davis and, for some reason or other, never managed to take advantage of those invitations.

"But he sounded like his old self whenever we spoke—and I know that, by then, drinking was no longer a problem for him. He also never discussed his stay at Menninger's, but then, I never asked him about it. And even though he talked a great deal about his sons, he *never* discussed Jennifer. It was a forbidden subject. He wouldn't dignify the sorry situation by discussing it, a decision on his part that I understood and respected."

Often, on weekends, Bob would drive the boys to Jim Henaghan's Malibu Beach house and relax on a stretch of white sand near the porch, keeping a close lookout while Michael and Bobby clowned in the surf.

Henaghan, looking back at that summer, said, "He wasn't remotely worried that he didn't have another film immediately on the horizon. He had such great faith in Schary, who was now at the helm at Metro, that he was confident that his career would continue on the upswing. His relationship with Kay was going smoothly—I don't think they ever had an argument—and he was now able to cope with his parents, as long as they remained at a safe distance.

"He bitched a great deal about McCarey's directorial shortcomings, but I dismissed his Leo-phobia as a normal occupational disease, and his expressions of disdain were always laced with good, healthy Walker humor. He was richly amused by McCarey's bombastic climax for the film, in which John Jefferson's (Bob's) former Commie comrades gun him down in the very shadow of the Lincoln Memorial. Called it 'corny, comic-strip symbolism.'"

McCarey, though, was very pleased with his creation, considering it a major contribution to the country's awareness of the Red

Menace. He was excited, too, by the strong performances he had elicited from his four gifted leads. Later, after he had won an Oscar nomination for his story, he'd say that if he hadn't had to make some unexpected revisions and resort to awkward patchwork for some sequences, "It might have been my greatest film."

Of Bob he'd reminisce: "I worked closely with him and learned to know him as a fine gentleman and a great actor.

"We had a working session together on Saturday [August 15]. At that time he showed no indication of being in ill health. On the contrary, he did his recording [the voice-over of John's recantation of his communistic philosophy] with great zest. I had just run a rough cut of the picture for him, and although a modest fellow, he fairly beamed at the results."

Although a few key scenes requiring his services still remained to be shot, Bob was informed he would not be on call for several weeks.

He drove out of the DeMille Gate in a jubilant mood and raced his Cadillac west on Sunset Boulevard, impatient to reach home before dusk in order to have a quick swim with Bobby and Michael before dinner. He'd granted them permission to spend a few days the following week with a couple of their buddies. Remembering the loneliness of his own youth, Bob went out of his way to foster his sons' friendships. After getting them to bed, he took off to Kay's, where they had a quiet dinner together, now a regular Saturday-night ritual.

Sam Marx recalls, "Years later, after she had married composer Leonard Rosenman and was living in Italy, I ran into Kay on a wintry day on the Via Veneto in Rome. We went to a charming café overlooking the Tiber and she reflected on Bobby, very sadly, admitting that although she was happy with Leonard, she had never forgotten that last night she had spent with Walker and often wondered about 'what might have been!'"

There'd be so many people who'd think about Robert Walker and wonder about "what might have been," the happiness he might have attained, the heights he could have reached: his sons, Jim Henaghan, Dore Schary, Barbara Ford, and probably even Jennifer Jones. If only . . .

23

The morning of August 28 was chilly under a pall of threatening skies. A deep fog rolled in from the Pacific, engulfing an area that extended from the beach to Beverly Hills. Unusual California weather for that time of the year.

It was an oppressive day, which became even more dispiriting after the torrential rain began.

Since he was not required at Paramount, Bob slept late. With his sons away, the house was morbidly quiet.

Emily Buck fixed him his usual light breakfast of juice and coffee and went about her household chores. Suffering the let-down that normally follows weeks of frantic activity, and confined to the house because of the weather, Bob became increasingly bored and restless. With Kay and Jim both at work and unable to get away, he was at loose ends.

At two P.M. he received a phone call from his business manager, Charles Trezona, with whom he had several minor financial matters to discuss.

Trezona recalled, "When we spoke, he appeared okay. Just fine. I don't believe he was drinking, and I'd known Bob long enough and well enough to be able to detect when he had had a few drinks."

The events of the next four hours of Bob Walker's life would forever be shrouded in mystery and subject to conjecture.

Was it possible that Jennifer Jones, preparing to leave for Italy, had called the house to bid farewell to her sons, only to discover that they were off visiting? If so, could Bob have spoken to his ex-wife, and if he had, would that have been enough to "set him off"? There was no evidence that such a call was made. Just a pos-

sibility. One thing is certain. He had no visitors that afternoon, no upsetting mail.

According to news reports, at six P.M. Bob's psychiatrist, Frederick Hacker, received an alarmed summons from Emily Buck imploring him to come to the house immediately, claiming—allegedly—that her employer was so distraught and out of control that she could not cope with him.

Hacker agreed to make the house call.

Such is the media version of the first of a bewildering series of events that culminated in the final agony of Robert Hudson Walker. Yet Jim Henaghan explicitly recalls, "On my way home from work, I dropped in on Bob for a drink and a quick hello. He was in the dining nook playing cards with his housekeeper, and he seemed quite normal to me . . . for Walker, *quite* normal.

"A few minutes later, Hacker entered the room. And I said, 'Oh wow! Listen, loony, if you're going to be seeing a crazy-doctor, I'm going to split.' And Hacker said, 'Please, please stay and help me get him into bed.' Hacker and I talked for a minute or two. Then Dr. Sidney Silver, an associate of his, arrived. The two doctors agreed that Bob needed a hypodermic shot of a sedative—sodium amytal—to calm him down and put him to sleep.

"Bob refused to agree to the injection, and he bolted outdoors. It was pouring, and I was in a hurry to get home.

"'Oh no, you don't,' he replied. And he took off his glasses and handed them to Dr. Hacker. 'And you're not big enough to make me.'

"I asked Hacker, 'Does he really need it?' and Hacker replied, 'Yes, he really needs it.'

"I picked Bob up, carried him struggling back into the house, and threw him onto the bed, pinning him down, and said firmly, 'Now, take this shot!'

"By this time, he was laughing. 'But I don't want it. It's not necessary.' Aside from resisting the medication, he didn't seem the slightest, the least bit disturbed to me. But the doctors began the injection, and he taunted them with 'You can't even find the vein.'

"But they found it, the fluid was injected, and Bob immediately passed out. I started to put a blanket over him, when Dr. Hacker noticed something was wrong and asked me to call Silver back into the room. Quickly.

"It was bewildering. Bob appeared to have stopped breathing." The doctors began artificial respiration. Jim called the fire department's emergency squad. It seemed an eternity before sirens were heard on the highway, but the truck veered off in the wrong direction. Jim ran half a mile up the road and caught up with the squad as they were turning around, and directed them to the house.

The squad went to work on Bob, but when Jim asked Silver and Hacker how things looked, they grimly replied, "Bad."

Jim refused to accept the gloomy assessment. In desperation he phoned Dr. Myron Prinzmetal, who was then considered one of the most brilliant internists in Beverly Hills.

"I asked him to come out immediately. He said he couldn't, and I replied, 'Well, I'm coming to get you, baby.' I drove like a maniac to his house and pounded on his door until he opened it. Then I shoved him into my car and sped about a hundred miles an hour back to Pacific Palisades. I left him in Bob's bedroom. A moment later the three doctors were in conference in the bathroom. When they emerged, looking defeated, I asked, 'Well, what's the matter? Can't you do anything for him?'

"Prinzmetal looked at me oddly and said, 'The man is dead. He's been dead for more than an hour.' It was now slightly past ten P.M.

"I broke the news to Emily. She had Bob's address book, and I asked her to contact Bob's parents at the Ben Lomond Hotel in Ogden. Then I phoned Dore Schary, told him Bob was dead, and asked him to come to the house immediately. It was too late to call Bobby and Michael. I planned to get to them before they heard the news in the morning from some other source.

"Then I returned to Bob's bedroom and uncovered his face. I spoke to him as if he could hear me. And I thought about the events leading up to his needless death. I saw it happen. And I had held him down. I could have stopped them. But I allowed it. I felt like a murderer. I sat there reflecting numbly.

"Hacker had been walking around the lawn without a coat, walking around in a daze, soaked to the skin. The other doctor, Silver, well, he was pretty shaken up too."

"I was filled with anger, crushed with sorrow. I poured myself a drink. Then I thought of that outrageous running gag Bob and I

had shared for so many years, the one in which we were always accusing one another of looting the other's possessions.

"I remembered that crazy night when he came to after sleeping off a binge at my place, and he said, 'If I was to die in my sleep, the first thing you'd do is rifle my pockets,' and I had laughed uproariously at the thought.

"I returned to the bedroom and went through his trousers. There was no money in his pockets. So I stole his watch and left.

"On my way home, I was sure I could hear him screaming, 'You bastard! I knew you'd do it!'"

At dawn Bob's body was removed from the house at 14238 Sunset Boulevard to a nearby funeral parlor. A few hours later, his mother and father boarded a plane to Los Angeles.

Jennifer and David Selznick, after being notified of Bob's death, canceled their trip to Venice and booked passage home.

Grief-stricken, Kay Scott was among the first arrivals at the mortuary. In a candlelit room she viewed the remains of the man she had hoped to marry. He had been conservatively dressed in a blue suit, white shirt, and dark tie. There were only a few persons Bob would have recognized among those who filed by. She remained with him for an hour, blinded by tears.

Dazed and tormented with guilt, Henaghan did not wish to view his friend's body for this one final time. Nor would he attend the funeral.

Charles Trezona and his wife met Bob's parents at Los Angeles International Airport and drove them directly to the mortuary, where, deeply shaken, they made arrangements for Bob to be buried at Forest Lawn Memorial Park at three P.M. Friday, September 1.

An hour after the senior Walkers had been picked up at the airport, Jennifer, in dark glasses, and David Selznick stepped down from their plane and, ignoring the reporters who bombarded them with questions, hastily strode to a waiting limousine and drove off to gather up her inconsolable sons and spirit them away to the privacy of the Selznick home. However, the grief that his boys, and all those close to Bob, would have preferred to suffer in private was already a matter of public concern and curiosity.

The MGM publicity department was being peppered with questions—questions that they were incapable of answering.

Dr. Hacker was called in. With the coroner, he had co-signed the death certificate, which stated that Bob had "died of natural causes after receiving a dose of sodium amytal and had been a victim of schizophrenia of an undiagnosed nature." With Dr. Silver at his side, he related to reporters his version of the tragic events that had taken place the night before.

"His housekeeper, Mrs. Emily Buck, called me about six o'clock last night. Walker was in a highly emotional state when I reached him. He kept saying, 'I feel terrible, Doc. Do something quick.'"

He said that he did not know whether the actor had been drinking.

"I called Dr. Silver to administer sodium amytal," he continued. "We had given him this sedative twenty-five to thirty times in the past without ill effect. The dosage was seven and a half grains. Often we have given him as much."

Almost immediately, the doctor said, Walker turned blue and there was respiratory failure.

Dr. Silver confirmed Hacker's explanation and added: "When Dr. Hacker felt a sedative was indicated, he called me.

"Walker was in a very emotional condition. We gave him an intravenous injection of seven and a half grains of sodium amytal. Many times before, we had given him a similar treatment, and he always reacted successfully and well, by falling asleep and waking relieved and refreshed.

"In this instance, however, the patient soon showed signs of respiratory failure. Not choking. We gave artificial respiration, then called the rescue squad.

"Fatal effect of the drug happens now and then, unfortunately. Perhaps once in ten thousand times it acts on the brain's respiratory center. While Walker had neither taken nor been given any drug from the time Dr. Hacker arrived at his home at about six P.M., neither of us knew whether or not he had taken any preparation of any kind prior to that hour."

Confirming Hacker's and Silver's assurance that a dosage of seven and a half grains was not excessive was the statement made by Coroner's Autopsy Surgeon Victor Cefalu. He said that "it

would require a dose of about fifteen grains of sodium amytal for that drug to become toxic. The normal dose—for sedation—is about three grains. However, seven and a half is not an abnormal amount to administer when the patient is extremely emotional."

When an autopsy was suggested, both Hacker and Silver agreed that the procedure was unnecessary and would not be performed unless Bob's family absolutely insisted.

Hacker was not queried about a cause for Walker's emotional upset. As for Emily Buck—presumably his sole companion before Jim and the doctors arrived—she preferred not to speak about the events that transpired on the afternoon of the tragic death.

Inexplicably, there was no mention of Jim Henaghan's participation in the events of that fatal evening. The fact that Jim had held Bob down while the injection was administered, or even his presence in the house when Bob died, was not put on the record.

Jim's story, however, has been confirmed by his ex-wife, Gwen Verdon, and other close friends.

In addition, though no reference was made to Dore Schary's appearance on the scene, in his autobiography, *Heyday*, the late Mr. Schary related: "One rainy night on my immediate return from a preview the phone rang and when I answered, a voice shouted, 'Dore—Bob's dead—Bob's dead. It was . . . Red Henaghan, who, through his tears and screams, told me he was in Bob's house. I hung up, got into my car, and rushed to the Uplifter's Ranch, only a mile away. The door to the house was open. Bob's doctor was standing there with his young assistant. They were both in shock. I pushed by them and went into Bob's bedroom, where Henaghan was sitting in a chair and sobbing. Bob was on the bed. He was wearing moccasins, slacks, a plaid woolen shirt with the left sleeve rolled up. There were bloodstains on his arm and the bed. Bob was dead.

"The doctors gave me the story. Henaghan had called because Bob had been drinking and getting violent. They had arrived and got Bob to lie down while they administered a shot of sodium penathol. [Author's note: It was definitely sodium amytal.] Some doctors choose not to run the risk of using such a drug in treating someone who has been drinking. It is not always a fatal risk, but according to some doctors, it is advisable to have oxygen handy when using the drug because of the danger that the depressive

effect of the drug, added to the depressive effect of a large amount of alcohol (which Bob had ingested), might cause a respiratory arrest.

"Metro's police chief, Whitey Henry . . . advised me to let them take over the rest of the unhappy details and go home."

Yet another anomaly was that no reports revealed that the eminent Dr. Prinzmetal had been brought into the case in that desperate but futile attempt to save Bob's life. The only time Prinzmetal's name appeared in print was in an "In Memoriam" magazine piece Jim wrote, "partly as a catharsis but mainly because I wanted the public to understand Bob."

What really happened? Here are three different versions. The last day of Robert Walker's life may always be shrouded in mystery.

On the morning of August 30 Jennifer accompanied her sons to Pacific Palisades and helped them gather and pack all their belongings brought to Bob's house when they had moved in for their happy summer vacation. She did not take them—nor allow anyone else to take them—to the mortuary. She'd later explain, in her only public comment, "I wanted them to remember their father the way he was."

Early in the afternoon of the same day, Horace and Zella Walker abruptly canceled all the arrangements that had been made for Bob's burial at Forest Lawn. In an announcement hastily released by Metro-Goldwyn-Mayer Studios, Mrs. Walker stated that Bob's remains would be transported to Ogden and that his final resting place would be the cemetery near the school he had attended as a boy.

Zella Walker further explained that the change of plans was "at the wish of Robert Jr. and Michael. We decided the ceremony should be where the boys wanted it to be. We want to do only what is best for our grandsons."

She didn't elaborate as to what might have inspired the boys to make such a last-minute request.

A few days later, David Selznick and Jennifer, together with her two sons, quietly flew back to New York, en route to Europe. Although their school term was due to begin in a few weeks, Jennifer was still undecided as to whether to return the boys to

Black Fox for another semester or to enroll them in a private school in Switzerland, since David's business affairs were still based primarily in Europe. Moreover, she was sensitive enough to know how much the boys needed a visible, tangible mother at this most traumatic time in their lives. And, indeed, that fall they enrolled in a Swiss school.

Bob's funeral was rescheduled for September 4, and Barbara Rabe remembers, "When they returned to Utah, I immediately went to see his parents. Aunt Zella and Uncle Horace were very closemouthed about the tragedy. I don't think either of them ever got over Bob's death. They had been so thrilled about his return to the screen—and then this!

"The public was welcome to take a last look at Bob, and there were mobs of curiosity seekers and young movie fans lined up for almost seven blocks. I suppose they had expected to see some of his Hollywood friends, but none of the people he had worked with was there. Perhaps they hadn't been informed. I don't know."

Only Charles Trezona was on hand to represent the movie colony and serve as a pallbearer.

However, Ogden had rarely, if ever, seen such a funeral. Some four hundred hometown folks crowded into the small chapel at Lindquist's mortuary to hear the services. Conducting the simple but often moving ceremony was Mormon Bishop David S. Romney, a former mayor of Ogden and a close friend of the Walkers'. Romney eulogized Bob as never having "lost the common touch, even though he had gained great fame."

It was stifling in the small chapel, with the heady smell of huge floral arrangements permeating the air.

Among the sprays were those sent by Spencer Tracy, the Alfred Hitchcocks, the Pat O'Brians, Dore Schary—and Mr. and Mrs. David O. Selznick.

Organ and violin music concluded the ceremony, and a hushed crowd remained seated as Bob's coffin was moved from the chapel and into the funeral car outside.

As it was lowered into the earth at Washington Heights Cemetery, Zella Walker, who had always prided herself on her ability to control her emotions, was heard sobbing, "What a beautiful, beautiful man. What a shameful, tragic waste."

Zella remained oblivious of the role she had herself played in the Bob Walker tragedy.

Others whose lives he touched throughout his brief span would always remember him with great admiration and greater love.

And the two who had dealt him the cruelest blow would be haunted by their memories of him and would pay, in time, a painfully high price.

AFTERWARD

--- ★

Jennifer talked openly about David's instability to me. She says it's almost as bad as her own. They are both in deep analysis.

—MONTGOMERY CLIFT

In shallow waters the dragon becomes the joke of the shrimp.

—DORE SCHARY (about the last years
of David O. Selznick's life)

Here's a man who was a genius and giant in the industry and he's lost it somehow. Watching him in those last years and admiring him as I did, it was terrible, just terrible.

—DANNY SELZNICK

Chapter

24

Neither Jennifer Jones nor David O. Selznick ever discussed Robert Walker publicly after his death, but it's unlikely they were ever completely capable of erasing the tragedy from their minds. Bob's sons, to whom he left his entire estate, were a constant reminder of their father's premature death.

Call it coincidence or poetic justice, but as John Huston so bluntly put it: "David never did anything worth a damn after he married Jennifer." Dore Schary was crueler still about Selznick, noting, "In shallow waters the dragon becomes the joke of the shrimp."

Jennifer fared somewhat better—for a while. After accompanying her husband on his European jaunts for over six months, she got an offer early in the spring from King Vidor, who had directed her in *Duel in the Sun*. He wanted her for the title role in his forthcoming Twentieth Century-Fox melodrama, *Ruby Gentry*.

Selznick was immediately attracted by the gutsy nature of the title role. Ruby, an apparently simple girl from the wrong side of the tracks, ditched by the young aristocrat whom she loves, marries the town's wealthiest man and rises to a position of power and affluence. Selznick felt that the part was just what his wife needed at this low point in her career and urged her to accept.

Before contracts were signed, however, Vidor extracted a promise from Selznick that the latter would not interfere with any aspect of the production. Since Selznick had business in New York during the months Jennifer was due before the cameras, there seemed to be little risk of his invading the set. Nevertheless, despite his promise and his distance, he still generated his share of memos about the script, about the musical score (the theme "Ruby" would

become a commercial hit), and he eventually persuaded Vidor to allow him to work on the final cutting and editing. Although contrived and trashy, *Ruby Gentry* did indeed revive Jennifer's stagnant career. With her two previous films in release in 1952, she was once more back in the public consciousness.

In December 1952 Selznick joined forces with Italy's revered producer-director Vittorio De Sica for *Stazione Termine*. The entire story of the final parting of a Philadelphia housewife and her Italian lover was set against the background of Rome's sparkling new Terminal Station. Montgomery Clift, who had recently completed Alfred Hitchcock's *I Confess*, played the agonized lover.

It was the collaboration between the two moguls, however, which proved the *most* agonizing. Selznick spoke no Italian; De Sica knew little English. The latter lovingly focused most of his film on the station and tampered with the script as the mood moved him. Selznick wanted a passionate love story and particularly Jennifer's role to receive the emphasis.

To add to the chaos, Clift was in constant conflict with both De Sica and Selznick, whom he called "an interfering fuckhead" behind his back. Clift was, however, sympathetic toward Jennifer, who he felt was still brooding over Robert Walker's death.

Later Clift would tell actress Patricia Collinge, "Maybe Walker haunts her, but Selznick's the guy she loves—in spite of his emotional hang-ups—which she talks about openly. 'Almost as bad as my own,' she says, and both of them are in deep analysis."

When the picture was finally completed, Jennifer gave Clift an expensive Gucci morocco leather briefcase. Its brass clasp perpetually kept unfastening. When Clift showed it to friends, he'd always note, "Jennifer Jones gave this to me. It's beautiful, but it doesn't quite work—how like Jennifer."

David Selznick brought the finished print of *Terminal Station* back to Hollywood, where he proceeded to eliminate most of De Sica's extraneous touches, which brought its running time down to a scant sixty minutes. He personally retitled the disaster *Indiscretion of an American Wife*, deriving some satisfaction from the fact that his wife now had the *title* role.

Jennifer stayed on in Italy when her friend and former director John Huston offered her the female lead in *Beat the Devil*, Truman Capote's biting satire about the bizarre adventures of a

motley group of mobsters. Wearing a curly blond wig for her role of Gwen Chelm, a whimsical, unmitigated liar, she had an opportunity to prove her flair for comedy for the second and final time in her career.

(*Time* magazine's critic applauded her performance, noting, "Jennifer Jones, her hair blonded for the occasion, does the best with the best part—she manages to catch the mystic fervor of the truly creative liar.")

Robert Jr. remembers joining his mother on location in Rome and Ravello, where he met the rest of the impressive cast: Humphrey Bogart, Gina Lollobrigida, Robert Morley, Peter Lorre.

"It was all pretty heady for a thirteen-year-old," he says. It was also a relief to be free of his studies, which bored him, as studies had bored his father before him, and in which, by his own admission, he did rather poorly.

However, unlike his father, Bobby wasn't the least bit interested in acting—then. Later he'd admit, "I went to fourteen or fifteen different schools in Switzerland, Hollywood, New York, New Jersey. I didn't like any of them, and I didn't participate in any of the school plays. Michael was the bright one in the family."

In 1954 Selznick, finally out from under his twelve-million-dollar indebtedness, was itching to get back into a production of his own, still dreaming of making a film that would equal or surpass *Gone with the Wind*. This successor epic would, of course, have to have a lead role suitable for Jennifer. Thinking big, as ever, he decided *War and Peace* was just the ticket, with Jennifer the quintessential Natasha Rostova. MGM had agreed to finance the project, and Selznick registered it with the Motion Picture Association. When both Michael Todd and Italy's Dino de Laurentiis declared they, too, were preparing versions of the Tolstoy classic, Selznick did not give up without a fight. However, when David had to admit there was no way he could get his epic to the theaters before his rivals did, Nick Schenck, president of Loew's Inc., MGM's parent company, withdrew his financing for *War and Peace*. Schenck, however, began negotiating a deal in which Selznick would produce two other large-scale pictures for the studio, but the two men were unable to reach an agreement as to the vehicles, and that deal also fell through.

With David's approval and encouragement, Jennifer accepted the title role in *The Country Girl*, Paramount's film version of Clifford Odets' 1950 play. She would be costarring with Bing Crosby and William Holden. George Seaton, who had written the screenplay of *The Song of Bernadette*, was now a prominent director and was convinced that Jennifer was the ideal actress for the complex role.

Despite the disappointing grosses of *Carrie*, Paramount was still high on Jennifer, but extracted the inevitable promise that Selznick would not "interfere." But interfere he did—in a most unexpected way. Shortly before she was due to report to work, Jennifer discovered she was pregnant again. She desperately wanted the role, but she wanted the baby more. She bowed out of the picture and was replaced by Grace Kelly, who went on to win an Oscar for her portrayal of Georgie Elgin.

The Selznicks settled down in their lavish home on Tower Grove Drive in Bel Air to await the arrival of what David willed to be a little girl. Everything that could be done was done to assure Jennifer complete tranquillity. Selznick had a small cottage constructed in back of the mansion to provide Bobby and Michael with their own living quarters. If they wanted or needed anything, he'd say, "Not to worry your mother. Tell me how much, and I'll write a check."

On August 12, 1954, Jennifer gave birth to the daughter Selznick had so desperately wanted. The arrival of Mary Jennifer sent him into such a euphoric state that he was able to forget both the dismal notices and the pitiful attendance accorded *Indiscretion of an American Wife*, released a couple of months earlier, and the overall mess he was making of his career.

David's world now revolved around Mary Jennifer, and with his fondest wish a reality, he didn't protest when Jennifer accepted an offer to make her Broadway debut as Isabel Archer in William Archibald's adaptation of Henry James's *Portrait of a Lady*, due to open in New York four days before Christmas. If the play, about expatriates in the Europe of the 1870's, was successful, David planned to turn it into a film.

Although apprehensive about the imminent challenge, Jennifer had regained most of her physical strength by the time rehearsals began in late fall.

Portrait of a Lady opened to a packed house on December 21. During the first act, however, the audience at the ANTA Theater began fidgeting in their seats. As the evening wore on, disappointment increased. There was the mandatory polite applause during the curtain calls, but the audience knew they had wasted their money. Although the cast included such talents as Cathleen Nesbitt, Douglas Watson, and, of course, Jennifer—and though each of them worked valiantly and resourcefully—there was no way to pump life into a poorly conceived script. *Portrait of a Lady* folded in a week.

And so Jennifer's dazzling childhood dream of "becoming a great Broadway actress" faded away with the old year. "I was bleeding from every pore," Jennifer admitted. "I wanted to run to Tahiti to hide." Ironically, *Variety* ran an article on the play, headed "Where Was David?" wondering why he had *not* chosen to get involved in the production. "Apparently I can't win," David later told friends, "either by interfering or not interfering."

Licking her wounds, Jennifer returned to the Selznicks' Tower Grove Drive mansion, resigned to concentrating solely on the role of mother and mistress of the house. And what a house it was: the living room, dining room, and bedrooms were lavishly furnished—but it was her bathroom that was the *pièce de résistance*, complete with wood-burning fireplace, crystal chandeliers, and plush carpeting. Three original Renoirs were mounted above the oversize tub. But one has to wonder if Jennifer hadn't been a great deal happier climbing that makeshift ladder to bathe in that Greenwich Village kitchen sink, back in a time when she still had her youth, her unshakable faith in the future—and Robert Walker.

Quite unexpectedly, early in 1955 Jennifer was offered a three-picture contract from Twentieth Century-Fox, the studio originally responsible for her stardom.

She felt she had come full circle when *Song of Bernadette's* director, Henry King, cast her as Han Suyin, the Eurasian doctor around whose real-life experiences the script of *Love Is a Many-Splendored Thing* had been written. Its exterior scenes were to be filmed in Hong Kong in Technicolor and CinemaScope.

William Holden was signed to play Suyin's ill-fated lover, an

American newspaperman, but in spite of their tender and touching love scenes, the two were in constant conflict. Holden was particularly annoyed by the rash of memos Selznick kept firing off to King and producer Buddy Adler commenting acidly on Jennifer's makeup, hairdo, accent, and a myriad of other details. Holden, a 1953 Oscar winner for *Stalag 17*, did have first star billing (which may have been the rub) and deeply resented being treated by the Selznicks as though he didn't exist. When his anger cooled down, he attempted to end the feud by presenting Jennifer with a beautiful spray of white roses. She threw them in his face and walked away. After that incident, contact between the two was confined to their scenes before the camera.

Love Is a Many-Splendored Thing, an outstanding critical and box-office success, would also garner an Oscar nomination as Best Picture of the year. To Jennifer it brought a fifth Best Actress nomination. (*Marty* and its male lead, Ernest Borgnine, were the surprise winners that year, and Anna Magnani was chosen Best Actress for *The Rose Tattoo*.) *Love Is a Many-Splendored Thing* had to be content with lesser awards, such as Best Song, Best Scoring, and one for Charles LeMaire's costume designs.

Despite her hostility toward Holden and her constant complaints during the shooting of *Love Is a Many-Splendored Thing*, Jennifer, eager to keep working, was delighted when Fox immediately cast her in *Good Morning, Miss Dove*, a sentimental story about a New England geography teacher who has sacrificed personal happiness in order to work and pay off her dead father's debts. The role of Miss Dove provided yet another dramatic tour de force, requiring Jennifer to age from a sparkling young girl to a hard-bitten, wrinkled, gray-haired schoolmarm on the brink of death. It was a role she played so well that even the fussy New York *Times* critic commented: "Miss Dove, in the person of Jennifer Jones, is a remarkable but believable character out of Dickens. Her carefully etched portrait of the dedicated teacher is a neat blend of pride, genuine gentility, and humor," and *Variety* noted, "Jennifer Jones gives a moving, throat-catching portrait."

In *Miss Dove*, Jennifer had no problems with her leading man; she had no leading man.

At home, however, she was deeply concerned about her private leading man's problems.

Daniel O'Shea, Selznick's former attorney, now president of RKO Pictures, signed his old boss to a three-year contract to provide prestige films for the ailing company. Although David announced to the "trades" that he intended to start no fewer than three pictures the following winter, and talked of later producing Selznick Company movies made specifically for television, the deal was abruptly canceled when General Tire, the owners of RKO, disbanded the company and sold the Gower Street lot and soundstages to Lucille Ball and Desi Arnaz.

Selznick was then seized with the inspiration to produce three hundred hours of film depicting the major events of the Bible, and entered into negotiations with General Motors to sponsor the mammoth weekly series. Complicated contracts were in the process of being drawn up when the giant auto company's ad agency decided the project would sit ill with a TV audience better attuned to Lucy and Desi than to Solomon and the Queen of Sheba.

Shortly thereafter, *The Ed Sullivan Show* ran a broadcast celebrating MGM's thirtieth anniversary, narrated by Dore Schary. Schary referred to *Gone with the Wind* as one of Metro's greatest achievements but gave no credit to David as the producer. Selznick threatened legal action but settled for a public apology. His once overwhelming ego was being chipped away bit by bit. At fifty-three he looked like a man in his late sixties.

Only in the company of his younger wife and baby daughter was he capable of displaying a flash of his former vitality. He had reached a point where his pleasure was derived from theirs.

This did not help free him from his obsessive ambition to surpass his *GWTW* triumph, however, or to display his beautiful Jennifer at her finest. He read every current best-seller, reviewed past literature, pestered friends and colleagues for suggestions, and rejected every idea offered.

He didn't disguise his disappointment when, for her third and final picture under her Twentieth Century-Fox contract, Jennifer was reunited with Gregory Peck in *The Man in the Gray Flannel Suit*. This film was the product of Nunnally Johnson's adaptation of Sloan Wilson's best-selling novel about the personal and professional trials of a fictional network's public-relations man.

Because of the machinations of the plot and subplot—Peck's adulterous wartime affair with a young Italian girl, whose baby he

unwittingly fathered—Jennifer's role as his wife, Betsy, could scarcely be considered more than a supporting role. Peck, of course, received first billing, and Johnson, who also directed, lavished the lion's share of his time and attention on his male star, answering Selznick's frantic memos about the way Jennifer was being treated with a curt "I have passed your notes on to Mr. Zanuck."

Between them, Jennifer and Peck, who had sizzled when they costarred in *Duel in the Sun,* now generated about as much warmth as a wet gray flannel blanket.

Following a preview, *Variety* complained: "Miss Jones allows almost no feeling of any relationship between her and Peck. She alternates between being the nagging wife and the frustrated lover, except that she rarely conveys the impression of being in love with her husband in the first place." The majority of the other critics were equally lukewarm.

Both David and Jennifer were determined that her next part would regain both the love and sympathy that she had forfeited by accepting this role. Ironically, their objective would be fulfilled by a film part which Jennifer never dreamed would be offered her, the real-life character she had adored most during her starry-eyed, uncomplicated teenage years.

Chapter

25

Early in the summer of 1956 Jennifer received a bid to go to London to star in Metro's remake of the 1934 production of *The Barretts of Wimpole Street*. A classic, the picture had starred Norma Shearer and Fredric March and had been an Oscar nominee. Producer Sam Zimbalist, eager to see the remake equal the success of the original, left nothing to chance. The original director, Sidney Franklin, now sixty-three, was called in for a repeat performance. The locales, all studio-built in the original film, were to be authentic—as was the cast, replete with fine English actors. Thirty-three-year-old Bill Travers was to be the romantic Robert Browning, and John Gielgud was cast as the tyrannical patriarch, Edward Moulton-Barrett. All this and Metro Color and CinemaScope too!

Dore Schary, Zimbalist, and Franklin all agreed a Hollywood star was essential to bolster the film's box-office appeal in the United States. However, on MGM's now shrinking contract list there was no one available with the qualities required to portray the dark-haired, big-eyed, thirty-eight-year-old semi-invalid poetess, Elizabeth Barrett.

Jennifer Jones, thirty-six, fit the bill on all counts.

Thrilled with the script, she signed the contract and flew to London, leaving David to his own devices. If he needed to talk with her, there was always the telephone, his second-favorite medium of communication.

David, every bit as enthusiastic as she about the film, couldn't resist reminiscing that he and Franklin had both started at Metro in 1926—Franklin as a full-fledged director, young David in the lowly position of "reader in the story department." And that eight

years later, when the Norma Shearer version was being filmed, Selznick was at work on a nearby soundstage as the producer of the classic *David Copperfield*.

He liked and trusted Franklin and was confident that Jennifer was in capable hands.

Jennifer was remarkably calm and exceedingly cooperative during the filming of *The Barretts of Wimpole Street*, and was the subject of considerable publicity and attention. Although the original Barrett no longer existed, she dedicated a plaque placed at 50 Wimpole Street, long a tourist attraction, and was flattered when her figure as Elizabeth was unveiled at Madame Tussaud's Wax Museum.

She worked effectively with both Gielgud and Travers under the patient direction of Franklin, who wisely did not attempt to have her emulate Miss Shearer's portrayal but allowed her to interpret the part in her own style. Tall, dark, and ruggedly handsome, Travers possessed a magnificently trained voice, as well as diction that belied his Newcastle origins, and their romantic scenes could not be faulted.

One can't avoid wondering, however, how often, as they performed, Jennifer's memories drifted back to the dreamy-eyed nineteen-year-old girl playing those same scenes, voicing those same words—words which then held a meaning for her that went far beyond mere acting.

With Gielgud and Travers, she would chat about the so-familiar lines, but neither Gielgud nor Travers recalls that she ever touched on the warm inner core of her memories—that she ever alluded to the boyish actor who, so ill-suited to the heavy Browning role, had risked his career at the Academy to let Jennifer's portrayal of Elizabeth show off her great talent.

When *The Barretts of Wimpole Street* was released the following February, the *Hollywood Reporter* raved: "Miss Jones has what looks like an easy role. She is the focus of attention at all times, and her dialogue can be drawn from some of the loveliest poetry ever written. But the role has its dangers. The performance must be muted, and much of the story and character can be shown only as gradually emerging from the icy chrysalis her illness and her father have put her in. Finally she must show—without shocking us too much—that she realizes her father's love is in reality poten-

tially incestuous, and her only hope is to risk her life and flee with the man she loves. Miss Jones does it with great warmth and skill. Her extreme achievement is to convince the audience that she is a person capable of having conceived Elizabeth Barrett's piercing sonnets."

And the less verbose *Variety* simply noted, "Miss Jones, while a surprisingly healthy-looking Elizabeth, plays the invalid literary figure with great skill."

Frustrated by his loss of *War and Peace* but still obsessively driven to produce a film whose dual themes of love and war would be in the tradition of *Gone with the Wind*, Selznick acquired the rights to Ernest Hemingway's *A Farewell to Arms*, long a favorite novel of his. Selznick had wanted to make the picture for several years, but Warner Brothers, who owned it, would never sell the rights to him. Warners bought the remake rights to *A Star Is Born*, but it was Selznick who owned the foreign rights to the picture, as well as the negative of the original production, and seeing his opportunity, he offered to swap them for the chance to make *A Farewell to Arms*. Finally, after a great deal of bargaining, and some additional cash from Selznick, the deal was made.

The story of a tragic love affair between an English nurse and an American soldier in World War I Italy had been successfully filmed by Paramount in 1932 with Gary Cooper and Helen Hayes. Selznick had also seen the butchered 1955 TV version of the tearjerker, featuring Diana Lynn and Guy Madison as the doomed lovers; but tawdry though it was, it still served to rekindle his interest in what Hemingway had called his *Romeo and Juliet*.

Once Twentieth Century-Fox agreed to finance the production, Selznick engaged writer Ben Hecht to create a screenplay that would not only provide spectacular battle footage but also, by enhancing the love story, would display Jennifer's talents to the fullest.

As director, he chose John Huston, now a close personal friend, with whom Jennifer had worked compatibly in *We Were Strangers* and *Beat the Devil*. He acceded to Huston's demands for a $250,000 fee and the freedom to film the picture as he saw fit, although Ray Klune, Selznick's former production manager, cautioned that the decision was a great mistake. "You'll kill each

other. It's the old 'law' of physics about an immovable object and an irresistible force."

Selznick envisioned Rock Hudson, Hollywood's newest romantic idol, as Lieutenant Frederick Henry, Nurse Catharine Barkley's passionate lover. In order to obtain his services from Universal, he was forced to guarantee Rock first star billing. Because of the then-thirty-year-old Hudson's dynamic box-office appeal, Jennifer graciously accepted a demotion.

A *Farewell to Arms* went into production in Rome early in 1957, and thereafter, whatever *could* go wrong *did* go wrong. Selznick and Huston were locked in constant combat over everything from script changes to Rock Hudson's hairstyle. Selznick kept deleting original Hemingway scenes from the script, feeling they did not play cinematically, and Huston kept adding them back in or inventing entirely new scenes altogether, often on the spur of the moment. Selznick wanted to emphasize the romantic aspects of the story, and Huston preferred to concentrate on the military, and the two visions of the film never meshed. Vitriolic memos flew back and forth, until finally, on March 17, Selznick dictated the memo to end all memos, making it clear that there was room at the top for only one genius, namely himself. At the time, Huston was on location in the rugged Northern Alps country around Cortina, where he was laying out his critical battle scenes. After barely scanning Selznick's prose, he dashed off to his room, packed his belongings, and wired his resignation, saying to reporters, "I not only hit the ceiling . . . I'm stuck up there."

Selznick explained Huston's vanishing act with a terse "I asked for a first violinist and instead got a soloist. I am the producer and must produce. I gave Huston the choice of either carrying out his contract or resigning. He chose to leave."

Huston was hurriedly replaced by Charles Vidor, a competent director who had chalked up such credits as *Gilda* and *Cover Girl* while under contract to Columbia Pictures. As shooting progressed, however, the Hungarian-born Vidor also became argumentative and explosive about David's persistent interference, stating, "He doesn't want a first violinist, he wants a piccolo player." At one point Vidor threatened to quit as well, and have Selznick direct the remaining scenes. The filming of A *Farewell to*

Arms continued through a brutal Italian summer, and everyone's nerves were at the breaking point.

Sensing a story for *Parade*, his professional instincts telling him that Jennifer might be overreacting to production pressures, writer Lloyd Shearer dropped in on the Cinecittà Studios in Rome and immediately started in pursuit of the preoccupied and elusive Selznick. Finally cornering his man, he said with deliberate irreverence, "For years Mrs. Selznick has given the impression that she is the most nervous, high-strung actress in the business. I wonder if you will tell me what kind of girl she really is."

Visibly nettled, Selznick replied, "It's nobody's business what sort of woman my wife is. If I didn't think she was a fascinating woman, I wouldn't have married her and remained married to her for eight years. Jennifer is extraordinarily sensitive. I have a feeling she was born out of her time. She has nothing in common with modern women. There is about her an almost Victorian quality, and she has a strange mystical sixth sense about things. She is extremely ambitious but for reasons completely different from those of other actresses. She has no interest in fame or money. All her awards, including the Oscar, have mysteriously disappeared from our house. She acts because she must act. It is a compulsion. As for her aversion to publicity, she has always had an ingrained feeling that the press wants to talk about her personal life. She just doesn't like being probed."

Later, observing Jennifer personally, Shearer wrote, "Her brown eyes are the saddest, most soulful eyes I have seen in a long time; nature fixed them so that she could look out but no one could look in."

Querying Jennifer about her press phobia, he received her standard reply: "I never know what to say when I'm being interviewed. Most interviewers pry into your private life, and I don't like it. I respect everyone's right to privacy and I feel mine should be respected too. . . . I'm just not good copy. . . . I love acting but not the limelight."

Principal filming on *A Farewell to Arms* was technically completed in mid-August. Exhausted, David and Jennifer booked passage on the *Queen Elizabeth* to unwind and devote more of their time to Mary Jennifer, who had been somewhat neglected in Italy.

They arrived in New York refreshed and relaxed, then flew home to California, where several interiors still remained to be shot.

David's concentration on editing his film was temporarily interrupted by the death of his former father-in-law, Louis B. Mayer, on October 20, 1957. When Irene Selznick phoned him with the news, David, according to Irene, arrived at once and took charge. When the important decisions were out of the way, "he took care of me and even carried me up the stairs."

The following morning, Irene received "masses of orchids" and an uplifting letter from her ex-husband. On the day of the funeral, David was caught hiding behind the bushes, because, as he later explained, he wanted "to make sure nothing went wrong until the services were under way." To David, life and death themselves were productions.

A month later, November 18 and 19, a rough cut of A *Farewell to Arms* was sneak-previewed in Burlingame and San Francisco. Audiences reacted favorably to most of the film, but were shocked and offended by an overly realistic ten-minute sequence devoted to Catherine's agony and subsequent death while giving birth to her illegitimate stillborn baby. Reluctantly David cut from the episode all but three minutes of what he considered Jennifer's finest acting.

Wildly but misguidedly enthusiastic about A *Farewell to Arms*—envisioning a potential Oscar winner—the top executives at Twentieth Century-Fox pressured Selznick to have the epic ready for Los Angeles release in time to meet the Academy's deadline, just before year's end.

Jennifer, spectacularly adorned in white ermine, diamonds, and December pearls, nervously accompanied her husband to Grauman's Chinese Theater on December 19 for the star-studded premiere of the first exclusively Selznick production in nine years.

In spite of her fear of pushy photographers, she smiled radiantly as they shot picture after picture of her with David and Rock Hudson.

The celebrity-packed audience gave the picture the rousing acclaim expected of them. The following day *Farewell* was released in other theaters in the L.A. area and grossed a then-whopping $350,000 during the first two weeks of its run.

Nevertheless, David was apprehensive about the reactions of the New York critics and flew east—without Jennifer—to be on hand for the Manhattan opening, set for January 24, 1958.

His apprehensions were well-founded.

Many years later, Danny Selznick told Stephen Farber and Marc Green, authors of *Hollywood Dynasties*, "The single most painful experience of my father's life has to have been A *Farewell to Arms*. . . . The worst moment actually was at the Roxy Theater when the film was opening. He wanted to sit there with me. I hoped to Christ that it would be wonderful. And I sat there in shock. Beginning with the excessive degree of hysteria in Jennifer's performance, everything was wrong. There was my father sitting with me waiting for me to tell him what I thought of it. I don't even know what I said. But the reviews were so harsh that whatever I said would have been mild in comparison. . . . He had been hoping for Academy Awards across the board, and I don't even know if there were any nominations. . . . [Author's note: There weren't.] Here was a man who was a genius and a giant in the industry, and he lost it somehow. Watching him in those last years and admiring him as I did was terrible, just terrible."

The *Farewell to Arms* reviews were more than harsh, they were abominable, and Jennifer was not spared.

Hollis Alpert in the *Saturday Review* was practically kind when he wrote: "Jennifer Jones has a great deal of skill as an actress, but she's a fairly mature woman now, the mother of children, and that big movie screen has a gruesome way of revealing the disparity between what might be termed screen age and actual age."

The New York *Times* cruelly observed: "Miss Jones plays the famous Catherine Barkley with bewildering nervous grimaces. The show of the devotion between two people is intensely acted, not realized."

From *Variety*: "Miss Jones imbues the nurse with a sense of neurosis and foreboding, but she only sporadically rises to the full challenge of this super-difficult role. As Miss Jones plays her, Catherine Barkley frequently lacks warmth."

The Seattle *Times*'s critic complained: "Jennifer Jones is not right for the role of Catherine. A fine actress in older roles, Miss Jones does not give this one the kind of freshness, the quality, a younger actress . . . could have."

And *Cue* magazine, brutally brief, observed, "Miss Jones as the nurse in love never quite makes it."

In a crushing anticlimax, the critics stood united in damning the 230-minute-long epic, not only as badly acted but as dated and altogether ineffective. As for Jennifer, they graciously allowed her to retreat behind the excuse of age—though Helen Hayes had been thirty-two when she superbly portrayed the twenty-year-old Catherine Barkley.

Selznick's black mood was deepened by the feeling that he had failed his wife, perhaps even ruined the career that had always meant as much to him as to her. Devastated by the notices, he mournfully told publicity man Marvin Houser, "God knows I gave it everything, and yet it didn't come off. Maybe my kind of picture is out of style.

"Maybe I'm an anachronism."

Chapter

26

To assuage Jennifer's hurt and as a means of salvaging his own shattered ego, David, the self-styled "anachronism," spent the early part of 1958 attempting to save *Farewell* from becoming a box-office disaster.

He fought for class bookings in London and other European cities, and if his methods of making motion pictures were out of style, his genius in promoting and marketing them was still potent. Despite its huge budget, the film would end up in the black, though barely, and eventually David sold his share of its take to Fox for a flat million dollars.

If, at any time during the difficult late 1950's, Jennifer harbored any dissatisfaction with her marriage, she kept it hidden. Never once were there any innuendos linking her name with another man's, nor was David's total fidelity to his wife ever questioned. The two appeared irrevocably bound to one another.

Professionally, however, David was a frustrated man. Because he was too proud to admit his lapses, whenever he was asked what he planned to do next, he would shrug and say, "I think I'll take some time off. I can afford to do nothing for a while. I need time to think."

He was still incapable, however, of thinking small. Although he had had no Broadway experience in his lengthy career, he was seized by the notion of producing a spectacular musical version of *Gone with the Wind*, which he planned to retitle *Scarlett O'Hara*, and approached some of the country's top composers and lyricists about writing the score. The project failed to get beyond the talking stage, however, as did a six-part TV version of the legendary classic.

Tormented by the fear that his wife's idleness was undermining her spirit, he read and reread the forty-odd properties he still owned. This intensive review turned up one property that electrified Selznick: F. Scott Fitzgerald's 1934 novel, *Tender Is the Night*, which dealt with young Americans living in Europe in the 1920's. The story—and especially the role of the psychologically ill Nicole Diver—enchanted Jennifer quite as much as it had David. Between them they decided that this was the vehicle to reactivate their failing careers. David was overjoyed that his wife's enthusiasm matched his.

He entered into negotiations with Twentieth Century-Fox's president, Spyros Skouras, to finance the major David O. Selznick Production, and began fashioning a script with Ivan Moffat. He ignored the reality that Jennifer had been damned for playing a young girl in *Farewell* and that Moffat's and his version of Fitzgerald's story takes Nicole from age twenty-four to age twenty-nine. In Selznick's eyes and heart, Jennifer was still the young girl with whom he had fallen in love.

Without warning, Skouras, plagued with financial problems caused by exorbitant expenses generated by Elizabeth Taylor's *Cleopatra*, asked Selznick to withdraw from the project. Skouras agreed to buy the rights, retain Jennifer's services, and assign Henry King directorial chores, but he could not risk Selznick's extravagances. For Jennifer's sake, Selznick agreed to the humiliating terms. According to Selznick, he was supposed to have had casting approval and approval of any changes in the script, but "they ignored my advice."

A former television producer, Henry Weinstein, basically inexperienced in moviemaking, took over. (In time, Weinstein would be best remembered as the man who fired Marilyn Monroe from Twentieth-Century Fox.)

Jason Robards, a fine actor, was badly miscast in the male lead, and Joan Fontaine, Tom Ewell, and Jill St. John were hired for other pivotal roles.

In late May 1961 the cast of *Tender Is the Night* left for location shooting on the French Riviera and Zurich, Switzerland, while David remained at home with Mary Jennifer, dashing off a stream of lengthy wires to King and Weinstein containing a barrage of suggestions, many inspired by nightly phone conversations with

his wife, about locations, lighting, incidental music, costumes, shooting schedules, and set decoration. ("It just makes me sick at my stomach . . . to see the sloppiness with which pictures are made today, including, I'm sorry to say, *Tender Is the Night*.")

They were filed and forgotten. Later Selznick would say that he worked harder and longer on *Tender Is the Night* than on *Gone with the Wind*—with but a fraction of the result.

When the company returned to Hollywood for interiors, Hedda Hopper talked with Jennifer. Freely discussing her long stretch between pictures, Jennifer insisted, "I was offered other things during the time of waiting, but there was nothing that interested me.

"I've always been a Fitzgerald fan, and of all his works, I like this one best. The *girl* is a wonderful character, and there are so few left.

"I've always loved the period of the twenties. *Tender* is a wonderful love story, with a most unusual relationship between Nicole and her husband. He is her lover as well as her psychiatrist, and it doesn't work out. She is healed, but, in the process, he is utterly destroyed."

Sensing that Jennifer regretted seeing the filming of *Tender* come to an end, Hedda casually asked what lay ahead in her professional future. Jennifer replied vaguely, "I'd like to do another picture soon, but it may not turn out that way. Many people think the big screen is a substitute for everything else and the story and character are not important as long as the screen is wide and in color. I'm an actress and I don't appreciate the technical things, but I do think the most important thing is still a good story.

"I read a lot and am sent numerous scripts, but I would still like to do another play before I settle back into domesticity."

Hedda concluded her story tamely: "The Selznicks are never seen at premieres or at restaurants where the stars gather. They prefer small dinners at home, followed by showings of new films. They were planning to show *Fanny* the day I was there."

Jennifer avoided discussing David's plans, or lack of them, with Miss Hopper, but did mention that Bobby Jr. had been studying with Lee Strasberg. Reading that, there were those who recalled that the tenth anniversary of Bob Sr.'s death was coming up within two weeks.

Despite Jennifer's optimistic expectations concerning *Tender Is the Night* and its meticulous production, the film was yet another fiasco.

The critic for the *New Yorker*, assessing its shortcomings, noted, "Miss Jones works hard at being Nicole but cannot embody her. The cast in every case is unsuitable. The chief objection to be made to them is that they are all too old—in the novel, Nicole is twenty-four."

A few reviewers were somewhat kinder.

Time magazine noted, "[Henry] King faced his biggest problem in actress Jones, and the problem wasn't only in age: in recent films the lady has limited her expressions largely to a toneless hysterical laugh and an alarming tic. But in *Night* she is well-cast as a neurotic and does her best work in a decade."

Bosley Crowther of the New York *Times* opined: "Jennifer Jones is quite proficient as the mercurial Nicole, proceeding from a state of mental anguish to one of rigid and heartless self-control," and Paul V. Beckley of the New York *Herald Tribune* admitted that "Jennifer Jones has it a little easier with Nicole, who is meant to be incomprehensible and psychotic, and she looks more comfortable in the last half-hour, when some shred of a sane dilemma confronts her."

Only *Variety* was unqualified in its praise: "Miss Jones, absent from the screen since *A Farewell to Arms* in 1957, emerges a crisply fresh, intriguing personality as the schizophrenic Nicole."

After the brief stir created by her performance in *Tender Is the Night*, however, Jennifer's career came to a complete standstill. She was a forty-two-year-old woman in an industry that was obsessed by youth and the likes of Natalie Wood, Sandra Dee, and Ann-Margret.

Unwanted by and disenchanted with the new Hollywood, the Selznicks spent the better part of the next two years abroad.

In Paris, in April 1964, David Selznick suffered the first of five heart attacks. He faked an "ankle injury" to explain his sudden immobility, and he revealed the true nature of his disability only to his former wife, Irene.

Although she was spared knowledge of the gravity of her husband's illness, Jennifer was alarmed by David's apparent exhaustion and made an effort to get him to let go and relax. They spent

most of the summer with the Louis Jourdans, first vacationing at Cap d'Antibes, then cruising the Riviera on novelist Irwin Shaw's yacht.

According to Bob Thomas, David confided in Louis: "I'm ready to go. Everything is settled. My only thought now is for my wife and daughter and my sons. . . . I want them to enjoy the best after I'm gone."

Returning to the States, he established residence, together with Mary Jennifer, at the Waldorf Towers in New York, where, with the exception of periodic visits to California, he spent most of the next nine months.

During one of his brief trips to Hollywood in late 1964, he granted his old friend Hedda Hopper a rare interview. Concealing his poor health and shrinking bank account, he brought her up-to-date with regard to his general activities.

Miss Hopper noted, "The Selznicks . . . rarely come off 'The Hill.' Several months a year they travel to New York, Europe, the Caribbean, the Mediterranean, and the Far East."

"It's a pleasant life," Selznick told her, "too pleasant to give up to make movies with the way things are in the industry these days." When Hedda suggested he write his memoirs, he insisted that he wouldn't do that until his old age, as it would be too time-consuming.

In mid-December Selznick was sent the script of *Goddess on the Couch*, a comedy about a psychiatrist's wife whose ideas don't coincide with her husband's. Both Jennifer and David felt it would provide a suitable vehicle for a return to Broadway.

A trial run was booked for March 22–27 at the Royal Poinciana Playhouse in Palm Beach, Florida, and at the Coconut Grove Playhouse in Miami from March 30 to April 11. If successful, David planned to bring it to Broadway later that spring.

The Man with the Perfect Wife, as it had been retitled by Danny Selznick, assistant producer, was little more than diverting summer-theater fare. Although Jennifer acquitted herself well in the part, the reviewers considered the play's third act weak and felt it lacked the style required for acceptance in New York. David attended opening night, but then detached himself altogether from the production.

Jennifer was still in Florida when David attended a dinner party

at the home of Bubbles and Arthur Hornblow in New York. The guest list included Leland Hayward and Irene Selznick. Midway through dinner, David, feeling ill, retired to the Hornblows' bedroom, signaling Irene to join him. She contacted her cardiologist, who advised her to keep David lying facedown. Irene and Bubbles Hornblow then took turns watching over the ailing man. After the other guests departed, Leland Hayward helped Irene to assist David back to his hotel. As he entered the Waldorf Towers he suffered what was later determined to have been a second heart attack and was taken to a nearby hospital, where he was quietly confined for ten days. When he was well enough to travel, he returned to the Coast to appear at a testimonial dinner for Alfred Hitchcock—past grievances now forgotten.

David spoke with force and emotion about the decline of the Hollywood that once was. But he didn't know when to stop, and, to the embarrassment of his peers, began to ramble pointlessly.

Garson Kanin remembers, "He spoke like a man who was dying."

After Jennifer rejoined David in California, he could no longer keep his illness secret from her. All devotion, she concerned herself exclusively with providing him with a stress-free life. But for a man who had always lived for activity, it was difficult to kick the habit.

On June 23 Selznick came down from the Hill to keep a noon appointment with his lawyer, Barry Brannen. An hour into their meeting, he put his hand on his chest and complained of feeling faint. Alarmed, Brannen called for an ambulance and then phoned Jennifer.

Selznick was rushed to Mount Sinai Hospital and placed in intensive care. He had arrived at the hospital at one P.M., and Jennifer appeared some twenty minutes later, then watched through a window for an hour, as, with the aid of a team of doctors, he fought for his life. At 2:33 P.M., at age sixty-three, David O. Selznick was pronounced dead as the result of a coronary occlusion.

The news of his sudden death stunned the industry. The dragon was no longer the joke of the shrimp. Tributes poured in from both friends and former adversaries.

Although confused and grief-stricken, Jennifer invited Irene

Selznick to fly west for the funeral. Irene thought it best not to, but she was pleased when Jennifer deferred to Jeff and Danny for the arrangements.

Anticipating death, Selznick had written a memo requesting his funeral be simple and brief, and the family attempted to adhere to his wishes.

Guests at the services held at the small Church of the Recessional at Forest Lawn cemetery were limited to two hundred. The pallbearers included William Wyler, Sam Spiegel, Samuel Goldwyn, Christopher Isherwood, William Paley, and Alfred Hitchcock.

Rabbi Max Nussbaum of Temple Israel read a short prayer. George Cukor read a eulogy written by Truman Capote. "His fantastic vitality was matched only by the profoundness of his sense of integrity, responsibility, honor, and loyalty, his good taste by his originality."

At Jennifer's request, Katharine Hepburn gave a moving reading of Kipling's poem *If*. Cary Grant read a tribute written by Paley which said, in part, "The one word that fits David Selznick better than any other is 'extravagance.' He was extravagant in every way, in his generosity, friendship, attention to those who sought him out for advice and guidance, and his love for those he loved. I cannot help but think our world will never be the same, nor will heaven. And if we are lucky enough to get there too, David will see that all arrangements are made."

And Joseph Cotten eulogized, "Greatness in a man usually makes him larger than life. This is not true of David Selznick. He was very much a part of life."

As Irene read the tributes to her former husband and lifetime friend, she recalled the evening when David had collapsed at Arthur and Bubbles Hornblow's dinner party, when he had gently turned aside his hostess's show of concern, saying, "It's all right, Bub. It's not much fun anymore."

And for Jennifer, although David had made her the sole beneficiary of his one-million-dollar life-insurance policy, during the next six years she too would find life "not so much fun anymore."

Chapter

27

For nearly five months following David's death, Jennifer rarely left the Tower Grove Drive mansion. Although she and David had been separated any number of times due to the demands of their individual careers, she found it difficult to reconcile herself to the reality that she'd never hear his booming voice or receive his moral support again. It was even more difficult for eleven-year-old Mary Jennifer, who was in all ways "daddy's little darling."

In the autumn, however, Mary Jennifer had her schoolwork at Buckley's to keep her busy. Jennifer had nothing. Occasionally she invited Charles Bickford and his wife, Beatrice, to the house for dinner, but essentially she was a lost and lonely lady. She was advised that the best therapy was a return to work, but the scripts sent her were unreadable and trashy.

When the moment came to reemerge into professional life, it came in a rush. Joseph E. Levine was about to produce a movie called *The Idol*, about an overpossessive mother who first detests her son's best friend and then has a brief affair with him that ends in tragedy.

Kim Stanley had been signed for the starring role, with Michael Parks costarring as the friend, and a young British actor, John Leyton, as the son. Three days before *The Idol* was due to begin, Miss Stanley fell ill and had to be replaced. In November Jennifer was sent a copy of the screenplay and given two days in which to decide whether or not to get on a plane to London.

In an interview given to Frank Watts, who was covering the European production for the New York *Times*, Jennifer revealed, "I liked . . . the script very much. Also it caught me at the psycho-

logical moment. Everything combined to make it a desirable thing to do. So here I am."

When asked how it felt to be acting again after three years, she replied, "Like riding a bicycle . . . once you've learned, you *know*." But a few days later, during another session with the writer, she revised that remark: "I realized I made it sound all too glib and easy. The truth is, with me it doesn't matter if the gap is three months or three years. I'm always taut with nerves for the first few days. The only thing that's true about the bicycle bit is that you know you've done it before, so you *must* be able to do it again, once you've got the rust out of your joints and get settled in yourself."

When asked about the rumor which had circulated before she signed for *The Idol*, that she had intended to retire completely, she just laughed. "How can one talk of retiring when one has been an actress since age six?" As for the term "comeback," she shrugged that off with, "It's been a long time between pictures, but it wasn't the first time that's happened. There have always been projects going, but for one reason or another they haven't materialized. Three in four projects I've been involved in never came to anything."

She would have been blessed if *The Idol* had also failed to materialize.

It was a distasteful flop, and although the New York *Times* conceded that "Both Miss Jones . . . and John Leyton give workmanlike performances," the film was unmercifully panned and quickly disappeared from view.

"*How can one talk of retiring when one has been an actress since age six?*" Jennifer had asked.

But what does one do when no one in the motion-picture industry wants you for anything decent? If one is Jennifer, one waits and withdraws. And so another eight months of reclusive idleness.

Then, in the summer of 1966, Lee Strasberg, the prominent drama coach and founder of the Actors' Studio, perhaps recalling that she had been the initial choice for the film of *The Country Girl*, offered her the lead in his version, to be staged by the City Center as part of its American Playwrights series. The role would bring Jennifer to New York for a limited but guaranteed run from September 29 to October 16, 1966.

Costarring with Rip Torn and Joseph Anthony, Jennifer was not reviewed well by the critics. "Her performance is cruel when it should be vital, and petulant when it should be angry," said the New York *Times*. Added *Women's Wear Daily*, "Miss Jones read most of her lines in a dull, listless fashion and appeared to be unconscious of the fact that she was playing with other actors."

Jennifer's desire for privacy was so firmly established that few outsiders attempted to see her. Film historian Douglas Mc-Clelland, however, ventured backstage, half-expecting to be turned away by a surly doorman.

"Instead," he says, "I was directed to her unpretentious dressing room, where I found her seated alone at the makeup table, still in her third-act costume, a sweater and a skirt.

"There was a fixed smile on her face, a vague look in her eyes when I introduced myself and complimented her on that evening's performance. When I mentioned that *Portrait of Jennie* was my favorite of all her films, she murmured softly, 'I've never seen it,' adding, 'Well, any quality that it may have is entirely due to my husband.'

"After a few more moments of small talk, I left, since I sensed she wanted to remove her makeup and change back into her street clothes.

"I noted sadly that there wasn't a soul waiting in the alley anxious to catch a glimpse of her or have their programs auto-graphed, the usual ritual when a movie star appears in the theater. That was odd and rather depressing."

Even more depressing—to Jennifer—was the fact that once she had completed her run in *The Country Girl*, no new offers came her way for other plays or films. In industry jargon, she was no longer considered "bankable."

She returned to the isolation of her home, once again a recluse. Suffering from insomnia, she began to rely on Seconal tablets to get her through her sleepless nights. She remained in limbo for a year, a middle-aged woman unwanted and unloved and unable to cope with life. There was no one who cared enough to fight for her, and at forty-eight she was incapable of fighting for herself. She'd never had to before.

On Thursday, November 9, 1967, Jennifer received the ex-pected by nonetheless devastating news that her dear friend

Charles Bickford had died of emphysema at UCLA Medical Center.

Later that evening, distraught and confused, she left her home holding a bottle of champagne and with a bottle of Seconal in her purse, and checked into an obscure motel in Malibu Beach. Shortly afterward, she phoned her personal physician, Dr. William Malley, from a public booth, told him she was somewhere in Malibu, had taken four pills, and intended to take more. The doctor immediately alerted the Malibu police to be on the lookout for a luxury sports car.

Sergeant Eldon Loke, who spotted the car at the top of a deserted cliff overlooking Point Dume, related that "her footprints wound down a thousand-foot-long path to within a few feet of the ocean. She was lying at the rock-strewn base of the cliff with the rising tide washing over her body. She wasn't breathing, but I heard a heartbeat through her back. After three minutes of mouth-to-mouth resuscitation, she began breathing again."

Jennifer was taken to Malibu Hospital to have her stomach pumped out and then rushed to Mount Sinai Hospital, where she lay in a coma for nearly six hours before regaining consciousness.

The following day, a spokesman for the hospital reported, "Mrs. Selznick is coming along very nicely. She's much improved, and her doctor says she is doing fine."

By Sunday night Jennifer was well enough to leave Mount Sinai quietly by a rear exit and return home.

During their investigation of the case, the police noticed that Jennifer had checked into the motel under the name of Phylis Walker.

Neither they nor the press who had headlined Jennifer's suicide attempt, accompanied by a morbid photo of the unconscious star with a tube between her lips, commented on the "alias," nor was she ever questioned about it.

Why Phylis Walker? If, in her confused state, she had wanted to conceal her identity, why not Phylis Jones or Jenny Isley? Or simply Jane Doe?

Did the giveaway alias represent a subconscious longing to be again, for a few, final moments, the girl she had once been— before Hollywood, before Selznick? Was she exorcising guilt? Was

this her way of reconciling, in death, with the father of her two sons? Possibly she, herself, never knew.

Years later, according to author Stephen Farber, Jennifer admitted that this had not been her only suicide try.

"I have attempted suicide three times," she acknowledged, "when I was at points of deep despair. It was a cry for help."

She found help by helping others, utilizing her early nurse's training and her money to work with emotionally disturbed and drug-addicted youngsters in a program called the Manhattan Project.

To be sure, this was a gratifying activity, but her need to act could not be denied. On February 17, 1969, she went before the cameras in the role of a former star of porno films who'd married for money. Based on a story written by Richard Thom, *Angel, Angel, Down We Go* was directed by the author and produced by American International. The "down we go" of the title could as well have applied to the state of Jennifer's career. Its dialogue was sordid, vulgar in the extreme—and, for those in the audience who carried an image of her as Bernadette, it was shocking to have to listen to lines such as "I've made thirty stag films and never faked an orgasm!" As the expression goes, David O. Selznick had to be turning over in his grave.

Both Jennifer and *Angel* were savaged. The atrocity was recalled, retitled *Cult of the Damned*, and reissued with an advertising campaign designed to emphasize its most lurid aspects. In a career that had had more than its share of mistakes, this was Jennifer's greatest by far, and it diminished the possibility that she'd ever again be offered a significant role in a prestige picture.

On May 29, 1969, Jennifer received a call from Phil Isley, now seventy-six, informing her that Flora Mae had quietly passed away in Dallas. Another bleak reminder for Jennifer that the figures of her past were dropping out of her life: Bob . . . David . . . and now her mother.

(Phil Isley would succumb in Dallas to complications following surgery on May 27, 1976.)

Realistically, Jennifer adjusted to the possibility that she might never work at her craft again. The thought of remarriage didn't enter her mind. Eligible men in her financial and age bracket

could have their pick of the young lovelies who populated Southern California, and the idea of becoming involved with a younger man, as was frequently the case with lonely fading film stars, was repellent to her.

Mary Jennifer, now fifteen, possessed neither the brilliance of her late father nor the beauty of her mother, but when she expressed her desire to pursue an acting career in New York after graduating from high school, Jennifer's attitude was the same as it had been with the Walker boys: "Do whatever you feel will make you happy."

Working on the Manhattan Project was making her happy, and she devoted most of her time and all of her energy to the program. She invited as many as a dozen youngsters at a time to her home on weekends for swimming, tennis, and conversation. Zealously she solicited funds from David's wealthy acquaintances, funds necessary for the construction of a new branch to be built outside Salt Lake City. Was it mere coincidence that Salt Lake City was also the birthplace of Robert Walker?

Although she still felt uncomfortable at large social gatherings, Jennifer accepted publisher Walter Annenberg's invitation to attend a lavish party at his California home on May 5, 1971.

Sixty-four-year-old Norton Simon, multimillionaire industrialist, art collector, and owner of the prestigious Duveen Gallery, was among the elite present. Despite success and wealth, Simon, at the time, was a lonely and notably unhappy man. A year earlier he had divorced Lucille Ellis, his wife of thirty-seven years' standing. The dissolution of the marriage had taken place shortly after their son, Robert—ill for some time—had committed suicide. Simon was a conservative Republican whose ambitions for a political career had been shattered when he had been defeated in the 1970 California Senate race.

Jennifer would later recall, "Norton knew I was an actress, but he had never really seen anything I did except, I think, *Portrait of Jennie.*"

His link to *Jennie* was—in the light of what was about to transpire—most intriguing. He had seen, and had been consumed by a desire to add to his collection, the Brackman portrait which Selznick had commissioned at the time of the filming. Unable to secure the painting, here he was at the Annenbergs' elegant home,

face-to-face with its model. Throughout the evening he monopolized her attention, finding her every bit as desirable as he had previously found her portrait.

As he later recalled that evening, "She happened to be going to Paris to visit the head of the Manhattan Project (who was on vacation in that city), and I happened to be going to the Caribbean and decided not to. Then we made up our minds on the spur of the moment to go to Paris together.

"There was great soul communication—great 'simpático' between us from the start. I found her soul more beautiful than her face, and you've got to admit her face is pretty nice."

Soon after their arrival in Paris, they found themselves falling in love, and at seven o'clock one morning, he proposed.

They were married early Sunday morning, May 30, 1971, by a Unitarian minister on a yacht off the coast of England.

Cornered by the press who met the boat, Jennifer didn't run. Asked about the impromptu wedding, she joyfully replied, "He walked me around Paris and London until I was so exhausted I couldn't resist him anymore. It was the most romantic thing that's ever happened to me."

Later she'd add, "Yes, we behaved impulsively. But, at our age, you're not exactly terrified of such things. Indeed, I'm convinced that, the older you get, the more risks you're willing to take."

When the Simons returned to America, they flew directly to Salt Lake City, where Jennifer helped open the new center for the Manhattan Project. Of that evening Simon said, "I'll tell you, Jennifer was fabulously good talking with the people of Salt Lake on the solution of their problems, and I was proud to be simply the husband of Jennifer Jones Simon that night."

Back in California, Jennifer packed her belongings and her treasures and moved into Simon's well-staffed Malibu mansion.

Mary Jennifer, shaken by her mother's sudden remarriage, moved east to study acting. Danny Selznick, son of David and Irene and thus Mary's half-brother, told a reporter, "It turned out she had a natural acting talent which I strongly encouraged her to develop through technical training, and I helped arrange for her to study with Uta Hagen in New York."

But perhaps because her mother had achieved stardom so

rapidly, Mary's concern with acting as a craft was tainted by her need for instant limelight.

Jennifer might have been able to talk some sense into her head-strong daughter, but, for now, she was committed to as difficult a role as any she had ever mastered: the role of being Mrs. Norton Simon, the queenly, gracious hostess to her husband's power- and influence-wielding friends—among them Henry Kissinger. And when the Simons traveled abroad, she couldn't afford to be an everyday tourist, gawking at Europe's great art treasures, guidebook in hand. She said, "I had always thought of museums as dreary, boring affairs. But because Norton expected it of me, I began to develop a 'good eye' and learned to discuss the masters with an expertise I couldn't believe was mine."

As Jennifer's third marriage thrived, she continued to be disturbed by the inability of her gifted but restless children to find themselves. It was as if her life were regulated by a malevolent system of credits and debits—with the black ink reserved for her, and for them the red. In 1973 Bob Jr., to the Simons' chagrin, decided to abandon acting and went to work as a $200-a-week chauffeur for a Los Angeles limousine rental company. To startled reporters he said, "For the first time, I really feel like a useful person instead of a show-business commodity." Apparently, in addition to his father's looks, his build, and his talent, Bobby had also inherited that unhappy man's rebellious nature. Then, within a month, he gave up being "a useful person" and returned to acting. Of Michael, little was heard—he'd lived in a kibbutz in Israel for a while, left because it "wasn't much fun," and moved to Paris, then made a few small television and film appearances.

Despite her unlimited wealth and social and charitable obligations, Jennifer still had a gnawing desire to return to the screen, a desire Simon, a large holder of Twentieth Century-Fox stock, may have helped make a reality. Early in 1974, after Olivia de Havilland rejected the sympathetic part of a lonely widow wooed by a phony bond salesman in Irwin Allen's spectacular disaster epic *The Towering Inferno*, Jennifer signed for the role.

The film, about the victims and survivors of a fire that erupts during the dedication of a 138-story San Francisco glass skyscraper, was budgeted at fourteen million dollars and designed to

attract a huge audience at a time when disaster movies were at their peak. After her previous two abominations, Jennifer cheerfully accepted the challenge, excited to be in a "class production" again after thirteen years, even though she was only billed after Steve McQueen, Paul Newman, William Holden, Faye Dunaway, Fred Astaire, and Richard Chamberlain.

With a beaming Norton Simon at her side, she even attended *The Towering Inferno*'s gala December 10 premiere and was pleased by her flattering reviews.

As, all through 1975, the big *Inferno* grosses continued to roll in, Jennifer might well have congratulated herself that she had played an important role in an outstanding box-office success. Certainly the audiences seeing the picture could not easily forget the scene in which her character, Lisolette Mueller, dangles for an agonizing moment inside a scenic elevator, loses her precarious balance, and plummets many stories to the street below.

While the glow of success still illuminated Jennifer Jones Simon, however, on May 11, 1976, her twenty-one-year-old daughter, Mary Jennifer, took a different elevator to the top of a different office building, in Los Angeles, stepped out on the roof, and jumped. Another credit. Another debit.

Jennifer's only comment was, "I was devastated when Mary died. She had gone through treatment, and, I thought, was at peace with herself. You never know . . . about the mind."

Simon made a superhuman effort to keep Jennifer from dwelling on the tragedy. In September 1977 he named her chairman of the directors of the Norton Simon Museum in Pasadena with its $250-million collection of masterpieces. That same year she worked as a commissioner on the Huntington's Disease Council. In November, while in Washington on behalf of the latter, she granted a rare interview to Nancy Collins of the Washington *Post*. Collins described her as "gracious, self-effacing, and upbeat." She talked freely about Simon and about David O. Selznick, saying of the latter, "I have always had a basic belief in my own talent, but obviously I was very fortunate to find David Selznick or have David find me. Every actress discovered or nurtured by him—and God knows we all need nurturing—well, every actress David helped was very fortunate."

She admitted that she still was looking for another good script,

wanted to keep acting, because, "It is what I do best," and claimed she was quite happy, and that, as far as she was concerned, she'd had a pretty good run.

"Actually, every time I stop to think about it, I'm really amazed. I think I've had an extraordinary life. And lots of times I can hardly believe it's me.

"Sometimes," Jennifer Jones Simon said, "I come home and catch Norton watching one of my old movies on television. He always seems kind of amazed that the woman he's watching is the same woman he's married to. But I just say to him, 'You're not really looking at that old thing, are you? Come on, Norton, you're looking at my past. Let's live in the moment.'"

To Jennifer Jones, the present was all that mattered. She required no image other than the one she saw in the mirror each morning, and to her it was a satisfying image.

When she was twenty-six, a reporter had asked her for her thoughts about the inevitability of aging, and she had casually replied: "I believe women should keep themselves young as long as possible.

"But I want to look forty when I reach forty and sixty when I reach sixty. I like to see well-groomed women who are aware of people and life and whose interest and activities give them great charm. They don't need endless massages and trips to the beauty parlor and face-lifts that give them masklike expressions."

Physically, the years had been kind to Jennifer. When she celebrated her sixtieth birthday on March 2, 1979, she could have easily passed for fifty. Her skin was flawless; her short-cropped hair remained raven black. Only a certain softness around the mouth and eyes gave so much as a hint of her years.

Due partly to a rigid regimen of exercise and her lifelong insistence on getting ten to twelve hours of sleep a night, she created an impression of boundless energy. In public or in the privacy of her own home, she was always impeccably dressed and groomed. And her varied interests and activities contributed to a productive life.

Although her name was absent from the movie pages, it was inevitably mentioned in the society columns whenever, exquisitely gowned, she graced the arm of her husband at the extravagant affairs hosted by California's elite rich and superrich. Invitations to

the Simons' formal and informal parties were rarely, if ever, turned down by Los Angeles' snobbish "old guard."

Jennifer Simon, to all outward appearances, was radiantly happy in her role of respected society matron, of art collector and connoisseur, and of benefactress to the mentally disturbed and the physically handicapped.

Simon worshiped her and had complete confidence in her judgment.

On April 15, 1980, unable to make the trip himself, he handed her a blank check and sent her to London's renowned Sotheby auction gallery to bid on a painting depicting the Resurrection of Christ, a 35-by-28 masterpiece by the fifteenth-century Dutch artist Dieric Bouts, which he wanted for the Norton Simon Museum.

In a heated bidding contest with London's National Gallery, Jennifer secured the painting for the then-record sum of 3.74 million dollars, although Sotheby's had estimated the work's value at approximately $440,000.

All that mattered to her was that she was able to help her husband get what he wanted.

She had everything money could buy. But she wanted more. She wanted to return to her days of acting glory. But she couldn't bring herself to carry her plans through.

Envisioning a comeback, she took an option on the film rights to Larry McMurtry's novel *Terms of Endearment*. Attracted to the poignant mother-daughter relationship, she consulted with writers about turning the book into a screenplay which would maximize her talents. Then, inexplicably, she abandoned the idea and sold the rights to Paramount. The film won an Oscar as Best Picture and Shirley MacLaine, who played Aurora Greenway, won the award for Best Actress of the year, ironic, since Jennifer had made no secret of the fact that, "Now, of course, if I won an Oscar, I'd be overwhelmed, thrilled to death."

Aware of his wife's craving to resume her career, Norton took an option on *The Jean Harris Story*, the heartbreaking drama of the elegant schoolmistress who killed her lover, Dr. Herman Tarnower, the best-selling author and creator of the Scarsdale Diet—but that project, too, was quietly dropped without explanation.

Early in 1984 Jennifer Jones made a surprise TV appearance at the American Film Institute's salute to Lillian Gish. Though she was no stranger to Miss Gish and had worked with her in *Duel in the Sun* and *Portrait of Jennie*, she was visibly nervous and barely audible during her brief speech paying tribute to the legendary silent film star.

Then, a few months later, the Simons disappeared from public view.

In May 1984 the seventy-seven-year-old Simon was felled by an acute attack of Guillain-Barré syndrome, an inflammation of the muscle nerves that results in paralysis and often death. (It was the same disease from which author Joseph Heller had recently recovered, after much suffering.)

Jennifer rarely left his side. In September 1985 she told society columnist Suzy, "In the early months, a team of ten nurses maintained an intensive-care facility in our home. Now, with his progress, they maintain a rehabilitative unit. The nurses are like family to us." Also in September, Jennifer was honored by the University of Pennsylvania's School of Nursing for her "efforts to promote a fairer, more compassionate society."

For a short period in 1985, rumors circulated along Television Row that Jennifer would return to acting on *The Colbys*, but before contracts could be executed, the deal fell through.

When Norton Simon passes from the scene, Jennifer Jones will undoubtedly inherit a fortune, but for the second time in her life, she will also be a woman alone.

She will still have her charities and her work with the Norton Simon Museum to keep her occupied. Perhaps such a labor—certainly one of love—will be sufficient to ward off the specter of loneliness. Perhaps. But through her lifetime, she has always needed a man to worship and protect her.

In spite of her insecurities and self-doubts, Jennifer Jones Simon is a survivor. The vigorous and aristocratic image she projects overshadows all personal defeats and tragedies—her three suicide attempts, the loss of a promising young daughter, the dizzying fluctuations of her career.

It's likely she will continue to survive.

She is wealthy enough to back either a play or a movie for

herself, should she fall prey to the desire to make yet another acting comeback.

She continues to avoid watching her old movies on television: *Since You Went Away* is a perennial Christmas-season attraction; *Duel in the Sun, Portrait of Jennie, Love Is a Many-Splendored Thing,* and *Love Letters* are frequently aired.

They are part of the "past" upon which she chooses not to dwell.

Yet, one must speculate whether Mrs. Norton Simon of Pasadena doesn't sometimes ponder what the fates would have ordained for her, for Robert Walker, for David O. Selznick, if a shy, big-eyed mother of two baby sons hadn't kept an appointment at 630 Fifth Avenue on July 21, 1941, to audition for the lead in *Claudia.*

The script cannot be rewritten.

Its final pages are still blank.

The Films of Robert Walker

Note: All dates are the New York openings. The directors' names appear in italics after these dates.

WINTER CARNIVAL United Artists, July 27, 1939. *Charles F. Riesner.* Ann Sheridan, Richard Carlson, Helen Parrish, James Corner, Robert Armstrong, Marsha Hunt, Virginia Gilmore, Robert Walker.

THESE GLAMOUR GIRLS. Metro-Goldwyn-Mayer, August 30, 1939. *S. Sylvan Simon.* Lew Ayres, Lana Turner, Tom Brown, Richard Carlson, Jane Bryan, Anita Louise, Marsha Hunt, Ann Rutherford, Robert Walker.

DANCING CO-ED. Metro-Goldwyn-Mayer, November 9, 1939. *S. Sylvan Simon.* Lana Turner, Richard Carlson, Artie Shaw, Ann Rutherford, Thurston Hall, Leon Erroll, Roscoe Karns, Mary Beth Hughes, Monty Woolley, June Preisser, Robert Walker.

BATAAN. Metro-Goldwyn-Mayer, June 3, 1943. *Tay Garnett.* Robert Taylor, George Murphy, Thomas Mitchell, Lloyd Nolan, Lee Bowman, Robert Walker, Desi Arnaz, Barry Nelson, Phillip Terry, Roque Espiritu, Kenneth Spencer, J. Alex Havier, Tom Dugan.

MADAME CURIE. Metro-Goldwyn-Mayer, December 16, 1943. *Mervyn LeRoy.* Greer Garson, Walter Pidgeon, Henry Travers, Dame May Whitty, Albert Basserman, Robert Walker, C. Aubrey Smith, Van Johnson, Victor Francen, Elsa Basserman, Reginald Owen, Margaret O'Brien.

SEE HERE, PRIVATE HARGROVE. Metro-Goldwyn-Mayer, March 21, 1944. *Wesley Ruggles.* Robert Walker, Donna Reed, Keenan Wynn, Robert Benchley, Ray Collins, Chill Wills, Bob Crosby, Marta Linden, Grant Mitchell, George Offerman Jr., Edward Fielding, Donald Curtis, William "Bill" Phillips, Douglas Fowley.

SINCE YOU WENT AWAY. United Artists, July 20, 1944. *John Cromwell.* Claudette Colbert, Jennifer Jones, Joseph Cotten, Shirley Temple, Monty Woolley, Lionel Barrymore, Robert Walker, Hattie McDaniel, Agnes Moorehead, Guy Madison, Keenan Wynn, Lloyd Corrigan, Gordon Oliver, Albert Basserman, Nazimova, Jackie Moran, Helen Koford (Terry Moore), Florence Bates, Craig Stevens.

THIRTY SECONDS OVER TOKYO. Metro-Goldwyn-Mayer, November 15, 1944. *Mervyn LeRoy.* Spencer Tracy, Van Johnson, Robert

Walker, Phyllis Thaxter, Tim Murdock, Scott McKay, Don De-Fore, Gordon McDonald, Robert Mitchum, John R. Reilly, Horace McNally, Donald Curtis, Louis Jean Heydt, William "Bill" Phillips, Douglas Cowan, Paul Langton, Ed Ames.

THE CLOCK. Metro-Goldwyn-Mayer, May 3, 1945. *Vincente Minnelli.* Judy Garland, Robert Walker, James Gleason, Keenan Wynn, Marshall Thompson, Lucille Gleason, Ruth Brady.

HER HIGHNESS AND THE BELLBOY. Metro-Goldwyn-Mayer, September 27, 1945. *Richard Thorpe.* Hedy Lamarr, Robert Walker, June Allyson, Agnes Moorehead, Carl Esmond, Warner Anderson.

WHAT NEXT, CORPORAL HARGROVE? Metro-Goldwyn-Mayer, December 25, 1945. *Richard Thorpe.* Robert Walker, Keenan Wynn, Jean Porter, Chill Wills, Hugo Haas, William "Bill" Phillips, Cameron Mitchell, Ted Lundigan.

THE SAILOR TAKES A WIFE. Metro-Goldwyn-Mayer, February 27, 1946. *Richard Whorf.* Robert Walker, June Allyson, Audrey Totter, Hume Cronyn, Eddie Anderson, Reginald Owen.

TILL THE CLOUDS ROLL BY. Metro-Goldwyn-Mayer, December 5, 1946. *Richard Whorf.* Robert Walker, June Allyson, Lucille Bremer, Judy Garland, Kathryn Grayson, Van Heflin, Paul Langton, Dorothy Patrick, Dinah Shore, Virginia O'Brien, Cyd Charisse, Gower Champion, Lena Horne, Van Johnson, Angela Lansbury, Tony Martin, Frank Sinatra.

THE BEGINNING OR THE END. Metro-Goldwyn-Mayer, February 20, 1947. *Norman Taurog.* Brian Donlevy, Robert Walker, Tom Drake, Audrey Totter, Beverly Tyler, Hume Cronyn, John Litel, Hurd Hatfield, Joseph Calleia, Godfrey Tearle, Victor Francen, Richard Haydn, Barry Nelson.

THE SEA OF GRASS. Metro-Goldwyn-Mayer, February 27, 1947. *Elia Kazan.* Katharine Hepburn, Spencer Tracy, Robert Walker, Melvyn Douglas, Phyllis Thaxter, Ruth Nelson, Edgar Buchanan, Harry Carey, William Phillips, Robert Armstrong, James Bell.

SONG OF LOVE. Metro-Goldwyn-Mayer, October 9, 1947. *Clarence Brown.* Katharine Hepburn, Paul Henreid, Robert Walker, Leo G. Carroll, Henry Daniell, Else Janssen, Gigi Perreau, "Tinker" Furlong, Ann Carter, Janine Perreau, Roman Bohnen.

ONE TOUCH OF VENUS. Universal-International, October 28, 1948. *William A. Seiter.* Robert Walker, Ava Gardner, Dick Haymes, Eve Arden, Olga San Juan, Tim Conway, James Flavin, Sara Allgood.

PLEASE BELIEVE ME. Metro-Goldwyn-Mayer, June 11, 1950. *Norman Taurog.* Deborah Kerr, Robert Walker, Mark Stevens, Peter Law-

ford, James Whitmore, J. Carroll Naish, Spring Byington, Carol Savage, Drue Mallory, George Cleveland, Ian Wolfe.

THE SKIPPER SURPRISED HIS WIFE. Metro-Goldwyn-Mayer, June 29, 1950. *Elliott Nugent*. Robert Walker, Joan Leslie, Edward Arnold, Jan Sterling, Spring Byington, Leon Ames, Anthony Ross, Paul Harvey, Kathryn Card, Tommy Myers, Rudy Lee.

VENGEANCE VALLEY. Metro-Goldwyn-Mayer, February 15, 1951. *Richard Thorpe*. Burt Lancaster, Robert Walker, Joanne Dru, Sally Forrest, John Ireland, Ray Collins, Carleton Carpenter, Ted de Corsia, Hugh O'Brian, Will Wright, Grace Mills.

STRANGERS ON A TRAIN. Warner Brothers, July 3, 1951. *Alfred Hitchcock*. Farley Granger, Ruth Roman, Robert Walker, Leo G. Carroll, Patricia Hitchcock, Laura Elliott, Marion Lorne, Jonathan Hale, Howard St. John, John Brown, Norma Varden.

MY SON JOHN. Paramount, April 8, 1952. *Leo McCarey*. Helen Hayes, Robert Walker, Van Heflin, Dean Jagger, Frank McHugh, Miner Watson, Richard Jaeckel, Irene Winston, James Young, Tod Karns.

The Films of Jennifer Jones

Note: All dates are the New York openings. The directors' names appear in italics after these dates.

NEW FRONTIER. Republic, August 9, 1939. *George Sherman.* John Wayne, Ray Corrigan, Raymond Hatton, Phylis Isley (Jennifer Jones), Eddy Walker, Sammy McKim, Leroy Mason.

DICK TRACY'S G-MEN. Republic, December 9, 1939. *William Witney, John English.* Ralph Byrd, Irving Pichel, Phylis Isley (Jennifer Jones), Ted Pearson, Walter Miller, George Douglas.

THE SONG OF BERNADETTE. Twentieth Century-Fox, January 26, 1944. *Henry King.* Jennifer Jones, William Eythe, Charles Bickford, Vincent Price, Lee J. Cobb, Gladys Cooper, Anne Revere, Roman Bohnen, Mary Anderson, Patricia Morison, Edith Barrett, Blanche Yurka, Marcel Dalio, Jerome Cowan, Tala Birell, Ian Wolfe, Dickie Moore, Linda Darnell.

SINCE YOU WENT AWAY. United Artists, July 20, 1944. *John Cromwell.* Claudette Colbert, Jennifer Jones, Joseph Cotten, Shirley Temple, Monty Woolley, Lionel Barrymore, Robert Walker, Hattie McDaniel, Agnes Moorehead, Guy Madison, Keenan Wynn, Lloyd Corrigan, Gordon Oliver, Albert Basserman, Nazimova, Jackie Moran, Helen Koford (Terry Moore), Florence Bates, Craig Stevens.

LOVE LETTERS. Paramount, August 26, 1945. *William Dieterle.* Jennifer Jones, Joseph Cotten, Ann Richards, Anita Louise, Cecil Kellaway, Gladys Cooper, Byron Barr, Robert Sully, Reginald Denny, Ernest Cossart, James Millican, Lumsden Hare, Winifred Harris, Ethel May Halls, Mary Field.

CLUNY BROWN. Twentieth Century-Fox, June 2, 1946. *Ernst Lubitsch.* Charles Boyer, Jennifer Jones, Peter Lawford, Helen Walker, Reginald Gardiner, C. Aubrey Smith, Richard Haydn, Margaret Bannerman, Sara Allgood, Ernest Cossart, Florence Bates, Una O'Connor, Queenie Leonard, Billy Bevan.

DUEL IN THE SUN. Selznick Releasing Organization, May 7, 1946. *King Vidor.* Jennifer Jones, Joseph Cotten, Gregory Peck, Lionel Barrymore, Lillian Gish, Walter Huston, Herbert Marshall, Charles Bickford, Joan Tetzel, Harry Carey, Otto Kruger, Sidney Blackmer, Tilly Losch, Scott McKay, Butterfly McQueen, the voice of Orson Welles.

PORTRAIT OF JENNIE. Selznick Releasing Organization, March 29, 1949. *William Dieterle.* Jennifer Jones, Joseph Cotten, Ethel Barrymore, Cecil Kellaway, David Wayne, Albert Sharpe, Lillian Gish, Florence Bates, Henry Hull, Esther Somers.

WE WERE STRANGERS. Columbia, April 27, 1949. *John Huston.* Jennifer Jones, John Garfield, Pedro Armendariz, Gilbert Roland, Jose Perez, Morris Ankrum, Tito Renaldo, Paul Monte, Leonard Strong, Roberta Haynes, Lelia Goldoni.

MADAME BOVARY. Metro-Goldwyn-Mayer, August 25, 1949. *Vincente Minnelli.* Jennifer Jones, Van Heflin, Louis Jourdan, James Mason, Christopher Kent, Gene Lockhart, Gladys Cooper, Frank Allenby, John Abbott, Henry (Harry) Morgan, George Zucco, Ellen Corby, Eduard Franz, Paul Cavanagh.

THE WILD HEART. Selznick/RKO, May 28, 1952. *Michael Powell, Emeric Pressburger.* Jennifer Jones, David Farrar, Cyril Cusack, Esmond Knight, Sybil Thorndike, Hugh Griffith, George Cole, Beatrice Varley, Edward Chapman.

CARRIE. Paramount, July 16, 1952. *William Wyler.* Laurence Olivier, Jennifer Jones, Eddie Albert, Miriam Hopkins, Basil Ruysdael, Ray Teal, Barry Kelley, Sara Berner, William Reynolds, Mary Murphy, Jacqueline DeWitt, Harry Hayden, Walter Baldwin, Dorothy Adams, Royal Dano, James Flavin, Margaret Field.

RUBY GENTRY. Twentieth Century-Fox, December 25, 1952. *King Vidor.* Jennifer Jones, Charlton Heston, Karl Malden, Tom Tully, Bernard Phillips, James Anderson, Josephine Hutchinson, Phyllis Avery, Herbert Hayes, Myra Marsh.

BEAT THE DEVIL. United Artists, March 12, 1954. *John Huston.* Humphrey Bogart, Jennifer Jones, Gina Lollobrigida, Robert Morley, Peter Lorre, Edward Underdown, Ivor Barnard.

INDISCRETION OF AN AMERICAN WIFE. Selznick/Columbia, June 25, 1954. *Vittorio De Sica.* Jennifer Jones, Montgomery Clift, Gino Cervi, Richard Beymer.

LOVE IS A MANY-SPLENDORED THING. Twentieth Century-Fox, August 18, 1955. *Henry King.* William Holden, Jennifer Jones, Torin Thatcher, Isobel Elsom, Murray Matheson, Virginia Gregg, Richard Loo, Soo Yong, Philip Ahn, Jorja Curtright, Donna Martell, Keye Luke.

GOOD MORNING, MISS DOVE. Twentieth Century-Fox, November 23, 1955. *Henry Koster.* Jennifer Jones, Robert Stack, Kipp Hamilton, Robert Douglas, Peggy Knudsen, Marshall Thompson, Chuck Connors, Biff Elliot, Mary Wickes, Jerry Paris, Richard Deacon, Virginia Christine, Dick Stewart, Betty Caulfield.

THE MAN IN THE GRAY FLANNEL SUIT. Twentieth Century-Fox, April 12, 1956. *Nunnally Johnson*. Gregory Peck, Jennifer Jones, Fredric March, Marisa Pavan, Ann Harding, Lee J. Cobb, Keenan Wynn, Gene Lockhart, Gigi Perreau, Portland Mason, Arthur O'Connell, Henry Daniell, Connie Gilchrist, Geraldine Wall, Dorothy Adams, Nan Martin, DeForest Kelley.

THE BARRETTS OF WIMPOLE STREET. Metro-Goldwyn-Mayer, January 17, 1957. *Sidney Franklin*. Jennifer Jones, John Gielgud, Bill Travers, Virginia McKenna, Susan Stephen, Vernon Gray, Jean Anderson, Maxine Audley, Leslie Phillips, Laurence Naismith, Moultrie Kelsall.

A FAREWELL TO ARMS. Selznick/Twentieth Century-Fox, January 24, 1958. *Charles Vidor*. Jennifer Jones, Rock Hudson, Vittorio De Sica, Alberto Sordi, Kurt Kasznar, Mercedes McCambridge, Oscar Homolka, Elaine Stritch, Leopoldo Trieste, Victor Francen, Joan Shawlee.

TENDER IS THE NIGHT. Twentieth Century-Fox, January 19, 1962. *Henry King*. Jennifer Jones, Jason Robards Jr., Joan Fontaine, Tom Ewell, Cesare Danova, Jill St. John, Paul Lukas, Bea Benadaret, Charles Fredericks, Sanford Meisner, Carole Mathews, Alan Napier.

THE IDOL. Embassy, August 10, 1966. *Daniel Petrie*. Jennifer Jones, Michael Parks, John Leyton, Jennifer Hilary, Guy Doleman, Natasha Pyne, Caroline Blakiston, Jeremy Bulloch.

ANGEL, ANGEL, DOWN WE GO. American International, August 19, 1969. *Robert Thom*. Jennifer Jones, Jordan Christopher, Roddy McDowall, Holly Near, Lou Rawls, Charles Aidman, Davey Davison, Marty Brill, Hiroko Watanabe.

THE TOWERING INFERNO. Warner Brothers/Twentieth Century-Fox, December 10, 1974. *John Guillermin, Irwin Allen*. Steve McQueen, Paul Newman, William Holden, Faye Dunaway, Fred Astaire, Richard Chamberlain, Jennifer Jones, Susan Blakely, O. J. Simpson, Robert Vaughn, Robert Wagner, Susan Flannery, Jack Collins, Sheila Matthews, Norman Burton.